"Dr. Siegel's work is a love letter to humanity—both a road map a⋯ appeal for us to understand the strength, basis, and innate connection that we all have and must become aware of in order to move beyond survival mode and into thriving mode. The reader of this elegant work will walk away with a deeper sense of intraconnection to all that exists and has ever existed in the universe. *IntraConnected* is a revelation, an awakening."
 —**Shelly Tygielski**, author of *Sit Down to Rise Up*, and founder of
Pandemic of Love

"*IntraConnected* completely redefines the word 'self' as we know it. We often hear 'we are all connected,' while the world shows us nothing but separation. Marrying modern science with indigenous wisdom, Siegel illuminates a doorway the world has desperately been trying to find. Walk through the door. Reading this book will change you forever. Dan Siegel has written another masterpiece. A balm for the difficulties we now face, *IntraConnected* cultivates hope for real positive change in your life, and the world."
 —**Justin Michael Williams**, author of *Stay Woke: A Meditation
Guide for the Rest of Us*

"In this personally engaging and philosophically illuminating work, Dr. Dan Siegel takes his unique explorations of the human experience of self and mind to a yet deeper level, revealing what he aptly calls the pandemic of solo-self to be based on a delusion, one at odds with both contemporary science and traditional wisdom. Eloquently and expertly, he guides us back towards our true nature, intra- and inter-being with all others and all that is."
 —**Gabor Maté**, MD, author of *The Myth of Normal: Trauma, Illness and
Healing in a Toxic Culture*

"In his latest book, Dan Siegel explores a pathway toward a more sustainable way of being humans facing the multiple pandemics of our times together. Synthesizing insights from a range of disciplines and ways of knowing, he argues for expanding, evolving the notion of the self, from an isolated and separate 'me' to a relational, awe-embracing integrated sense—called, in his intriguing coinage, 'MWe.' I know of no more encouraging prescription for what ails us at this time."
 —**Rhonda V. Magee**, MA, JD, professor of law, University of San Francisco School of Law, and author of *The Inner Work of Racial Justice: Healing
Ourselves and Transforming Our Communities Through Mindfulness*

"In an amazing dance of intellectual brilliance, heartfelt caring, and wise embrace, Dan Siegel invites us into the depth of his and our human story of development in order to examine, reflect, and melt the nature of the separate self. A new possibility of humanity arises when we authentically allow the possibility of intraconnectedness into our lives."
—**Thomas Hübl**, PhD, founder, Academy of Inner Science, and author of
Healing Collective Trauma: A Process for Integrating Our Intergenerational and Cultural Wounds

"What a joy it is to be alive in a time when neuroscience, rooted from within the body, offers us liberation, illuminating our inescapable belonging to each other and the living Earth. Dan Siegel's groundbreaking work here is of revolutionary, and indeed evolutionary, importance."
—**Joanna Macy**, author of *World as Lover, World as Self*

"In a world riven by polarization and division, Dan Siegel offers a compelling and timely gift to our hearts and minds, an awakening to non-duality that is innate to us all. Dan's deep practice and studies take the reader to a place where they can see anew, where the overstimulated mind can recognize the biological and ancient truths of our inseparability from each other and all of life."
—**Paul Hawken**, author of Regeneration: *Ending the Climate Crisis in One Generation*

IntraConnected

THE NORTON SERIES ON INTERPERSONAL NEUROBIOLOGY

Louis Cozolino, PhD, Series Editor
Allan N. Schore, PhD, Series Editor, 2007–2014
Daniel J. Siegel, MD, Founding Editor

The field of mental health is in a tremendously exciting period of growth and conceptual reorganization. Independent findings from a variety of scientific endeavors are converging in an interdisciplinary view of the mind and mental well-being. An interpersonal neurobiology of human development enables us to understand that the structure and function of the mind and brain are shaped by experiences, especially those involving emotional relationships.

The Norton Series on Interpersonal Neurobiology provides cutting-edge, multidisciplinary views that further our understanding of the complex neurobiology of the human mind. By drawing on a wide range of traditionally independent fields of research—such as neurobiology, genetics, memory, attachment, complex systems, anthropology, and evolutionary psychology—these texts offer mental health professionals a review and synthesis of scientific findings often inaccessible to clinicians. The books advance our understanding of human experience by finding the unity of knowledge, or consilience, that emerges with the translation of findings from numerous domains of study into a common language and conceptual framework. The series integrates the best of modern science with the healing art of psychotherapy.

IntraConnected

MWe (Me + We)

AS THE INTEGRATION OF SELF, IDENTITY, AND BELONGING

DANIEL J. SIEGEL

W. W. NORTON & COMPANY
Celebrating a Century of Independent Publishing

Diagrams by Madeleine Welch Siegel, copyright © 2018 Mind Your Brain, Inc., used with permission and first published in Daniel J. Siegel: *Aware: The Science and Practice of Presence.*

For information about permission to reproduce selections from this book, write to Permissions, W. W. Norton & Company, Inc. 500 Fifth Avenue, New York, NY 10110

For information about special discounts for bulk purchases, please contact W. W. Norton Special Sales at specialsales@wwnorton.com or 800-233-4830

Manufacturing by Lakeside Book Company
Production manager: Gwen Cullen

ISBN: 978-0-393-71169-1

W. W. Norton & Company, Inc., 500 Fifth Avenue, New York, NY 10110
www.wwnorton.com

W. W. Norton & Company Ltd., 15 Carlisle Street, London W1D 3BS

2 3 4 5 6 7 8 9 0

To each of us, siblings in the intraconnected
family of the whole of nature

Contents

Acknowledgments

Gratitude fills this moment as I type these words to you. I am grateful for you, dear reader, for considering the adventure of taking your time and energy to read this book, to join me in this conversation about who we are in our contemporary world. The reason this book exists at all is to connect with you, as a reader, and invite us to dive deeply into a journey reflecting on where we've come as a human family in our present place on this precious, fragile home we've named Earth.

If you've already read *IntraConnected* and are now turning to this acknowledgment section, I hope the book was a meaningful journey for you and will provide the ideas and the practices to enhance your personal well-being, professional work, and the greater good of our world. If you are just starting here reading this section, I hope the exploration of this book into how we've come to narrate the story of who we humans are in modern times—what our self, identity, and belonging are made of—and what we might do, individually and collectively, will be both meaningful and helpful in our finding the way to live a more free and fulfilling, health-promoting way of being in the world.

I am also grateful to the land upon which I live and work and the Indigenous people who were stewards of this land taken from them without their permission here in Los Angeles: the Chumash and the Tongva of modern day North America. The Indigenous knowledge from these groups, along with so many others from around the world, have informed the explorations in this book of how we might regain a way of living with respect and reciprocity in our shared world.

Surrounding the life of this human body called Dan have been numerous ancestors across hundreds of millions of years of the evolution of life on our planet. As we'll explore in this conversation, to open to our deeply intraconnected lives is to become filled with gratitude, compassion, and awe—the emotional states that help us transcend the small, separate, isolated sense of self so often dominating our modern construction of the experience of who and what we are. Contemplative teachings from a range of traditions and Indigenous knowledge from around the world have independently come to similar conclusions about a relative, "close-up" aspect of reality, and a universal, timeless realm of connection. I am grateful for these ancient wisdom traditions and appreciate that Western science in which I am trained is catching up with these insights in our contemporary studies.

In the steps to create this book, I chose to invite certain individuals from a wide variety of backgrounds in our culture to join me in a "pre-book" bookclub, a kind of think-tank about what a book on self, identity, and belonging might include. I set out seven chapters that spelled the word SIBLING: Self, Identity, Belonging, Love, Intraconnection, Noesis, and Gnosis, these latter two being factual knowledge and wisdom from experiential learning. Each month we'd discuss that chapter's topic as if the book had already been written. In those wonderful gatherings were the following individuals, many of whom continued on beyond the initial book club to become a part of what has come to be called our MWe Council. Some have also gone on to become Garrison Institute Fellows. Here is a list of our book club members whom I thank immensely: Alex Vesely, Andrew Villamil, Angel Acosta, Ashley Kim, Barnaby Willett, Elizabeth Folie, Gia Naranjo-Rivera, Jackie Ivy, Jennifer Bloom, Justin Michael Williams, Kasey Crown, Luthern Williams, Matt Khoury, Masi Ngidi-Brown, Mindia Gabichvadze, Mona Rich, Nichol Chase, Nico Cary, Orlando Villarraga, Rian Doris, Sará King, Selma Augusta Quist Moeller, Shane O'Donohue, Shelby Alsup, Shelly Tygielski, and Trevor Cobb.

We were honored with the guest appearances of a number of writers and scholars at various times to discuss the book, including

Joanna Macy, Mary Pipher, john a. powell, and June and Alan Sroufe, whose invaluable ideas and life's work were deeply inspiring for us all.

Over the years, the input from my fellow Board members of the Garrison Institute have been immensely helpful, and I thank them all, especially Paul Hawken, Diana and Jonathan Rose, Sharon Salzburg, and Jonathan Weisner. Together we try to bring "timeless wisdom" to "timely action."

Over the twenty years since the initiation of the professional books series at W. W. Norton on Interpersonal Neurobiology ("IPNB"), my relationship with vice president, Deborah Malmud, has given me the challenge, opportunity, and support to oversee the creation and production of a wide range of practical books in this interdisciplinary field of IPNB. For *IntraConnected*, I especially thank Deborah not only for our frank and direct lines of communication that helped the idea of this book move from an extensive rhyming fictional account of lifespan development to a comprehensive but too lengthy scientific discussion to the current version of this shorter, more focused work on self, identity, and belonging. To help with this transition, I had the great fortune of having two magnificent editors. One is Trish Watson, whose excellent work to find the core ideas within a lengthy initial manuscript helped to create a tighter, more accessible core presentation of the material. The second is Julie HawkOwl who served as copyeditor extraordinaire, finding the most subtle ways in which language can be inadvertently misleading and to help, in a fun and inspiring way, to find clarity in the suggested changes. I'm thrilled with how these two editors served to make the book tighter and with less ambiguity and am grateful for our professional collaboration. At Norton I'd also like to thank Mariah Eppes and Jamie Vincent for such careful attention to the final production of the book, and to Kevin Olsen and Emma Paolini for supporting it's release into the world. For any errors that remain in the wording of these complex ideas in the final manuscript, I take full responsibility.

I am also deeply grateful for how these ideas could find a visual mode of expression in the excellent drawings and diagrams of Madeleine Welch Siegel, graduate student in environmental sciences and engineering, my old roller blading partner around the block, and my wondrous daughter. Thank you, Maddi, for these fabulous visual images and our profound discussions about science, self, and life! Maddi's brother, Alex Siegel, has composed a musical library that was my auditory source of inspiration and creativity during the writing of this book during these several years. Over the decades since these two were born, our family conversations with Maddi and Alex, and their grandmother, Sue, have filled our lives with illuminating explorations of these ideas about what and who we truly are and where our wider human family might go in these challenging times.

My extended personal family members, Jason Siegel and Alice Davis, Jamie Davis-Siegel and Erin Siegel, Katherine, Sean, Phoebe, Lexi and Dylan Eskovitz, and family-by-choice Jenny Lorant and Ken, Lily and Leo Grouf, are an endless source of family fun and connection in this journey of life. My sister-by-choice, Diane Ackerman, has been a writing soulmate for years, and I thank her for her continual reminder to me of the challenge of birthing a book into the world. I also am grateful for the friendship and professional support in the nurturing of these *IntraConnected* ideas from a wonderful group of colleagues: Doug and Rachel Abrams, Lou Cozolino, Elissa Epel, Dacher Keltner, Jack Kornfield and Trudy Goodman Kornfield, Joanna Macy, Sally Maslansky, and my MWe Council faMWely members.

My life and work partner, Caroline Welch, has been a steadfast supporter over the four decades of our life together. Professionally, we are supported at the Mindsight Institute by a fabulous team including Kristi Morelli, Ashish Soni, Andrew Schulman, and Jane Daily. Together, our mission is to make the mindsight work of interpersonal neurobiology accessible online and in person to a diverse audience from around the world. Our motto, "Integration made visible is Kindness and Compassion" reminds me every day of the work we need to do in the world to synthesize science and find practical applications to help the world become more integrative while connecting with the ancient wisdom of our Indigenous and contemplative traditions.

At home, as well as at work, Caroline is a constant reminder by example of how to live fully in the present moment and to consider each day, as our dear family friend, poet, and philosopher John O'Donohue would say, as a mystical gift—to honor the thresholds of sunrise and sunset as the bookends of a precious life for which we can be deeply grateful. We all miss him dearly. I thank John for our friendship and hope he would have enjoyed the journey of this book as a way of making the "invisible visible" as I hope you have, or soon will, as well.

SYNOPSIS

Weaving the internal and external, the subjective and objective, *IntraConnected* reveals how the wiring in our brain, as well as the messages of modern culture, may reinforce a way of living and a belief system based on the view that our fundamental nature is one of independence, of separation—a life to be lived as a solo, isolated self. Yet a wider perspective, revealed in new views of contemporary science and echoed by the wisdom of generations of Indigenous and contemplative traditions, unveils that who we are, our deeper reality, may actually be something more than isolated individuals interacting with one another—one's mind and the experience of self it creates are broader than the brain, bigger than the body: Each are fundamental to the social systems and the natural world in which we live. Investigating the nature of how our experience of what we often call "self" and of how the related experiences of identity and belonging emerge across the lifespan, from twinkle to twilight, this exploration combines personal reflections, lessons from contemplation and Indigenous knowledge, and findings from immersive meditative practices with scientific discussions of how the mind, brain, and relationships shape who we are and who we can become. Our body-based self—the origin of a Me—is not only connected to others but also connected within these relational worlds themselves: a We, forming the essence of belonging and a broader sense of self that forms our identity. Who we are is both within and between: Me plus We equals MWe, the reality of an integrative wholeness of our intra-connected lives.

IntraConnected

WELCOME

Belonging in the world—feeling membership, an experience of joining in our connections with people around us and with
nature—is shaped by our identity, the defining features of our center of experience of being alive, our sense of self. I invite you to join
me in the conversational journey of this book, a way we con-verse or
"together-turn" our attention in exploring the experience of becoming
who we are—how we develop a sense of self, identity, and belonging.

But what exactly is this self truly made of?

A range of scientific approaches to this question leads to a suggestion that the term "self" generally refers to how we experience the
subjective sensations of being alive, the perspective we have on the
world, and the agency we assert in shaping our behavior and interactions. When we use the term "self," we broadly mean our sensation,
perspective, and agency.

Yet there are many approaches other than science for exploring
reality. Science is a term we use to generally denote a rigorous way
humans observe patterns in the world and create hypotheses about
what that world is like. In Western science, we test those ideas with
experimental paradigms to challenge our viewpoints and confirm, or
disprove, our proposals on the nature of nature; on the way reality
functions. I have been trained in the Western educational system,
as a scientist as well as a physician, and this "scientific method" of

hypothesis-testing and refutation has been the foundation for what I've learned as a researcher and clinician. Some of these Western scientific explorations of what the self is involve heated debates, animated discussions that will naturally continue, about the nature of who we are—about what the "self" is. We won't be solving these disagreements here, but will, hopefully, find a way to build on the disparate insights in helpful ways.

In their breadth across a range of disciplines, from neuroscience and psychology to anthropology and philosophy, these Western perspectives contain an array of empirical and theoretical approaches to identity and belonging, as exemplified by academics such as Baumeister (1998), Breger (1974), Clark (2016), Damasio (2010, 2018), Godrey-Smith (2016), Kegan (1982, 1994), Kelly (1995), Markus and Sentis (1982), Marsella, DeVos, and Hsu (1985), and Stern (1985). While we will build on these scientific foundations, this will not be a discursive academic review; however, it is an invitation to build on fields of knowledge to find their common ground, illuminate relevant implications, and then suggest practical applications for how we might come to live in more generative, health-promoting ways in contemporary times. While we will draw on the overall insights of these various scientific explorations in our conversation here, we will build a framework that incorporates many other perspectives as well, with the intention of engaging in a discussion about who we are, individually and as a human family, and where we might choose to go in the immediate future. With consciousness opened up to these ideas, choice can become possible. It is my hope that joining together in this immersive exploration will give us a foundation for intentionally shaping our experience of self, identity, and belonging in ways that enable us to thrive in this wondrous world we all share.

This Western bias of my training has also naturally shaped how I have been practicing as a psychotherapist for over thirty-five years. While looking for answers from science and medicine was a place to start, my search needed to be expanded by turning to wisdom traditions and immersive experiences of helping others as distinct but equally important "ways of knowing" about the nature of our lives.

Within the human endeavor to make sense of the world, non-Western approaches to a disciplined way of understanding reality—including forms of Indigenous science in the careful observation of nature as well as contemplative insights from extensive meditative practices into the nature of the mind—offer important perspectives on the world and how life unfolds. These disciplined ways of studying reality may not use the Western hypothesis-testing approach and peer review process, but they offer crucial and distinct ways of rigorously observing and exploring the nature of our world—and of our "self."

In these pursuits of understanding of this self, known as Dan, I have come to appreciate that our sense of self sometimes becomes distorted and misleads, constricts, and limits our well-being in life. Our subjective sensations may become filled with suffering experienced as chaos and rigidity; our perspective limited or distorted by filters beyond our awareness; our agency hampered by paralysis or overwhelmed by impulsivity.

In modern times, an experience of self—what is sometimes called a "sense of self"—that is defined only by our individual body as a center of identity and belonging can lead to the sadly common experience of disconnection, disillusionment, and despair. The ensuing anxiety, depression, and even suicidal thoughts and behavior are painful outcomes that are steadily increasing in our modern societies. But if you, like me, live within a culture that subscribes to this perspective of "identity equals body," isn't the "self" truly based solely in this bodily center? Akin to the statement that the mind is only the activity of the brain, questioning self as body alone is often not even a part of our inquiries into the nature of life. It is a modern construction, rarely challenged, that the individual is the center of self-experience. It may even seem inevitable, through this particular lens on identity, to say that our sensations, perspective, and agency come only from an individual, bodily source.

If you live in a modern culture, when you ask who or where or what you are, you likely point to your body, or perhaps your head, and say, "Here I am. This is me." You might ask, from this common vantage point of contemporary life, how else would we see what the self is other than the individual? Yet by understanding the true nature of ourselves and how our identities and belonging actually can be expanded beyond the body as a center of sensation, perspective, and agency, we come to a wider view of how we are in fact connected with one another as human beings and within nature as members of a broader belonging, an identity that is integrated with more of the world than the body alone, a self that is a part of a synergy of systems much bigger than the individual. It is the hope of this journey, *IntraConnected*, that together we can transform our experiences from disconnection to connection and come to live a healthier, fuller, freer life, with enhanced personal flourishing, public health, and even with shared planetary well-being.

A tall order, you may think—to move from the experience of an individual's identity to the health of life on Earth. But consider this: When we examine how the actions of our human family are influencing so many aspects of living systems on this precarious and precious planet upon which we live, from the impact of human endeavors on our shared air, water, and land to the social injustices and racism rampant in our civilization to the loss of fellow species with whom we share our biosphere, we can see that those consequences are each driven by the human mind. And it is this mind—so rarely defined yet so profoundly influential—that is at the heart of how well-being, or suffering, arises in our lives. I've spent the last four decades obsessed with questions of what the mind is and what makes for a healthy mind. This focus on self, identity, and belonging is a natural extension and application of this exploration to some of the most pressing challenges we face today: the health and flourishing of life on Earth.

These explorations of combining various ways of knowing into a common-ground framework called interpersonal neurobiology have led to the idea that well-being emerges when distinct aspects of our bodily lives, our relationships, and our planetary systems become linked together as an integrative, adaptive whole. We clearly define integration as the linkage of differentiated components of a system. When this system's components are interacting and interdependent in their flow, the system is called complex and has self-organizing features that include being adaptive and able to learn. These complex systems, as we'll explore throughout our journey, are within the body and its brain, within families and communities, and within all the ecosystems that form the intricate personal, social, and natural environments in which we live—these inner and inter sources of our experience of identity and belonging, our experience of self, shape our lives and are, in turn, shaped by us.

We are all busy in our lives, so in this book, I'll try to be as succinct as possible; I'll put a suggestion or an idea we can ponder together upfront, then follow that with support for, or background on, that notion. Here is one for us to start with: A complex system is composed of interacting parts, often called nodes, and each node interacts with other nodes via their linkages. This is how the system functions. If a node functions as if it is the totality of its identity, that it belongs only to its nodal part in the system, it will behave in a disconnected way, interdependence will shut down, and the whole complex system will lose its ability to adapt and learn. Its self-organization toward harmony will be compromised, and instead the system will move toward chaos or rigidity. If the human mind has constructed a view of the self as separate, it may be that the body (a node) has come to identify itself as the whole self—rather than the self also including the whole of the systems in which that node (the body) exists. In medicine, when this happens to renegade cells in the body that grow without regard to the complex living somatic system, we call it cancer.

In the journey we are undertaking together, as you, in the body with your inner identity, read this book and I, in this body, write it, we will explore how these systems shape our identity and belonging across the human lifespan. I'll be inviting you to reflect on your own experience, to differentiate and define it, and then link it to what I'll be sharing with you from my own personal reflections. We'll also be differentiating and then linking various ideas and ways of knowing as we distinguish them and then connect them to one another—as we integrate them. We'll be drawing on a range of ways of knowing, seeking out the consilience, or overlap, across these often-distinct approaches to making sense of reality to reveal the ways of living that support not confusion or constriction but a generative, health- and connection-promoting outcome—ways by which we can honor the complexity of what we experience as self, identity, and belonging and enable these to develop in a positive, integrative direction.

Challenge and Opportunity

We live in remarkable times and face many challenges to our well-being that can often feel overwhelming and insurmountable. It's not uncommon these days to hear people describe a sense of despair and hopelessness when facing the social injustices and environmental destruction that surround us. Yet this challenging moment in the history of life on Earth, of humanity and of all nature, also provides an opportunity, a motivation for us to reimagine how we might live, individually and as a human and nature family on Earth, in ways that actually might serve as collective inspiration for growth. In this book I invite you to join me in asking the fundamental questions of what self, identity, and belonging truly are. Then we will be in a position to ask, "What has gone wrong and how can this be changed?" so that we might illuminate how the modern pathway has strayed from what we—individually, humans collectively, and the natural world—need to be and do to live as sustainable, generative systems on Earth. I invite you to explore, express, and then consider ways to engage your selves, your identities, and your belonging in fundamental changes that will promote health on our planet.

If the human mind is responsible for the difficulties we now face, then the human mind can be responsible for the awareness of these conditions and the actions that are possible to transform a destructive path into a constructive one. This is how we can transform challenge into opportunity. While in this moment we might feel despair and hopelessness, guilt and confusion, we can work together, with knowledge and skills, to move beyond these states of paralysis and fear into ones of choice and change. We can learn to dance with challenge rather than dread it.

The human mind is open to growth across the lifespan. And it is the mind that creates human culture. If modern culture has been creating a distorted, constricting, and unhelpful notion of self, this may be the mental construct our minds, now awakened to this error, need to change. Cultural evolution proceeds much more rapidly than genetic evolution; we have the potential to make the urgent changes we need to make if we can accurately identify the issues at play and the helpful practices we can now enact to transform how we live in the world. If how we have constructed what the self is, what our identity and belonging are based upon, is the source of many of the troubles we now face—then we can now change this pattern and move in a more integrative pathway forward.

The mind shapes belonging, identity, and self. If we clarify the mental lens through which we see the self and deepen our understanding of identity and belonging, we may be able to shift how we live and then create a path that cultivates more personal, public, and planetary health for us all. We are proposing that many of the challenges to global health we now experience in multiple ways across humanity—what can be called pandemics, a term that means involving all people, something affecting humanity—are caused by a limited and limiting view of "self."

One form of pandemic we currently face is infectious disease—COVID-19, caused by the novel coronavirus SARS-CoV-2. But many pandemics affect us now. Another pandemic we face today is social injustice: the dehumanization and marginalization that emerges from in-group domination over out-groups that are subordinate in the social hierarchy. A third pandemic is environmental destruction: we now live in the Anthropocene era, when human activity is having devastating consequences for life on Earth and the environments that sustain us. A fourth pandemic is of misinformation and polarization, made rampant with the internet's capacity to create self-sustaining bubbles of isolated information sharing. A fifth pandemic is of attention addiction, the draw of our attentional focus toward compelling states of endless comparison and competition and the ensuing feeling of inadequacy, inferiority, and incompleteness.

And there is a sixth pandemic, one addressed in great depth in the pages that follow: the modern cultural, or what some might call Western, view of an isolated, separate identity—the solo-self. While this perspective may have originated in the West—in European-originated colonialist nations—it has now spread around the globe so extensively that a geographical indicator may no longer apply to this wide-spread cultural construction of self. This solo-self is not just the inner, private aspect of who we are but rather the concept and belief that the totality of our identity is separate from others, especially other, not "like-me" people, as well as separate from other nonhuman species—apart from nature. The consequences of this excessively differentiated identity and the disconnection from belonging that it creates are responsible for much suffering, both as the chaos and rigidity we may experience internally and as turmoil in our relational lives—states that arise from a nonintegrated way of being in the world. By "relational," I mean the way the bodily, inner self is connected to other people and to the planet, the whole of nature. These connections, involving patterns in the exchange of energy and information, may not be as visible to the eye as is the body, but they are equally real. When we live as a solo-self and ignore these important yet invisible connections, we experience our identity as centered predominantly in the body, and we feel relationally connected only to those who are like-me.

This solo-self pandemic, one of the main topics of our journey, clearly has a negative impact on each of the other five pandemics—and may be a fundamental source of them. In this book, we will explore the nature of our modern experience of separation, of the solo-self, and then consider pathways that offer the potential for large and lasting positive impacts on how we construct our sense of self, identity, and belonging that can help us in our individual, interpersonal, and planetary lives as citizens on Earth.

This is the mission of our journey. If this is something that intrigues you, if it is something that feels compelling and relevant to your life and to your work, I hope you will find the expedition ahead meaningful, interesting, and useful.

The solo-self is our mind's construction; it develops through key developmental milestones, alongside and within us, as we mature and move out into the world. For this reason, in this book we will take a lifespan approach to these foundational aspects of our lives and how they emerge as we examine how we might turn these challenges into opportunities for growth to harness ways to develop a more helpful experience of self in the world. Windows of change in human development are not only moments of vulnerability but potential invitations for transformation in life. This is true for both our individual lives and for this collective moment of upheaval in how our modern societies are evolving. The acronym VUCA has been used to refer, initially by the military and later by journalists, to the volatile, uncertain, complex, and ambiguous nature of the times we live in. It is understandable that anxiety, despair, and depression can arise from the challenges these VUCA conditions present. But we can find a path to transform those increasingly present reactive states into more receptive modes of being as we move, together, toward a healthier way of living. In many ways, this is how we can "get our acts together" in both meanings of that phrase—to awaken our minds individually to the importance of liberating a more integrative sense of self, and to collaborate in facing the shared challenges ahead by addressing the fundamental mental processes at their root.

Social activist and author Bryan Stevenson has stated in his film, *Just Mercy*, that "Hopelessness is the enemy of justice." And we can state the corollary of that wisdom: Hope is the steward of justice. When we aim to shape our individual and cultural evolution, reflect on the nature of self, have agency, work together and follow a pathway with a purpose, we generate hope and cultivate positive changes in the world. Challenge becomes an opportunity for learning and growing together.

If the perspective of the solo-self—the concept and belief that the totality of one's identity is separate from others, or others who are not like-us—is indeed at the root of many of the difficulties we now face, we can harness the potential of our individual and collective minds to construct our experience of self in a broader and more integrative way to cultivate lasting positive change.

Language Can Liberate

It may be helpful to reflect briefly on the terminology regarding what has been named the "modern" societal view of a solo-self. In the study of cultures, group dynamics, information processing, brain function- ing, and even physics, we discover that, broadly speaking, we can view reality by focusing on its component parts, and we can see real- ity as comprised of the relationships among these parts. While it may sound simplistic to divide our human perspectives in this way, it is consistent with much of what researchers see, and it is a useful place to start identifying differences in how we construct not only our per- ceptions of the world, but also the belief systems and ways of living that follow those views of reality.

If our goal is to clarify how we tend to perceive the world, we will be able to see opportunities clearly and make conscious choices to act and move forward in life as members of a truly global family if we have an intraconnected sense of self, identity, and belonging. Using words in a book is a challenge in that these linguistic symbols—how we communicate in this literary format—are themselves limiting; on the other hand, words can be liberating. They are limiting in that they become static terms, printed in a format that sometimes is not rela- tionally engaging, open, or receptive to change. Yet words can free us to name something and then see it, together, in a frame of perception that gives us the power to change how we have been living, should we choose to make such intentional changes, individually or even col- lectively as a modern human culture. Cultural evolution is driven by such changes in perception, belief, and ways of living.

In putting language to perception, belief, and behavior, we can say that when we narrow our focus of attention to the parts of a system, we are "reducing" reality to parts rather than seeing the whole. In this way, we are "analyzing"—literally down-breaking (ana-lyzing); or breaking down—the whole to study its components. That reduc- tionist view, or what some might call a linear perspective, has great utility even though, if taken as the totality of reality, it can be quite limiting. Taking a linear perspective, we may lose the context of a moment and instead see only the separate part or parts. In contrast, we can also have a wide perspective, take a more contextual view, and see the relationships among the parts, and even focus on the patterns of how those relationships reveal an interdependence in their interactions. Perceiving patterns of interactions is part of what can be called a systems view—in contrast to a nonsystems, or linear perspective. Some would say that a nonlinear, contextual, systems view reveals how something emerges from the interactions that is greater than the sum of the parts— a synergy arises, like the wetness of water that is not experienced with individual molecules of water. The mathematical study of complex systems reveals that emergence is a fundamental part of nonlinear, chaos-capable, open systems. Such complex systems have diverse parts, connections among those components, and interdependence of the parts to one another, and from these features arise the self-organizing, emergent processes of adaptation and learning.

With the human brain's processing of energy flow into information, we do see these wholistic, contextual, pattern-recognizing, relationally focused systems perceptions unfolding in different neural network calculations than the individualistic, noncontextual, detail-driven perspective of separation. These distinctions in neural processing may help us understand how such different worldviews—one of systems or one of separation—may be held in mind with a purity and conviction that make the belief system have a sense of completion; of being true and the whole story. This distinction may offer insight into the contrast of the separate-parts perspective of modern Western medicine and science compared to a wider view of consciousness and mind as emergent aspects of complex systems. One worldview sees the identity of the part as fundamentally complete, a closed system; the other perceives a part as one aspect of a set of deeply interwoven relational connections, an open system. Some researchers would cringe at the suggestion that these distinct perceptual frameworks occur in completely separate areas, on one side of the brain or the other; others would concur that there truly are distinct "modes" of perception, wherever their neural processing occurs. With perceptual mechanisms that appear dominant on the right side of the human cortex, we can suggest that a "right mode" of information processing sees the context and relational connections whereas a "left mode" narrowly focuses in on details of the parts. Both modes have an important role to play in being in the world and each contribute to a way of living with wholeness. The key is to differentiate them and link them both—to integrate them—so that a synergy arises and the self-organizational capacity for seeing both the parts and the whole emerges. In this way, we can highlight the importance of integrating these two distinct ways of knowing as one of a narrow, closed, disconnected, independent, individualistic view compared to that of a wide, open, connected, interdependent, collectivistic perspective. They are distinct modes of perceiving, however they may be constructed within the brain, and likely underly the different modes of constructing the experience of self.

You can choose whichever terms most resonate with your way of understanding things at this moment in our journey, and this may change as we move along in our conversation. Some might see the disconnected, closed perspective as dominating the "Western" view of what is historically termed a colonialist, settler stance; this is in contrast to the knowledge of Indigenous peoples and their practices along with the independent discoveries of the contemplative perspectives of what some might call an "Eastern" point of view. I once presented a question using this East versus West terminology in a meeting with His Holiness, the Dalai Lama, who then vehemently—but mindfully—pushed back and urged me not to use what, in his view, was an outdated and no longer appropriate geographical distinction given the influence of this "modern" thinking on those in both the western and eastern parts of the planet. For this reason, I'll use the term "modern" to indicate this narrow focus of attention on individual parts in contrast to the contemplative or Indigenous perspectives that broadly focus on the relationships among the parts: contrasting the mental construction of a closed, separated, disconnected view of reality with one of an open, systems, connected sense of the world.

Separation and systems; disconnection and connection; closed and open: Each are important in our lives. The deep dive into the details enabled by a narrow focus of our attention can yield much about the world, allowing us to analyze a virus, for example, and decipher its nucleic acid composition to construct a vaccine to protect billions of lives. The narrow focus of the left mode is vital for living in our world. The wide perspective of our right mode lends a distinct but equally important way of perceiving aspects of reality. A broad, systems view, however it is processed neurologically, enables us to perceive patterns in systems and reveals, for example, how marginalized individuals are unjustly impacted by not only the effects of a viral pandemic, but also the impact of environmental degradation. These systems perspectives can empower us to see the interdependent whole and how we, individually and together, can then act to create a flourishing and fair world for all.

I'll be speaking directly to you throughout the pages ahead, inviting you to reflect on how you sense, perceive, and act on issues related to your own experience of self, identity and belonging as we move along. Hopefully our sharing these ideas will help us draw on both a narrow and wide focus of our attention and the language we use will liberate us to create the life we then can consciously choose. In order for me to be fully present in this experience too, I'll try to offer my own reflections on these experiences as we go along, with the intention of inviting you to be fully present in this exploration as well. Once, language left me, and my own experience of self was shattered the summer just before my twentieth birthday.

Losing to Loosen: Personal Identity

The experiences of me, this person called Dan—the person who is typing these words as your companion along the journey of this book—began in the cultural setting of the United States in the second half of the twentieth century. I am struggling now between writing "I" in the first-person way, to speak of "my" experience, or as "Dan," in the third-person perspective, as if you and I could refer to him and "his" experience. Let's start with the third-person perspective here, and then switch back to first-person after this initial exploration. Dan was born in a body with an XY chromosomal make-up, a genetic male, and happened to identify mentally as male, so one might call him "cisgender"; Dan had a heterosexual orientation—he was sexually attracted to females—and had pale skin, and in this way was identified with the mental and social construction of race often known as white. Dan was born into a social context that had the features of the dominant grouping, a privileged position in the United States in which he felt his identity—a white, heterosexual, cisgender male, born into a middle class family—was accepted. The family and body that Dan was born into—the context, the "positionality" of this person called Dan—and the fact that his identity aligned with where he was situated, meant that he did not need to think about his position in society nor whether it might limit anything he might wish to do. That is privilege.

Right at this moment, inside this body, is such a push to avoid using words like I, me, or my. It feels as if these words contradict one of the premises of our journey: the importance of a broader, intraconnected sense of MWe. Yet to embrace the integrated components of me and of we, the differentiation of each is necessary—and so it now begins to feel right to offer a first-person perspective on self, identity, and belonging and see where MWe can go with that. Moving back now to a first-person perspective, I thank you for being together in this exploration and invite you to reflect on your on positionality in life and the social worlds in which you grew and now live.

I was a child filled with curiosity and wonder about our world, excited as much to be with people as I was with the various animals and plants that populated our backyard. After public primary and secondary school—in which my proclivity toward dance and my aversion to competitive sports may have made me not fit in with the expectations of a young American boy, my empowerment to act on these preferences demonstrated my privilege: I was accepted when I applied to enter the girls' modern dance class in high school. I attended a private university (where my father was a college professor and my mother had received her master's degree in education before becoming a vice principal at my high school—after I left). So, you can see we were and are an educated clan, filled with ideas and trained in modernity through the lens of Western education. This is the positionality and the perspective on reality in which I grew. My experience of self, my sensation, perspective, and agency (which I like to refer to as my "SPA of self" to readily recall these core components) was shaped by the context of the culture in which I was born and raised. In a position of privilege, I never felt that my identity would limit how I might pursue what had meaning in my life.

Just as in my earlier education, in college I did well academically, learning in a linear, reductionistically-oriented way how to analyze, from the viewpoint of Western science, the components of whatever topic we were focusing on in narrow detail. I'm sure that mental exercise activated my left mode a great deal. I majored in biochemistry and did my honors research on chemical reactions in fish that enabled them to move to their new saltwater surroundings after hatching in freshwater. While the larger question was "How does this species of fish survive in the new, oceanic world?", the work focused on how an oxygen molecule was added to a trimethylamine molecule by an enzyme, which we were desperate to find in the kidneys and liver... and did. But even in the excitement of that linear expedition where details about the molecules mattered, I had a nagging feeling that there was something more, a bigger picture view. With that burning curiosity filling my belly, I took a tai chi chuan class, studying how the symbolic movement of this ancient dynamic mindfulness practice could embody the philosophical principles of Taoist thought; at the same time, I worked on a nighttime suicide prevention hotline and joined the ballroom dance team. But even with all those attempts to broaden my experience in college, likely trying to access and exercise my right mode to balance out my life, I had the painful feeling of not belonging at the school or with my fellow students. The predominant thought seemed to be, find a job that pays well and move along. Something didn't feel quite right; and perhaps that, too, was my privilege, to even question that commonly accepted line of thinking. I was intensely doubting what I was told, and I tended to question everything, which bothered teachers a bit, I imagined, and seemed to alienate me from many of my classmates.

Where did I belong in life? Ever since I became a teenager, I felt I belonged by the side of the creek, way up in the canyons carved through the hills of West Hollywood, miles from my small Spanish style home in the flats of Los Angeles, where I lived with my parents and brother, who was three years older than I. Even before I was an adolescent, when I was out in nature, I felt deeply relaxed and at home. I identified as a living being and felt the animals and plants were my siblings. Though I knew I was a person, not a mushroom or mulberry bush or mouse, I simply felt at home with the newts and birds along that creekside more than I did with the teenagers in junior high or with my high school or college classmates later on. I loved all living things, including people; I just felt disconnected from my peers and didn't quite understand how to engage in the social setups that seemed to dominate adolescent life. I was so fascinated with the world and living beings that I chose to study biochemistry after high school. My love for fish landed me a research assistantship looking for that enzyme that let them survive their development from river to sea. I suppose on some level I was looking for answers to questions I couldn't even articulate then: how we live in one state, and then how we survive the transition from that state to where we are growing toward—the fundamental question of development. My son, Alex Siegel, composed a song called "Good Leg" that expresses this sentiment exactly: "I had too many questions for all the answers I was told." In many ways, this is what our conversation is about—how do we grow and change in changing times?

In college as a biology student, I took a class on video ethnography—studying other cultures through the lens of documentary film. I was fascinated to become immersed, even at a distance, in the various world views and ways of living that the human mind could construct in the different social settings that we call society and culture. I was so inspired by the anthropology teacher of that course that I chose to sign up for a summer project with him to study the impact of modernization on the Indigenous cultures in rural Mexico. The

Miguel Aleman Dam was to be expanded, and the loss of land and livelihood for the local people in the surrounding villages was of concern to the United Nations and its World Health Organization. I was intrigued by my teacher's invitation to leave the safety of the classroom, to go out and live in another culture. Under my professor's leadership, a group of us went to study various aspects of community life in Mexico. My team focused on health care—we were to investigate the healing practitioners and how they interacted within the medical care system of the region. We arrived and met in Tuxtepec, a large town hundreds of miles south of the huge metropolis of Mexico City, and then two of us on the "folk healer" team—a colleague from the UN and I—were transported to a small village, dozens of miles away, deep in the foothills of the mountains that divide the country down the middle, with the Pacific Ocean to the west and the Gulf of Mexico to the east.

The hills were glistening green, summer just arriving in this old community in which people from the Zapotec and Chinantec cultures lived together peacefully. I found the local village health center, which was run by a Western medical doctor from Mexico City. I interviewed this physician and several of the foot doctors, as they called them: local members of the community who served the roles of paramedics and nurse practitioners. My next task was to investigate how the dam's influences had interfaced with the more traditional approach to medical care, the curanderos or folk healers, since the dam was constructed.

One healer, La Reina de los Hongos, the queen of the mushrooms, was widely known and lived a few mountain ridges away in the neighboring state of Oaxaca; we arranged to borrow some local horses to make our way to interview her the next day. At around five in the morning, a band started playing outside our window—a group of musicians entertaining the farmers who would come weekly for a local market. By six in the morning, it was time to rustle out of bed, have some eggs and chorizo for breakfast, and then head out to the horse ranch down the road to get set up to set out for our trip to see the mushroom queen.

I remember seeing the three horses they brought out from the corral. My UN colleague and the fifteen-year-old boy from our house took the first two, older and larger, horses; I got on the smaller, younger horse, and off we went. When we left the main road and headed up into the hills, I saw a wide trail, flat at first, bordered on one side by the lush brush and on the other, a ravine. I recall the excitement of the adventure, loving being back on a horse, going on a journey of discovery. Our young companion yelled out, "Vamanos!" And away we went.

The next thing I remember is the image of a large syringe, which the medical director was holding up to my face, and being in the clinic that I was studying. The doctor laughed and said, in Spanish, that I could get some gold teeth to fill in where my teeth had been broken, and they would try to fix my nose and repair my arm.

I would later piece together, from what the doctor said and then what my colleague told me, that while my horse was at a full gallop, the saddle loosened and my whole body turned to the horse's belly, and he apparently ran even faster then, with my feet caught in the stirrups and dragging my head across the stones that lined the road, for over a hundred yards. They thought I must be dead—or, when they heard my moans, that I had at least broken my neck with all the banging along the rock-strewn path.

I did break some bones and lose some teeth, which ultimately got fixed up. But I also lost something that sparked a lifelong shift for me: I had broken my sense of personal identity—I had no idea who I was! And I had no idea what anything was! For about the next twenty-four hours, although I was wide awake and I could eat and drink (even past the broken teeth and swollen face), I was immersed in a wordless world.

I remember being served a meal that day in the back room of the clinic that they had set up for recovery. The round object that I now call a plate shimmered at its edges. The colors of what I'd now call vegetables were bursting from their origins—reds were red gone wild, greens melted into purple hues. Their flavors were hilarious, intense, almost shouting out with a music of taste, texture, and smell. The water was wet, filling the mouth, smooth going down into the body. Resting there, feeling a fullness, sitting back just watching the colors streaming through the window—dots, then lines, that for some unknown reason made laughter arise. And you might think that, with all these injuries, I'd feel pain, but somehow I felt joy. It's hard to describe this now, but for those twenty-four hours things just . . . happened—things were just things being things, happenings happening.

I recall, after a dozen or so hours, asking my UN partner who I was. It's strange now to write this, but how could I even know there was someone to be known if I no longer had an "I" that had a name as knower? Whatever allowed that state to exist, I kept repeating the question, "Who am I?" I recall that my companions didn't think this was amusing at all, just confusing for them—and they had the patience to tell me: "You are Dan. You had an accident. You will be okay." And then, moments or minutes or hours later, I'd ask the same question again and receive their same patient response, but it just didn't seem to sink in.

That is, until the next morning. I woke up back in the room where I'd been staying, with light streaming through the same windows where, early the morning before, the local musicians had woken me up before that ill-fated horseback ride. "Ill-fated or a gift?" I wonder now. I once again had the experience of knowing my name: Dan. And I could recall the history of who I'd been, how I got to Mexico, and a bit of what they told me had happened beneath the horse's belly.

But when I got back home, I wasn't the same. Researchers would later discover the role of a circuitry located mostly at the midline of the brain: the default mode network, or DMN. It is possible that the repeated knocking of my head against the stones along the path temporarily shut down this integrative network, disallowing any constructive, sense-making efforts of my life narrative. Studies would later reveal that there is a mutual inhibition between these midline "me" circuits and the side sensory channels of the brain: The more we let go of the preoccupations with personal identity, the more we are open to the free flow of sensation. We also later learned that both mindfulness meditation and certain medical interventions, such as the careful and controlled use of psychedelics, can promote a sense of connection and awe and also markedly reduce the DMN's activity, even when it has been overly active, as in states of depression and anxiety. Having a family member who suffered from addiction, I had a psychological "allergy" to the use of any mind-altering substances. But through this accident of being dragged over the rocks, I guess you could say I had accidentally fallen into my own version of getting "stoned."

IntraConnected

After that head injury, I somehow had a more open sense of who "I" was—a sense of self that felt more fluid, more flexible and receptive to things that arose in my unfolding life, and that strangely felt freer, more present, more connected to whatever was going on. Perhaps it is more accurate to say that I had a different sense of who I wasn't: The name, Dan, almost felt like a joke if it was how others, or my now opened sense of self, would try to indicate the totality of my identity—of who I was. After my bones and teeth were repaired, I may have looked the same from the outside, but inside there was a kind of freedom that for decades I would attribute to some quirk of a knock on the head, or perhaps some existential "wake-up call" to live life with less worry and fewer preoccupations after nearly escaping more serious injury, or death.

I went on to finish college, and then attended another private institution of higher learning, Harvard Medical School. There I continued the life of privilege that comes with having a body with the features of a white, cisgendered, heterosexual male, journeying a life further down the road of living without worry about my identities of gender, sexual orientation, or race. Even in the positionality of my education, I had the opportunities of privilege—being trained, now, to become a physician at an esteemed research institution. Whatever blind spots I inevitably had from such a position of privilege, I was blind to them; I had, and still have, blind spots for my blind spots—the ultimate challenge of not being challenged because one identifies with the majority.

Yet even in this situation, I still felt I didn't belong. Perhaps the lack of focus on our inner mental life of that medical culture made me feel even more alienated. As I would describe later in several books, including *Mindsight* and *Mind: A Journey to the Heart of Being Human*, after my second year I dropped out of medical school because of this feeling that something just wasn't quite right. I didn't think much about that horse accident back in Mexico, but as I share this with you now, that shift in a sense of personal identity likely underlay that restless feeling I had that something did not feel real, did not quite fit with the deeper reality beneath the surface of how people seemed to be going about living their lives. After considering a number of alternative professional pathways, from salmon fishing to dance, and coming back to Los Angeles to reflect on where life had brought me, I decided to return to my medical training. I made up the term "mindsight" to help me remember that the subjective life of our mind is quite real and very important. Perhaps with that word in place, I'd be empowered to not cave in to the pressure to conform to what seemed to be a mindsightless world of medicine at the time.

After medical school, I trained initially in pediatrics—pursuing my interests in human development—and then switched over to psychiatry to deepen my understanding of being human, how the mind shapes our sense of self, and how we become who we are. Years later, I would join up with a team that was studying how to develop a "systems awareness" and move beyond the linear, narrow, disconnected way I had been trained to think in college and medical school. One outing of that group was a week-long field trip out in nature.

High up in Colorado's Rocky Mountains, John P. Milton's "Way of Nature" program offered an exploration of Indigenous wisdom teachings from around the world, combined with discussions of nature and our relationship with the environment. As part of this experience, we spent several days in silence, each of us in our own isolated spot along the mountain trail. During this time I experienced the sense that my separate, personal identity had vanished—the sensory flow of the water of the creek, the wind through the leaves, the sun, the clouds, the turning of day to night, I experienced all of this as a flowing whole, and this bodily self that was called Dan was only one aspect of the totality of the identity that was somehow much bigger than the body and that encompassed the trees, the creek, the clouds, and the whole of the flow of reality.

In stark contrast, sometime the next morning as I was in that blissful state, a colleague trotted by and exclaimed, "Hi Dan!" In an instant, my personal identity swooped back in, along with a shift in feeling that my body was now an isolated container of "my" experience. Although I cherished the prior silence, when I envisioned him disturbing our other colleagues further down the trail, I decided to use my voice and called out, waving him back. I reminded him of the rules—no contact with others, no communication, and no leaving our separate, designated camping areas.

For most of the rest of that day, my sense of being isolated from the forest, from nature, remained—until the sun hit the tops of the distant trees. The rays poured through their waving leaves, and the glorious rainbow of colors filtered into dances with the wind; the gurgling of the small waterfall at the creek's edge became woven with the sounds of the breeze; the light slowly dimmed as the sun set, and the stars appeared—expanding the sense of being across space, across time. And the feeling of just being there, just being, remained for the rest of the time. It was, truly, a time of rest from the exhausting illusion of separation that living as a solo-self can often be in our modern, everyday lives.

When those enchanting, awe-filled days came to an end, I wandered back down the trail to join our group as we came together to share our experiences. Instead of feeling alone, for each of us, the independent experience felt more like "all-one." The trees, the sky, the water of the flowing creek, these were not separate from identity—these were who we were in those days at one with the world. Though terms like "interdependent," "interconnected," "interrelated," "interbeing," "interactive," "interwoven," and "interlaced" are sometimes used to describe this way of being a fundamental part of nature, it was a struggle to find words to describe it that actually felt right.

Just days before that retreat in Colorado, I had been with a group in the Fishlake National Forest in Utah, where we became immersed in a grove of 47,000 quaking aspen (Populus tremuloides) trunks. These trunks—which on the surface appeared to be distinct, separate trees—were actually sprouting from a common root ball, that of a massive singular organism. DNA testing has revealed that these trunks are a single tree, commonly known as Pando, and it is among the largest, and oldest, living beings on Earth.

And so, as I tried to find words to express this experience of identity I had alone in the wilderness in Colorado, after the Pando immersion in Utah, the term that seemed to feel right was not "inter," as in betweenness, but "intra"—a withinness of identity and belonging, It was the feeling of being intraconnected, linked within a fabric of life—not a sense of a separate "me" that is connected to the trees, but rather a sense of connectedness within a whole.

I wouldn't find out, until I typed that word, "intraconnected," into a Word document and the word processor continually changed it to "interconnected," that it was, in fact, not a word in the English language. It's best to avoid creating new words unless we need them; and here it seemed we needed some term to capture the connectivity within the whole—and so the term "intraconnected" was born.

Over the many years since my accident, I had become deeply committed to understanding the nature of our minds and how a sense of self emerges in our lives to shape the experience we have of identity and belonging. The conversation I invite you to join me in within the pages of this book is an exploration of how we might come to discover, or perhaps recover, how to regain our sense of wholeness, how to live with a more integrated identity and a broader belonging than that of the contemporary, disconnected sense of solo-self, how to reclaim our intraconnected place in the world—how our sense of self can become intraconnected, linked within a fabric of life.

Certainty in Identity as Entity

My parents named me Daniel when I was born. They called me Danny, and in school my friends used that name, as did my teachers; but my driver's license had the birth certificate name Daniel and, later, so did my college degree and tax forms. I was rewarded for being certain: certain of my name, certain of how to spell words and how to add numbers, certain of how to repeat facts, grammar, science, history. Certainty must have aligned with my brain's reward circuitry, because it became an unquestioned place of familiarity and comfort.

Certainty also meant predictability and safety, so my deep survival circuits may have felt quite relieved, too, to have a firm name designating this certain belonging and identity, the certainty of a self I could rely on. This center of perception, this something we come to call "self," comes to have a name, a specific way to identify itself as an identity and in this way, in the drive to experience belonging, to become a member of some group in our environment.

Our brain is an anticipation machine, feeling safe in its capacity to predict what is likely to occur next. This brain seeks out patterns, extracting fundamental features of what we see. This "top-down" processing lets us learn from the past to shape what we anticipate will happen next, in the future, based on these patterns we've detected in the past, whereas our "bottom-up" processing more directly senses things as they are for us at this moment. From these bottom-up sensations, we construct myriad forms of perception and cognition—our thoughts, memories, and beliefs about the world. These constructions in turn exert top-down influence. In this way, we come to perceive what we believe, the result of the top-down layering of our mental constructions affecting how we experience reality.

The self can become one of these top-down constructions: We believe the self to be what we have learned it is, and this belief then shapes our perception of the self—our sense of self is based on what we believe it to be. This is called self-reinforcing (no pun intended).

If we learn to perceive the world with a narrow focus on the details of the individual only, our self will be constructed from this narrow view and will then be experienced as an entity—a separate thing, a noun. Not only will we experience our self as emanating from the body alone, but the "environment" in which our body exists may not be sensed as a living, breathing, broader source of belonging in which the self is intraconnected; instead we will perceive it as a container outside our self, and agency will not be in service of the welfare of that external container. Nature would not be included in how we would define or experience our self. If instead we learn to perceive the world from a broad focus of attention on the relationships among parts and on the patterns that emerge from these relational connections, then we'll experience a self that emerges from the systems in which we live: the body, the interpersonal relationships, the whole of nature. We'll have a subjective sensation, a perspective, and an agency—our SPA of self—centered in these layers of interacting systems, as unfolding, connected verb-like events, not as a noun-like separate entity, alone in a disconnected world. MWe are personal, public, and planetary.

In these ways, our perception of the world and construction of self are molded by what we've learned to anticipate and predict based on how we've come to focus our attention, narrow or broad. The self that is reinforced and repeatedly shaped by this narrow or broad attention is experienced as separated or as connected. From a view of the individual, I—my identity and the reference point of my belonging—am me, this body, this center of sensation, perception, and action which in modern culture we tend to have named as "self." Yet from the view of the system, I am the whole that this body is just a part of: the whole system is my self, the body only a node in that larger whole. If sensation, perception, and agency are the defining elements of what we are naming as self, then how do these become formed in our lives? This we will explore through the lens of human development. Here we can begin with the notion that the top-down, learned, constructive process is a self-forming and self-fulfilling way in which my experience of myself is construed, created, and perhaps at times constricted by the very anticipatory processes that reinforce their own predictions— they are self-organizing entities. How we construct this self will continually reinforce its own features, as isolated and disconnected, as an aspect of interdependent, interconnected systems, or perhaps as self being the intraconnected whole system of reality.

Let us, you and I, keep this question in mind: Is the sense of self always a construction? Is simply being, or simply being aware, a flowing experience of sensation, perception, and agency that is not constructive, but instead arises as a self-experience that emerges in a bottom-up manner? If this is true, then would this be a "true self" that sometimes lays hidden beneath a learned, top-down constructive mechanism? Was this the basis of the experience I described after the horse accident, and in the all-one time in the forest in Colorado: a losing of the top-down and a liberation of the bottom-up experience of self? Is a sense of an individual personal identity (in this case, a person named Dan) a top-down construction, and the experience of intraconnected wholeness of identity a more direct bottom-up realization?

If, instead, both the inner self and the inter self are each comprised of both a bottom up flow, as through a conduit we can name "conduition," as well as construction, so that the subjective sensation is a direct flow of conduition and the perception and agency are outcomes of construction—in both our internal flow and our relational flow—then we can see that self-experience has a constructive element to it. The fundamental question, then, is how can we construct the most integrative experience of self possible to promote well-being in our world?

One possibility is that a self-reinforcing loop becomes automatic, persistent, and tenacious as the top-down construction of a separate, personal identity. With such a separate identity, there is a quality of being contained in, controlled by, and enclosed within a cloak of individuality that has the qualities of predictability and stability, the qualities we attribute to entities that, in the English language, we might refer to as "nouns." There may even be a "holding-together" quality, a feeling of something being cohesive. This may be proposed to be the underlying origin of a solitary, separate solo-self. This sense of self has a solidity to it, the sense of being an entity, something with boundaries defining and surrounding it: a cohesive, separate, independent thing that we linguistically name as a noun. Dan I am.

I was not raised to think in more bottom-up ways of experiencing the self as a "verb," as an action instead of a thing, as dynamic instead of fixed and certain. This more connected aspect of a verb-like self has a distinct sense of less predictability and control—it is not closed in separation but open and ever-changing in dynamic, interactive ways. Instead of this more fluid sense of self, we often live in what we can identify as the disconnected view of modernity: Who I am, what I am, how I am, are all reinforced as a noun-like thing—something I can hold, an entity, a thing with the appearance of top-down certainty. That constructed sense of certainty has a benefit in that it helps me feel safe in a world that holds certainty in such high esteem. This is the world in which I grew up in the United States of America, a land that, anthropologists tell us, hosts the most "individualistic" culture on the planet.

In contrast, some studies have described other cultures, such as the traditional way of living in Japan, as "collectivistic." In fact, one study by psychologists Richard Nisbett and Yuri Myomoto (2005) compared Japanese born-and-raised individuals with those whose parents were from Japan but were raised in the United States and revealed that the groups had distinct ways of perceiving a photograph of an aquarium scene. One group consistently noted the features of a prominent fish, identifying its various fins and their textures and colors. The other group saw the whole scene, noting the big picture elements of plants and rocks that made up the aquarium environment. Which group do you think was which? Culture shapes how the brain learns to decode incoming information, the top-down ways we construct what we perceive are what we call the mental construction of perception: Individualistic ways of seeing lead to seeing individual features with a narrow focus of attention; collectivistic cultural practices lead one to construct a perception of the whole with a wide focus of attention.

In Indigenous cultures throughout the world, as we'll soon discuss, life is viewed more as interdependent interacting elements across the continuum of space and time. The cultural passage of both knowledge and ways of perceiving through the oral tradition itself enables a sense of self to become embedded in systems of deeply interwoven parts and the individual is often seen as woven into the tapestry of a larger whole, a whole broader than the body alone. Though these Indigenous practices, found around the world, grew in geographic isolation from one another, they often share common ground in seeing humanity as woven within all of nature—not owning the landscape nor dividing it into parts, but as custodians of the living system of nature as a whole.

These cross-cultural findings reveal how self, identity, and belonging are constructed aspects of human life and how the human mind, as it creates culture, directly shapes its own sense of self-experience. We can express a question that emerges from these findings directly this way: Is the narrow focus that creates a noun-like solo-self producing a constructed sense of self? In contrast, is a wider focus yielding access to a more flowing, verb-like SPA experience of sensation, perspective, and agency? In other words, is isolation an outcome of a constructed filter of perception and self-reinforcing agency, whereas interdependence is sensing reality more clearly, felt with a bottom-up sense of coherence, sensing directly from the "ground-up," even before the constructive processes of perception and agency? For this body called Dan, immersion in a family, educational system, and then larger society each emphasized separation and the appearance of a solid, solitary, noun-like self—Dan—that was not in question. And then, that horse accident changed this constructed illusion of noun-like existence for this body and immersed the ensuing perception in a verb-like unfolding, without solidity, that ironically felt more grounded in reality, albeit fluid and flowing without closure or certainty. This sense might correlate with a systems reality of deep intraconnection and would feel coherent, consistent with the deeply connected nature of the world and "our place" within it.

The Western-derived, now-modern, global, contemporary pressure, this cultural push to perceive self only as a noun, makes us vulnerable by its inaccuracy, its error in perception and conception, which may be more than misleading, as we will explore throughout our journey in this book. This seeing ourselves only as a discrete noun may be an outright blunder; it may even be a lethal lie, a misguided and dangerous story that we unwittingly tell our selves and live our lives by, to our own detriment.

But the good news is: If the mind's constructions create this perception of the solo-self—this isolated sense of identity that struggles to recognize connections that it cannot see even though they are already there—the mind's capacities can also identify this mistake and course-correct, in both our personal and our public lives. This is how we can turn this VUCA moment of challenge into an opportunity for change.

The compelling feature of the contemporary emphasis on a solo-self construction is its promise to fulfill the longing for certainty, the drive for predictability that creates clear boundaries and a belief in an illusion—that is, "I" am a solid, noun-like entity with features and definitions of who and what I am that are essentially predictable. Yet that illusion of certainty, as attractive as it may be to our anticipatory, prediction-driven brains, is also a trap compelling us to desperately attempt to live lives with an unfulfillable fantasy based not on reality but on a contemporary consensus about a noun-like nature of the self, leading us down a destructive path of disconnection and delusion. "A delusion?" you might ask, hearing these words, as you are, from a psychiatrist. Yes, a belief not consistent with reality. Disconnection and the delusion of self as separate, self as noun alone. Perception and belief are constructions, and if the mind makes a deep error in this constructive process, the result would be distorted perception as illusion, or false perception and belief as delusion. If this delusion drives the plotline of our autobiographical narratives, as I see so often in my psychotherapy practice, we can get caught up in the cloud of confusion the delusion creates as we base our life's decisions on erroneous reasoning and make misguided choices. This is true not only for individuals but for our modern societies and their schools, businesses, and governments as well.

You may be thinking that viewing the experience of self-as-separate as a delusion is too strong a position to take; a psychiatrist overstating his clinical assessment of our cultural situation. Yet this view is consistent with thousands of years of teaching in Indigenous and contemplative traditions, and a scientific conclusion from one of our leading scientific thinkers. In helping address the grief of a father who had lost a child, these were Albert Einstein's words (1972):

> A human being is a part of the whole, called by us, "Universe," a part limited in time and space. He experiences himself, his thoughts and feelings as something separated from the rest—a kind of optical delusion of his consciousness. This delusion is a kind of prison for us, restricting us to our personal desires and to affection for a few persons nearest to us. Our task must be to free ourselves from this prison by widening our circle of compassion to embrace all living creatures and the whole of nature in its beauty. Nobody is able to achieve this completely, but the striving for such achievement is in itself a part of the liberation and a foundation for inner security. (*New York Times*, March 29, 1950, p. 1)

In modern life, these narratives of separation often close us down, and we cling to our expectations and a "flimsy fantasy of certainty," as multidisciplinary artist Kameelah Janan Rasheed names it, in order to maintain our sense that all is right in our world: Certainty is predictability; predictability ensures safety; safety means survival. This drive for certainty as safety and survival is especially true when we are young, profoundly vulnerable, and dependent on others to live. The phrase "flimsy fantasy of certainty" is part of a quote in the entryway to the Brooklyn Public Library, where I first saw Rasheed's words: "Having abandoned the flimsy fantasy of certainty, I decided to wander." Are you open to wandering with me in exploring the nature of the reality of who we are?

My purpose in our conversation here is to awaken us from our slumber, from the separate solo-self's autopilot, its noun-like self-reinforcing isolation, and to rejoice in our revelation of the reality of a self that is broader than any one individual as we integrate our identity and broaden our belonging into the wider world of our life on Earth.

Wisdom Traditions

This journey exploring how the self is constructed in our lives invites us to focus not only on what we know, but how we come to know. In the travels of this person called Dan, my starting place—that is, being taught by my parents in the culture of the United States—lead to an implicit, unquestioned view of self as separate—the noun-like, entity-identity, restricted-belonging that emerges from living as a solo-self. The I of that life perspective moved beyond family and friendships that were also immersed in this view of self into professional education; Western science became my focus and worldview. I was fascinated with how the world of empirical knowledge—what we could learn from close observation, experimentation, hypothesis testing, idea challenging, and theory generation—constructed our sense of what reality is like; my fascination with life lead me to study biology, focusing on biochemistry and the molecular mechanisms underlying living beings. Years later, psychologist and author Adam Grant (2021) would explore the value of such a scientific approach—which always keeps a doubting mind active and challenges our own assumptions—in his book, *Think Again*. In adult development, this stance of being open to shifting our own perspectives is part of the evolution of the self which is described by researchers Robert Kegan and Lisa Lahey (2009) as a self-transforming mind, one with the "mental complexity" to consider the value of even conflictual points of view. I loved and love living with such an open, curious mindset in approaching how we come to understand life and reality. A truly scientific stance welcomes challenge and invites continual assessment of the accuracy of its own observations and ideas. In our conversation, we are asking our selves, and the larger modern culture, to "think again" about how we've come to construct the self-as-separate and how this solo-self is shaping our identity and belonging.

Yet once that horse accident shattered my unquestioned sense of a solo-self, I found nothing in biology, or later in the study of medicine, that illuminated how we come to have a self, the ways we create identity, or how we come to belong in life. The shift from a noun way of living as an entity to realizing a verb set of patterns of energy flow that were deeply interconnected seemed to have no place in the linear views of science that I was learning—until I came across two fields of study. One was the nearly one-hundred-year-old discipline of quantum physics; the other was the new science of complex systems that was emerging in the last decades of our prior millennium. The lessons from physics' exploration of small units of energy, of quanta, revealed a world of verb-like happenings that were deeply connected. In this "quantum realm" of small quanta, such as electrons and photons, there were no nouns—no "things"—only verbs—emerging events— where time and space did not exist as dimensions of separation. In the domain of larger entities, the noun-like objects we call matter, the "macrostate" realm that Newton had studied, the Newtonian principles of classical physics reveal separate entities interacting with one another across the classical separations of time and of space.

In the mathematical study of systems in which three characteristics exist—being open to influences outside of the system; being capable of chaotic, or random, behavior; and being nonlinear, in which a small input leads to large and difficult-to-predict outcomes—there is an emergence of phenomena in these complex systems in which the whole is greater than the sum of the individual parts. This recent Western scientific understanding of complexity reveals insights into the verb-like nature of emergence—and the ways in which a synergy arises from the parts that can appear, to a linear, simple, reductionist view, to be magic and implausible. Systems awareness enables us to sense the connections among parts and to observe the patterns in how those connected parts interact. Systems thinking is all about relationality, not individuality alone.

But the positionality of this body of Dan, as a person of privilege, trained in the methodology of empirical Western science—even if it was at first linear scientific reasoning and now is expanding to a systems science view—means it is my responsibility to acknowledge my blind spots, as best I can, and be open to equally valid ways of understanding the world. Those views can come from deep inner reflection we call contemplative insights and from the wisdom passed along most commonly in the oral tradition as Indigenous knowledge. Since these Indigenous and contemplative approaches are often rigorous ways of understanding our world, we could choose to apply the general term "science" to their observations of perceived patterns of reality. However, Indigenous, or what is sometimes also termed "traditional," knowledge is considered to be quite distinct from Western science in that it involves a view of the whole, a sense of both the secular and the sacred, and an emphasis on wisdom. Some might prefer that we reserve the term "science" for experimental studies and the knowledge derived from them, an approach often attributed to the European Renaissance and including what is known as the "scientific method." If you and I are attempting to understand reality deeply here—the reality of self, identity, and belonging—it seems to me, even as a Western-trained scientist, that it is important to extend our conceptual reach beyond experimental approaches and include many sources of knowing and wisdom. David Graeber and David Wengrow's opus, *The Dawn of Everything: A New History of Humanity*, explores the importance of the contributions Indigenous peoples have made in the emergence of our life as a human species. Jeremy Lent's *The Web of Meaning* provides further support for how wisdom traditions offer great insights into our world. Western science is only one way to know about reality. Our task will be to harness the scientific invitation to "think again" and continually challenge even the most basic assumptions we may have, while at the same time extending beyond Western scientific knowledge to include insights from distinct rigorous and disciplined ways of understanding the world.

In preparing for this exploration, I turned to examples of contemplative and Indigenous sources to see if there might be a consilience, a common ground, with Western scientific insights that might inform a broader, more inclusive view of how self, identity, and belonging form in our lives. Using the process that sociobiologist E. O. Wilson (1998) calls "consilience," these discoveries and their similarities among Western, Indigenous, and contemplative explorations of reality can be woven together to form a basic cross-disciplinary framework, one that underlies the perspective, known as interpersonal neurobiology, we are drawing upon.

At various times along our journey together, it may be helpful to pause, take a breath, and consider and challenge these ideas; to contemplate what they might mean for you in your personal life, in your professional work, and for the planet. And it might be helpful to consider how they might feel, open your perspective, change how you act in the world; to imagine how they affect the various SPA facets of your self—to try them on for size in your life. At points when I think taking a brief pause from the reading might be especially helpful to consider, challenge, and contemplate what we are exploring, I have inserted the traditional Celtic symbol of air, to symbolize the breath: . Of course, you may choose to ignore these suggestions and continue reading, and you can take such pauses naturally at any time of your choosing. I will note particular moments in our conversation when three intentional, long breaths or a mindful pause, however it arises and feels right to you, may be appropriate for you to consider.

The systems science and quantum physics view of the interconnection of all things may be new for Western science, but hardly new for humanity. This teaching has been around for millennia, found in philosophical, Indigenous, and contemplative knowledge, yet in modern times this systems perspective is often hidden from view, absent from our education, not part of our everyday conversations. We can refer to these ancient ways of knowing collectively as "wisdom traditions," acknowledging their range across time and across our planet and their diversity in both origin and content. In the ancient philosophy of Confucianism, Taoism, and Stoicism, for example, this view of the interconnection of all things was a fundamental teaching, as it also has been in contemplative teachings from meditative practices, such as in Buddhism, Christian Centering Prayer, and Hindu traditions, as well as in the Indigenous knowledge of groups such as those of North America, including the Inuit, Lakota, Chumash, and Tongva (on whose unceded traditional lands I now reside and work); those of South America, including the ancient Inca and the contemporary Tayuna; those of the Polynesian Islands; as well as the Māori of New Zealand and the Aborigine of Australia. In the tradition of southern Africa known as Ubuntu, the notion of "I am because we are" is at the heart of living; in the Zen Buddhist tradition of Thich Nhat Hanh, we "inter-are" in what he calls interbeing. This view of a common ground of wisdom traditions is part of what has been called the perennial philosophy.

At the beginning of the COVID-19 pandemic, two Dutch film makers, Ingeborg Ertenger and Thomas Roebers, organized the contributions of Indigenous wisdom traditions from around the globe. This traditional knowledge had lessons to remind humans of what we may need to course-correct how our species had come to live on the planet. And what is so striking about hearing these words directly, in the oral tradition, the frequent medium through which many of these insights are conveyed across the generations, is how they share such consilience—a common ground, a similar set of principles—though they come from people whose populations have lived in distinct regions, without communication with one another, for thousands of years. Our human family is a deep resource for wisdom passed along through the generations, a wisdom still present, but in modern times it is often heard only as a whisper, rarely given attention or turned into action.

In the face of a viral pandemic spreading around the globe and the shutting down of transportation and manufacturing as people were urged to stay at home to curtail the spread of the disease, the living ecological systems of Earth seemed to breathe a sigh of relief, the pollution and excessive speed slowing down across the globe virtually in an instant. Through the Rooted Messages project, Ertinger and Roebers reached out to 16 wise teachers from their traditional lands and then compiled their teachings into short videos that were made available to the wider world to disseminate insights regarding what we might learn from this moment of a collective shut down— and what we might do to make a positive difference going forward. If humanity could give the Earth a breather from its virtually nonstop carbon emission modern life, might we not listen to what the natural world, Mother Earth, is needing us to hear?

With permission, I include a few relevant excerpts that I transcribed from their oral sharing in their contributions to Rooted Messages (rootedmessages.com).

Beginning in the southern hemisphere, Te Ngaehe Wanikau of the Māori people of New Zealand says:

> It's about our connection. . . between us and the cosmos, between us and every single thing in the environment, and us to each other. We know that to go back to what we were prior to COVID-19 would only be a testimony to our collective stupidity. Be the generation that said, "No, enough." We're not lost anymore; we're finding our way home. (Ertinger & Roebers, 2020, Te Ngaehe Wanikau)

Imagine what "our way home" might look like. What is this "home" really about? Letting go of the separate, solo-self and seeing the truth of our deeply intraconnected reality?

Tyson Yunkaporta (2020), an arts critic and researcher who belongs to the Apalech clan in Queensland, Australia, describes his journey across the continent to explore Indigenous ways of knowing in his inspiring text, *Sand Talk: How Indigenous Thinking Can Save the World.* Though published in book form, the audiobook version enables the reader to soak in the more customary vocal transmission of cross-generational wisdom, which focuses on the connections among parts of systems that make up our world. In describing how a local elder could detect patterns within living systems, Yunkaporta (2020) states, "His process is all about seeing the overall shape of the connections between things. Look beyond the things and focus on the connections between them, he says. Then look beyond the connections and see the patterns they make" (p. 77). Highlighting the deep systems wisdom of aboriginal teaching, he goes on to state:

> Preindustrial cultures have worked within self-organizing systems for thousands of years to predict weather patterns, seasonal activity, and the dynamics of social groups, then manage responses to these complexities in nonintrusive ways that maintain systemic balance. While interventions are possible from within these dynamic systems, they cannot be controlled from the outside. Systems are heterarchical—composed of equal parts interacting together. Imposing a hierarchical model of top-down control can only destroy them. (Yunkaporta, 2020, p. 82)

Inherent in the participation of agents of change is the central importance of respect: "Respectful observation and interaction within the system, with the parts and the connections between them, is the only way to see the pattern. You cannot know any part, let alone the whole, without respect" (p. 83).

As we move through these lessons of wisdom traditions, it may be helpful to keep this stance in mind. Yunkaporta (2020) suggests that

> Each part, each person, is dignified as an embodiment of the knowledge. Respect must be facilitated by custodians, but there is no outside-imposed authority, no "boss," no "dominion over." While senior people ensure that the processes and stages of coming to higher levels of knowledge are maintained with safety and cohesion, there is no centralized control in Aboriginal societies. (p. 83)

What is the challenge, then? To bring the wisdom of systems thinking into our modern-day cultural view? If a "pervasive leadership" that enables each person to serve as a custodian of the whole, in whatever ways their individual capacities allow, may be the way forward, how might we invite a shift toward broad participation as custodians of life on Earth? Let's move on further, around the globe, and see what other preindustrial, Indigenous teachings of Rooted Messages might guide us to consider in humanity's next step of evolution.

Moving west from Australia to South America, Vandria Borari of the Borari Indigenous people of the Tapajos region of the Amazon Rainforest in Brazil says:

> For us, the Mother Earth is Sacred . . . the river, the forest, and the animals, they complete our lives, and they are the reason for our existence . . . . So it is urgent that all the people of the planet need to reconcile and connect with nature. We need to value all the forms of life . . . . We need more love, we need more humanity, and we need to accept our differences so that then we can combat planetary inequality. (Ertinger & Roebers, 2020, Vandria Borari)

Her words, "We need to value all forms of life," honor diversity within our unity (Ertinger & Roebers, 2020). In this perspective, the connecting of differentiated elements—what we have specifically named "integration"—seems to be a fundamental position of respect. Robin Wall Kimmerer—a distinguished teaching professor of environmental biology, director of the Center for Native Peoples and the Environment, and member of the Citizen Potawatomi Nation of North America—in her transformative text, *Braiding Sweet Grass: Indigenous Wisdom, Scientific Knowledge, and the Teachings of Plants* (2013), states

There are layers upon layers of reciprocity in this garden between the bean and the bacterium, the bean and the corn, the corn and the squash, and ultimately with the people.... The beauty of the partnership is that each plant does what it does in order to increase its own growth. But as it happens, when the individuals flourish, so does the whole. The way of the Three Sisters reminds me of one of the basic teachings of our people. The most important thing each of us can know is our unique gift and how to use it in the world. Individuality is cherished and nurtured because in order for the whole to flourish, each of us has to be strong in who we are and carry our gifts with conviction so they can be shared with others. Being among the sisters provides a visible manifestation of what a community can become when its members understand and share their gifts. In reciprocity, we fill our spirits as well as our bellies. (pp. 129–130)

Heading north, we come to Chief Phil Lane, Jr., of the Ihanktonwan and Chickasaw Nations of North America and Canada (Ertinger & Roebers, 2020):

Each one of us has within us those potentialities, those capabilities, those gifts that if shared in unity and respect and kindness and compassion, will transform the world we live in. (Chief Phil Lane, Jr.)

We'll explore soon a science perspective on that kindness and compassion through the lens of a systems view of being intraconnected—having a self, identity, and belonging as fundamental to the whole, of which these bodies we are born into in this time and place are simply a part. The journey to find that shift, as Chief Lane continues to suggest, is within us:

To understand oneness also means to understand we're related to all living things. That's the fundamental foundation of the Indigenous worldview. Even to the point where now science is proving what Black Elk said so beautifully: The center of the universe is everywhere. Everywhere. That means we're intimately related.... For in this process of integration and disintegration, there is disintegration unfolding everywhere. At that same time, we can choose to be part of that disintegration or be part of the integration. (Ertinger & Roebers, 2020, Chief Phil Lane, Jr.)

As science also suggests, within the part is the whole, within the whole are the parts. How we find our way to remembering such truths is an inspiration of the various attempts to articulate them in words, words that can at times feel too concrete in their proclamations—yet pointing in a direction we can feel as well as come to know conceptually. In the foreword to John G. Neihardt's classic text, *Black Elk Speaks* (2014), Vine Deloria, Jr. states:

Reflection is the most difficult of all our activities because we are no longer able to establish relative priorities from the multitude of sensations that engulf us. Times such as these seem to illuminate the classic expression for eternal truths and great wisdom comes to stand out in the crowd of ordinary maxims .... The very nature of great religious teachings is that they encompass everyone who understands them, and personalities become indistinguishable from the transcendent truth that is expressed. So let it be with *Black Elk Speaks*. That it speaks to us with the simple and compelling language about an aspect of human experience and encourages us to emphasize the best that dwells within us is sufficient. (pp. xiiv, xvi)

The inspiration of the North American Oglala Lakota visionary and healer, Nicholas Black Elk, reveals a view that each individual belongs to the whole of humanity and humanity in turn to the whole of nature.

This wholeness, imbued with a reverence, respect, and responsibility for our interdependence, is an eternal truth found throughout Indigenous teachings.

We'll be heading west now, all the way to the Far East, to Asia, to further explore these rooted messages. Ayan Ayangat of the Chonos people of Mongolia states that Indigenous people are

> Rooted in their ecosystem because they are deeply and closely connected with the nurturing environment, they have their own unique lifestyle, education, and cultural heritage.... Current mainstream culture is not able to see the value of the Indigenous lifestyle and its heritage. Our vivid Earth needs diverse cultures to sustain its brilliance...their unique and close connection with Mother Earth. (Ertinger & Roebers, 2020, Ayan Ayangat)

Each lesson reminds us that we are woven within Earth's wholeness—a tapestry that includes different strands intertwined to make a magnificent whole. In many ways, these teachings are consilient with the more recent perspective illuminated in the study of complex systems, those systems that are open, chaos-capable, and nonlinear: They are comprised of differentiated but linked components that are connected through interdependence. This complexity gives rise to emergence; one of those emergent properties is the adaptation and learning inherent to the self-organization that arises innately from the complex system. This, too, is consilient with Buckminster Fuller's writings about synergy—the whole being greater than merely the sum of its parts.

Continuing westward from the Far East, Patrick Dacquay (Ertinger & Roebers, 2020) from the Celtic people of France, states that to deal with the fear people are now experiencing, to have a relationship in equality with all things, "It is within this wholeness, when all vibrates well, that the harmony and the symphony are perfect. The song of life is perfect."

Singing life in harmony. From a systems perspective, harmony emerges when differentiated parts become linked, just as a choir expresses its emergence through the different singers' voices and the creation of harmonic intervals while also singing the same song. How might such integration at the heart of harmony become our shared goal for living on Earth? Perhaps broadening our belonging emerges as the integration of our identity as a me—the differentiated body—and a we—our relational self—helps us live with a self, identity, and belonging as "MWe."

Heading north to Greenland, Angaangaq Angakkorsuaq of the Eskimo tribes says:

> When we don't relate to each other . . . we don't celebrate each other's beauty. Only by melting the ice in the heart, you and I will have a chance to change. And when we change, we will see that path where we get home to our self. Thus, mankind has a chance to come to the next level of reality of consciousness and realizing that there are the yellow people, the white people, the red people, and the Black people and we all belong in the same circle. (Ertinger & Roebers, 2020, Angaangaq Angakkorsuaq)

The ice of the heart. What might we do to create conditions that melt that ice, that free our compassion to liberate our connection? In science, the head, the heart, and the intestines literally process information. To connect head to heart may mean linking the logical reasoning of the head with the compassionate feelings of relational connections of the heart. To melt that ice, we may need to inform and transform, to realize the relational fields that connect us, even if the logical eye cannot yet see. How does that feel in the fullness of you?

As Tyson Yunkaporta (2020) suggests in his learnings from Indigenous elders, we first bring spirit (respect), then heart (connect), then head (reflect), and then hands (direct) as we join in the work of being a custodian of our shared belonging to one another and to the lands upon which we live. This is how he suggests we can bring the Indigenous wisdom of embracing the systems in which we live into helpful ways of transforming our current challenges and change the ways we can now live in our shared world.

Heading back to the Southern Hemisphere, Don Sebastian of the Inca people in Peru states:

> We have to restore our harmony with Mother Earth in order to enjoy a harmonious and full life . . . . We should live in harmony, like brothers, like one family with respect for each other . . . . Why not be united and all walk together as a single force? (Ertinger & Roebers, 2020, Don Sebastian)

A family filled with siblings? How might we have the love of family and move beyond sibling rivalry? If we see all humanity as one such family, and the family of all living beings as an even broader belonging to the family of nature, we may be able to imagine how that membership within the whole might emerge. Siblings may have their rivalry for fear of lack of protection, lack of resources—this feeling of scarcity increases our distrust. Imagine a world where we might live with an attitude of abundance and experience a reciprocity and mutuality of belonging in our widening family circles. That is a world of harmony we not only can imagine, but one we may be able to move our modern lives toward.

Headed east to the west of Africa, Fadimata Walet Alassane (Ertinger & Roebers, 2020, Fadimata Walet Alassane) of the Tuareg people, Burkina Faso reminds us, "The Earth has always come first, and now

comes last .... Compassion was there at first, and it is no more ... "
When we come to embrace a larger sense of who we are, our mental well-being and our experience of self, identity, and belonging can change.

Once, while visiting a San tribe in Namibia, I noticed that the villagers we met seemed so happy despite the presence of an epidemic of disease, famine, and a drought. When asked about that observation, a leader of the village said, "My people are happy. We are happy because we belong. We belong to our village community. And we belong to nature." He then went on to ask me, through the translator, if we in America were happy, did we belong? I paused; and sadly, after reflecting, came up with a no to both inquiries. Despite material wealth, research showed that those in the United States, our most individualistic- and material-oriented of countries, has some of the highest levels of loneliness and mental health challenges on Earth.

A colleague of mine from South Africa received his PhD for his studies of the Ubuntu cultural practices of Southern Africa. He told me that there, the fundamental principle of the way of life is found in the phrase, "I am because we are," a shared humanity. After reading his seven hundred-page dissertation, it was clear how this sense of connection within community and caring could shape the feeling of a cultural environment in a school, business, or community. I asked him if this philosophy of living embraced both the connection and the individuation that were each a part of integration. He said he found that the individual often becomes lost within the collaboration as a whole. Ubuntu, in his analysis at least, was not MWe—a way we honor the differentiated inner individual experiences as me while also belonging as a relational we.

In contrast, scholar James Ogude (2019) says,

Ubuntu is rooted in what I call a relational form of personhood, basically meaning that you are because of the others. In other words, as a human being, you—your humanity, your personhood—you are fostered in relation to other people. (para. 4)

Yet the individual has a voice, Ogude (2019) suggests, and there is a place for differentiation:

> People will debate, people will disagree; it's not like there are no tensions. It is about coming together and building a consensus around what affects the community. And once you have debated, then it is understood what is best for the community, and then you have to buy into that . . . . There's a sense in which ubuntu as a concept, and the African communitarian ethos, imposes a sense of moral obligation regarding your responsibility for others even before you think of yourself. You must, as the Russian critic, Bahktin would say, look into another person's eyes and have that person return the gaze. When the gaze is returned, that recognition is what humanizes you. (paras. 5, 9)

Robin Wall Kimmerer's description of coming to know your gifts as an individual, having conviction in these, and then offering these in service to the greater whole may parallel the ethos of Ubuntu and capture what we are looking toward: a way of living, symbolized by the simple symbol of MWe, as a synergy of self that is not at the extremes of individualistic or collectivist cultures, as anthropologists have classified them in their studies, but as integrated self, identity, and belonging that honors differences while promoting compassionate, collaborative linkages.

MWe as an integrated identity might fit well with a sense of broader belonging, as it is widened from an individual alone but does not leave the individual out of the cultural relational field. What this synergy of self suggests is that we might find a way to have both a broad belonging and an integrated identity, which would allow for the wide focus of attention on our overall world while at the same time honoring the importance of the individual's focus on inner experience. MWe invites the integrative linkage of connection and the differentiation of individuality.

In modern cultures, this balance is often skewed toward the individual alone, pushing for the solo-self in isolation. We are turning to the long-standing wisdom of Indigenous teachings to explore how ancient knowledge systems of how we can be linked within all of nature may help us return to this balance of an integrative life in contemporary times. Careful application of these teachings is advisable, as illustrated in the following story: I once ran a conference in which the first set of speakers and I were on a panel describing the importance of Indigenous teachings that remind us of our experience of being "all one" with nature, all one in the universe. It was a beautiful way to begin our three-day gathering on "Timeless Wisdom, Timely Action"—the phrase we use at the Garrison Institute, a nonprofit organization where I was and am still on the board. The next panel was focused on the history of racism and the importance of social justice in America. One of the speakers on that next panel raised the concern that before we can move to an all-one linkage in our lives, we need to fully honor the differentiated experiences of distinct, individual groupings, such as the genocide of the Indigenous of North America and the enslavement of and systemic racism against Black individuals in the United States. Without such honoring of differences first, this wise faculty member suggested, movements toward the all-one mentality would be an act of aggression against the marginalized.

This powerful and insightful reflection, right at the beginning of our time together, was a crucial reminder that integration is not about blending, it's not about being all-one without first knowing, honoring, and sharing our individual features, including our ancestral histories.

A parallel experience arose in some community work I participated in when the group discussion facilitators of a local conference in our city, a collection of individuals who represented a wide array of cultural backgrounds, came together before the event began to prepare for our work. There was a stagnation of the air in the room at first, and then outright hostility one could feel. I offered an overview of integration and suggested that before we might work collaboratively as a group, we needed to share our individual backgrounds and aspirations. One by one, each person communicated to the group their own histories: One was a woman who had come from Cambodia's genocide and found the United States unwelcoming, her family's adolescents now finding street gangs their only opportunity for belonging; one was a Black man whose grandparents had been sharecroppers who came west to escape the Jim Crow laws of the south, only to find continued racism in California; and my own history of a grandmother who was sent away at the age of 12 to escape the pogroms of Russia that had killed her father in the small Ukranian village they had lived in. On and on, each of us opened up, sharing our own painful personal pasts. Once the individual sharing was welcomed into the room with respect and gratitude, then the joining could begin: We could become a group without losing our individuality, open to receiving the joyful hopes for a new community life.

Our human belonging, as Indigenous knowledge passed down for millennia suggests, is even broader than our connections within humanity—it extends to embrace all of nature. As we continue to soak in these words from Indigenous knowledge stewards, we can keep in mind that the goal here is not to idealize the past—there has been, in many cultures throughout the ages and throughout the world, violence against out-groups and great hardship and, perhaps, a lack of honoring of the individual. Our common stance can be to see how we might learn from these cultures what in modern times we have lost: a way of belonging to a greater whole—to humanity and to nature. Our aim here might be to rework that balance, to bring connection back into our lives while not losing the equally important ways we thrive with the diversity of our individuality.

Heading south again, now back to Australia, we discover more rooted messages. Anne Poelina of the Aboriginal people from the Martuwarra Country (Fitzroy River), Professor and Chair of Indigenous Studies, University of Notre Dame, had these powerful words to say:

> Indigenous wisdom right across the planet is grounded in law of the land..... Earth-centered governance .... Look at where greed has taken us and severed our relationship with nature...
>
> We are coming with a gift of knowledge ... a gift to humanity ... this ancient wisdom has relevance in modernity.... It's time to relearn the values, the ethics, the principles of care and love that we as First Nations, as Indigenous Wisdom Holders know, that we must continue to have this relationship with the natural world. We are not separate. .... We need to realize that this is a world of relationship, of an ethics of care, and of love ... this wisdom, these laws, this knowledge is Indigenous science which must be factored into the way that we start to do business differently with our planet. (Ertinger & Roebers, 2020, Anne Poelina)

How do we start doing business differently? How would you contribute to a world that might be based on "a world of relationship, of an ethics of care, and of love"?

Imagine that. Instead of isolated competitive actors in a game of winner takes all, consider how we might see the world as a web of mutual beneficence and sing the song of life into this collaborative belonging as an intraconnected whole. Living our way into the life of the whole makes the term "greater good" come alive as a win-win-win way of being: Individually we will thrive with such belonging; the community will benefit from the altruism and care that arise; and our home, Mother Earth, will breathe a regenerative sigh of relief as we come to our senses and recognize—remind our conscious minds—of the reality of our intraconnected nature.

If we get our act together, we can act together.

MWe can do this.

Heading north and east, we come to the islands of Hawaii. The linguistic symbols of words can hold much in the concepts and categories they communicate. MWe can choose our words wisely to cultivate the integration at the heart of intraconnected ways of life that are possible for humanity on Earth. Kuu Kaulia of the Native Hawaiian people offers two words from his heritage to help us along our collective way:

> Aloha in Hawaiian means unconditional love. . . . Ho'oponopono refers to making a "wrong" right. . . . Our message from my people to everyone is to love one another and to make things right now in this life in order for us to move on and live a healthier life amidst the many different challenges in the world today that we're facing. (Ertinger & Roebers, 2020, Kuu Kaulia)

Indigenous knowledge reminds us that deep learning invites an evolution, perhaps a revolution, in consciousness. We start with our individual lives and access a potentiality that rests in each of us. The universe in a grain of sand; the infinite within the finitude of these bodily lives we lead. Though we might not ever see the fruits of our labor nor resolve the seeming paradoxes of these polarities, we can know that the eternal lives within the transience of these bodies we are born into.

With the internal embraced, we move to the relational; we integrate identity, broaden belonging. What arises is a synergy of self, an emergence of something from the Me and We that is integration made visible: kindness, compassion, love.

In a meeting with the activist Joanna Macy and some wonderful MWe colleagues (or should it be "MWonderful" colleagues?), Joanna inspired us to consider how bridging activism and spirituality could be done with deep love, deep compassion. Her suggestion that we travel "gloriously" on this challenging journey together to bring healing into the world, and that, whether we succeed or not, we feel the gratitude and love in the effort, ignited a fire in each of us.

If our conversation here is contributing anything to the larger human conversation, it is the underscoring of the importance of these philosophical, Indigenous, and contemplative sources of systems wisdom to the contemporary narrative and the noting of the potential fundamental mechanism of integration and its practical implications, which underlie how systems function well in our world to promote harmony and health. By delineating the differentiation and linkage components of integration, we are given a science-informed, practical pathway to identify what might be creating the chaos and rigidity in our lives—individually, socially, ecologically—and then take action to liberate the various levels of impaired integration at the root of these sources of suffering. While wisdom traditions from Indigenous knowledge holders and from contemplative practice may not explicitly use the concept of integration itself, nor that of emergent self-organization, it seems they are implicitly consilient with these views from Western mathematics and science and they knew them deeply for millennia before science began to explore the synergy that arises from interacting parts.

In addition to adding the lens of the science of systems and of energy to this perennial wisdom, we will also be exploring key highlights of the developmental stages of human life, which may help shed light on how modern culture may mold the modern mind toward linear thinking and away from systems wisdom across the lifespan. Both forms of thinking—linear and systems—have important contributions to make for us to see the world fully and act wisely in the world. Whatever our place in life, our positionality, our developmental stage, we can participate in this move toward integration. Each of us has the invitation; and those in a position of privilege have the duty of integrity—the duty of bringing more integration into our waiting world.

We can choose to live a life of love, awareness, and connection—to move beyond a business-as-usual way of being on this planet that we all share. As Indigenous scholars La Donna Harris and Jacqueline Wasilewski (2004) suggest:

> Structured dialogue processes have provided culturally resonant means through which Indigenous peoples have been able to identify and articulate their core values to broader audiences, especially the four R's (Relationship, Responsibility, Reciprocity and Redistribution). These four R's form the core of an emerging concept, Indigeneity. The dynamic inclusivity of this value cluster has much to contribute to global discourse as we go about the task of constructing global agoras, the dialogic spaces of optimal mutual learning of the 21st century. (p. 489)

They contrast these four R's of Indigeneity to the two P's of modernity: power and profit.

We can suggest a consilient notion that these core values of connection are manifestations of a foundation of integration as health. We can choose to take on these integrative ways of living in relationship with responsibility, with a mutuality of reciprocal influence, and in ways that redistribute and share our gifts—all driven by the innate force of love. Imagine coming to these spaces of conversation, our modern agoras across our shared systems of belonging, with love, connection, and the open awareness of showing up, fully present, for one another, for humanity, and for all living beings.

With these consilient approaches of wisdom traditions from thousands of years of living on Earth, we can draw new ways of being and behaving that have connection and collaboration at their core. Moving beyond the extremes of the separation of individualism and the loss of independence in collectivism, an integrated approach might be to combine the inner aspect of identity, I or Me, with the inter aspect of belonging, an Us or We, in the simple integrative self as MWe.

What a loving world MWe can choose to liberate, a world we can intentionally nurture with a wider sense of what the self is, an integrative identity, and a broadened belonging. MWe are each at once members of a personal, human, and planetary family of all life on Earth. To re-mind ourselves, to bring back to mind these broader ideas of what the notions of "our" and "self" can truly mean, is the intention of our initial steps on our journey.

An Integrative Self

Long before I was exposed to these ancient teachings from Indigenous knowledge or to the questions that challenged the modern view of a separate self found in many contemplative practices, such as the Buddhist focus on interdependence and the lack of a concrete self, I had been a young adolescent focusing my attention on studying biology in college. Then I came across those fascinating documentary films of other cultures in a general education course on anthropology. The following summer I worked in Mexico on that project with my anthropology teacher—the same trip where I accidentally "lost my self." I didn't understand until many years later that what shook me most about the academic aspect of that project, was how I had expected to learn about their separate, isolated, Indigenous ways of healing from a linear view of reducing something into its parts, analyzing or breaking down things as if finding the fundamental units would reveal the essence of something. I had been learning to see with a simple view: take things apart to understand the whole. Yet in my immersion in interviews with the various Indigenous healers, it seemed they saw things through a different lens, a way of living that focused on interconnection, not separation. And then, as a misfortune or not, I "fell into" the experience of knocking that default mode-mediated experience of a separate self right out of my worldview. My immediate, direct experience was one of awareness without separation, a fullness of experience as a verb, without the overlay of an identity as a noun of separation. Though I came home to repair the bodily damage I sustained during that accident on the horse, the "damage" to my linear, self-is-body view remained. As I try to convey these experiences to you now, a feeling of gratitude arises, one with a sense of awe that somehow, in the course of life's unfolding, there could be such an immersive shift in the feeling of identity, such a timely blow to the linear lessons of a limited sense of self in the midst of adolescence.

Indigenous teachings—such as those offered by the knowledge holders described earlier and those I've had the privilege to learn about directly from individuals living in the cultures of the Tayuna of South America, the Lakota and Inuit of North America, the San of Namibia in Africa, the Māori of New Zealand, and the Aboriginal people of Australia—each have in their core principles the notion that humans are fundamentally connected to each other and to nature, that we are part of, not separate from, everything and everyone around us. Similar insights are offered in the ancient philosophical teachings and contemplative practices of Buddhism, originating in India, Taoism and Confucianism in China, and the Stoics of Greece. In the religious traditions of Christianity, Hinduism, Islam, and Judaism, a larger sense of belonging within the human family is often fundamental to their original teachings.

Yet now, in a trend that perhaps began in the West but seems to be growing throughout the world, in the East and West, in the Northern and Southern Hemispheres, the view of "modern culture" emphasizes individuality and disconnection—the solo-self. From the perspective of integration as health, this is an assault on well-being, as it overemphasizes differentiation over linkage. Anthropologists and social psychologists suggest that this modern cultural tendency toward a "self-construal" of individualism and independence is at its most extreme in the United States of America, my home. The culture here emphasizes separation rather than connection, independence rather than interdependence, individuality rather than a shared identity. There is often a pervasive attitude here that feels something like "pull yourself up by your own bootstraps" rather than a mutuality of belonging to each other and to some greater good, some larger whole of which we are a part. Instead, we are apart from one another, finding our own way, it often feels to me, even in this body with white skin, a heterosexual orientation, and economic and educational privilege. From this position in this particular culture, I may try to understand but can only listen deeply to friends and colleagues who do not share this position of the majority, a position of privilege. And this culture of separateness is contributing to, if not causing, many, if not all, of the pandemics we are experiencing today, including those of social injustice and racism, and the assaults on the vitality of our natural world.

Over these years I've learned from my relationship and my teaching with Jack Kornfield about the contemplative tradition of Buddhism. And I've had the honor of teaching at various times alongside the leader of Tibetan Buddhism, his Holiness, the Dalai Lama. This contemplative tradition is not my own background nor personal in-depth training, but these years of learning, especially from these two individuals, about Buddhist thinking and practice have given me insights into some of its contemplative—that is, learning from meditative reflection—and philosophical points of view. In these years, too, I have had the opportunity to teach with John O'Donohue, a former Irish Catholic priest, philosopher, poet, and, in his own words, mystic—someone who believes in the reality of the invisible (O'Donohue, personal communication, October 15, 2003). These direct relationships and experiences have woken my mind to the value of seeing beyond the academy, beyond the research approach my own training in science and medicine had led me to rely solely upon in constructing a worldview.

When we invite into our experience the reality of the connections among parts of a system and open to the patterns of these connections across time and space, we can realize how these invisible system connections are in fact real. When we add to this the understanding that the ways in which we've learned to perceive reality, including how to construct a sense of self, turn back to filter what we sense into what we perceive in a top-down construction of our view of the world, then we are further humbled and inspired to do the hard work of being open to learning from different ways of seeing, different ways of knowing, than what we were initially taught. It is important to recall the statement, "the more we know, the less we see," so that we can come to let go of conceptual knowledge that may filter our sensations into limited perceptions; we can, with intention, open our minds to new ways of knowing.

As a science trained, Western educated physician, the challenge for this body has been to let that educational top-down filtering move to the side in order to attempt, as best as I could, to listen receptively to patients, students, colleagues, and the wisdom of contemplative practice and Indigenous teachings. This approach has invited the weaving of these ways of knowing into a consilience with the foundations of science and, in turn, has opened the doors to conversations with those in a range of many religious traditions, including Christianity, Islam, Hinduism, Judaism, and the Bahá'i faith. As a child, my own experiences in my personal family were with the Quaker American Friends and with the Unitarian Universalists. In each of these new conversations and experiences, it seems that sensing a self that is larger than the body has been at the heart of the teachings, even with the various and quite distinct ways this principle is expressed in day-to-day religious practices. Was there a way to bring these approaches to knowing together, to bridge the worlds of science and of spirituality? While the notion of being "interconnected" is at the heart of many of these perspectives, might there be a way of moving from this perspective of a part that is connected to other parts to a view from the experience of the whole as intraconnected? Could there be an experience of the sensation, perspective, and agency—the elements from a science approach to self—that might be consilient with this sense of being the whole, not just a part of it?

As a white-identified person in the majority social grouping in the land I live in, trained in the privileged educational systems of science and medicine, I need to be open to the many blind spots I am blind to knowing that I have. Even as I write these words to you, I remind myself to realize that the journey of this self, of this individual named Dan, may speak to these idealistic notions from the naïve position of not being marginalized, of not facing the suffering and pain of being dehumanized because of the identifying features of this body—its looks, its beliefs, its background, on some levels, fit into the majority groupings. One state of mind in this body says, "What right have you to write about belonging or identity when you come from a position of such privilege where you never had to question identity, never felt excluded because of that identity?" There have been many days when this doubt has kept me stuck. I wonder, "Is there anything useful from this place of privilege that might be of service to the world?" What arises in this doubtful questioning is an inquiry into bridging worlds. Is there a way to accept blind spots and respectfully offer something that may provide a path to linking some of these often-separated ways of knowing? When the news of global struggles continues to reveal the mounting suffering the various pandemics create in our world, the doubts are overcome by the drive to provide something that just might spark a light in our collective efforts to change course.

With these limitations and concerns in mind, I feel that the journey toward a consilience of knowledge, that common ground of a set of discoveries derived from independent ways of knowing, might be a useful and respectful attempt to see the whole elephant picture of our situation on Earth, rather than relying on only one particular way of studying a part of the whole. If we try to find the common ground across ways of knowing, to not only illuminate a perhaps deeper sense of the truth of the world, we might also be able to build helpful bridges across what seemed like insurmountable divisions, bridges that offer an effective pathway for cultivating a healthier world in which we all can live. "And maybe," the doubting mind of this body says, "just maybe, that could be of benefit to our individual and collective journey ahead."

What are we adding in our conversation here that hasn't already been addressed for thousands of years in wisdom teachings? We are acknowledging, with deep respect and gratitude, these ancient teachings—and we are offering to not only remind ourselves of this wisdom but also to add to this focus on self. We are connecting the teachings from Indigenous knowledge and of contemplative practice to the contributions of empirical science in hopes that weaving long-standing insights with modern views may bring a consilient strength to our human narrative, our ongoing conversation, about who we are and where we are going.

From the framework of interpersonal neurobiology, it seems consiliently clear that health is based on integration—the honoring of differences and the cultivation of linkages. We are using the linguistic term "integration" to name this balance of elements as being unique, specialized, or differentiated on the one hand, and then connected, interwoven, or linked on the other. Within the linkage there is no impeding of the differences. If we are adding anything to this ancient topic, it is to name integration directly as the process of well-being, to identify the chaos and rigidity that arise when integration is not facilitated, and then to suggest ways to cultivate integration to achieve states of well-being, of harmony, of health.

Opening to this consilience across ways of knowing brings up the scientific notion, paralleled by contemplative and Indigenous teachings, that an excessively differentiated self in modern culture may be at the root of our most pressing challenges today. We can state the science-based notion this way: Modern culture is not promoting an integrative self, identity, or belonging. This impairment to integration is leading to the accelerating chaos and rigidity in our personal, public, and planetary lives.

This is the impetus for our journey here, to dive deeply into self, identity, and belonging. We can say that neither of the extremes of the original ways researchers have identified this construction of self—an individualistic, independent approach to self-construal that overemphasizes differentiation over linkage nor an interdependent, relational, or collectivistic approach that focuses on linkage at the peril of differentiation—lead to integration. A broader building of identity might be wider than the two forms of relational or collective interdependence, of being connected to other people or to groups, features of our "self-aspects" explored by Emiko Kashima and Elizabeth Hardie (2000), and perhaps be similar to the more recent academic proposal of a metapersonal self-construal that sees one's self as related to all of humanity and to nature—not just particular people or groups of people. In the original study of DeCicco and Stroink (2007), lower levels of anxiety and depression were found in those in this metapersonal grouping compared to those in the original two self-construal categories—independent or interdependent, whether relational or collectivistic. Questions that explore this more universal view of self include items related to one's personal existence being purposeful and meaningful; a belief of not being separate from others; and a kinship with all living things. Some studies suggest that those individuals of contemplative and Indigenous backgrounds may reveal this metapersonal self-construal more often than that those with other backgrounds. Factors also included in this grouping are valuing an inner sense of peace, taking time to quiet the mind, and acknowledging the benefits of intuition. With this wider self-construal, enhanced well-being was found in further studies by psychologists Constance Mara, Teresa DiCicco, and Mirella Stroink (2010) who state:

> The most relevant finding was in regard to the Metapersonal Self-Construal. Higher Metapersonal Self-Construal scores predicted higher emotional intelligence scores. . . . Additionally, higher Metapersonal Self Construal scores alone predicted higher scores on two of the three subscales of the TMMS [Trait Meta Mood Scale]: Mood Repair and Attention to Feelings . . . . The Metapersonal Self-Construal scale was also a stronger predictor of greater well-being. Thus, the Metapersonal Self-Construal was meaningfully differentiated from the independent and interdependent self-construals as a predictor of wellbeing and emotional intelligence scores. (pp. 7–8)

Overall, these findings suggest that broadening our sense of belonging, expanding our identity, enabling ourselves to have an experience of self that extends beyond the body and even beyond just our personal relationships and beliefs, and having membership in "something more" that connects us to one another as a humanity, to nature, and to the reality of the universe are both possible and beneficial. While the specific details of the empirical measurement of self-construal may be actively debated in the academic literature, as discussed, for example, by researchers Timothy Levine and colleagues (2003) and further elaborated by Tom Giraud and team (Gibas, 2016), the concept itself—that we have various ways we construct a sense of self—has important value. We will build on this concept of the construction of self, acknowledging that the details of how to measure and delineate the nature of these inner and relational identity processes is actively being debated.

One basic premise we will suggest is that the journey toward a widened sense of self does not need to leave our inner bodily experience out of this extension of who we are—we can live a life that is both the inner, individual me and the relational, connected we. This integration of self is what our conversational journey is all about.

A consilient proposal is to see how human cultural evolution might move itself in an integrative direction, honoring both differentiation and linkage, cultivating and combining both the inner identity of me and the inter identity of we as an intraconnected, integrative identity of MWe.

An Ancient Invitation for Modern Times

Our journey is an invitation to join together in addressing key issues about our self, the experience of identity and belonging. In some ways, these questions have been a part of our human dialogue in Indigenous cultures and contemplative practices for thousands of years. So, you might wonder, why focus on such ancient issues right now? We've seen that the major challenges we face today, individually, as families, as communities, and as a global system of living beings, may be fundamentally related to how we humans view what the self is. It is the sense of self that may directly influence our individual and collective well-being. And for this reason, addressing an ancient question, perhaps with some new insights from science, may be quite timely.

You may also be asking, even if these are interesting issues, what can we do to make an effective and lasting impact on our well-being beyond just discussing ideas? If the proposition from the wisdom traditions of Indigenous and contemplative teachings is true, that we are all part of a larger whole of nature and not merely the individual bodies we are born into, what further impetus would we need to accept that timeless invitation to be aware of our larger self and now turn that insight into timely action? How can we make a difference in the journey of humanity in the immediate years ahead of us?

One approach to these questions is to consider how we grow and change. We'll examine our individual development—highlighting particular aspects of developmental science that may be especially relevant to understanding how the mind and the construction of the experience of self, identity, and belonging develop across the lifespan. And we'll explore how we change in large groups of people, how culture and community grow and change. Cultural evolution can initiate deep shifts in how we live together on Earth. This cultural growth in the self can be initiated and maintained through the ways we intentionally choose to construct a sense of self. You are reading and I am writing, and together, honoring the inner of you and of me, yet acknowledging the deeply real—if sometimes not readily visible—relational connections of we, MWe can consider new ways of living into the wholeness of being intraconnected in our shared world. The way we communicate—with one another, and within our internal reflections—shapes how we become immersed in new ways of feeling into our experience of self. Symbols, too, the language we use, can support ways of sharing and deepening that directly felt shift in how we perceive reality. Perhaps it is idealistic, perhaps naïve, perhaps wishful optimism—yet when we add the broad fields of science, especially the sciences of energy and of systems, to this timeless invitation to push back on our vulnerability to perceiving only as an individual, we may come to see that naming this challenge allows us to frame its parameters and then initiate wise action in the service of cultural evolution. We can, with awareness, openness, and intention, move beyond the understandable drive for certainty yet inherent confusion of individualism and embrace the less visible, less certain, and less controllable reality of our integrated nature, the intraconnection of the whole of which these bodies, this you and this me, are just one component.

We are interconnected, you and I. We share many things between us: air, ideas, economy, language, humanity. This betweenness is what we express with the prefix "inter-." This is where all those inter- terms, like "interconnected," arise; something very real exists between entities. The idea and experience of intraconnection, in contrast, expresses a withinness of identity and belonging, linked within a fabric of life. It emerged as a term to describe a sense not merely of being connected to trees and people and place but rather of a connectedness within a whole—a sense of wholeness experienced from within.

This type of connection suggests that the wholeness of our self may actually be different from the modern solo-me self we've so often been taught. From an intraconnected perspective, the term "self" is more than merely the brain, the body, the person that creates these words—bigger than the body that empowers us to write and read these words. From this perspective, the self encompasses the whole of the systems in which we live. A system is composed of parts; and it may be that instead of seeing the living system as the self, we've come to see only the part as the self. It may be time to correct this illusion, this misguided perception—to widen our lens and see the self not only as these bodies but to include the living system as an intraconnected whole.

I invite you to join me in exploring how we might more deeply know what comprises the experience of self, perhaps opening up our understanding of how that self emerges, widening our perspective on how we identify the self as we integrate our identity and broaden our sense of belonging. I invite you to see inside the sea inside and to be open to what may not at first be visible to the eye: a withinness that happens not just in your body but within the wholeness of life itself. John O'Donohue might suggest this then is a mystical journey, a quest to see the reality of the invisible. Indigenous teachings would suggest this is ancient knowledge. Contemplative insights might see this as the realization of the reality of interdependence. And recent findings in science, from physics's study of the microstate properties of energy to the mathematical implications of the emergence of complex systems, would support the movement from the simplistic, closed, linear Newtonian view to a more complex, open, dynamical systems perspective of not only the connections among parts but the patterns of the whole that are observed with a different way of perceiving the nature of reality—equally real, simply sensed with a different lens.

This perspective may build a bridge to new ways, for many of us in modern times, to experience a wider, more integrated identity, a broader belonging that incorporates all of humanity and of nature, not only those like-us, letting the experience of self open up to live more fully in life.

One way to symbolize this intraconnection, how individually we become part of something larger than merely our inner selves or our connections to individuals like us, is with a simple equation:

$$Me + We = MWe.$$

While I first introduced this term in prior writings (Siegel, 2014; 2017; 2020), here we are exploring, expanding, and expressing its features and implications for how we might, as a human family, approach the many pandemics that both challenge us and afford us an opportunity to embrace the Indigenous wisdom of coming to respect, connect, reflect, and direct our efforts to shift cultural evolution toward a more integrative way of living together on Earth.

MWe is perhaps a funny and awkward word for some. Yet for others it is a simple and useful term that reminds us of our integrated identity, the features that characterize us as individuals (Me—our individual, inner self), our wider belonging in humanity and within nature (We—our relational, inter self), and the intraconnected, integrated experience of self in the relational wholeness of MWe.

MWe symbolizes the ways we join as part of something larger than our inner selves, larger than our connection to those who are like us: We join with people and the planet; we are intraconnected within nature. Within this intraconnection, we do not lose our individuality; MWe embraces both the me and the we of our identity. MWe reminds us how we can integrate our identity and broaden our belonging to stretch beyond a limiting, separate, solo-self.

A truly scientific stance entails not only curiosity about the true nature of reality but also an inherent understanding that there is much beyond what we can sense directly. When we open to that wonder about the world, we leave behind the noun-like illusion of certainty that the solo-self shrinks into. A wider sense of self fills us with wonder, opening to the verb-like nature of unfolding.

As MWe move along in our journey here, I offer you an opportunity, within the framework of this book, to creatively experience more than just a factual exploration of things and events—the noun-like cognition of things. I am also offering an experiential way of knowing—a verb-like dynamic happening—as you pause, wonder, and explore this inner connection of self within an intraconnected whole, which may be invisible to our eyes yet is equally real. These two ways of knowing are captured by the Greek terms "noesis," meaning intellectual knowledge, and "gnosis," meaning knowledge gained from direct experience. Noesis and gnosis each provide foundational ways of gaining new insights, understanding, and ways of being.

The developmental approach we will take on our journey will invite both types of knowledge: Through the lens of lifespan growth and learning, from before conception through mature adult, we will explore core issues and key aspects of the growth of our experience of self, identity, and belonging. You may find yourself reflecting on your own history as you take this journey. You'll find two forms of immersive experiences that focus on the personal process of integration in the Appendices, should you choose to try these out: a Wheel of Awareness reflective practice, which I'll discuss more soon, and an Integrative Movement Series, which enables the embodiment in motion of nine domains of integration, each relevant to our journey here. You may find it helpful to reflect, in a journal or in your inner mental explorations, on how these ideas and immersive experiences expand your understanding of your own personal pathway in life and how they help link the experiential knowing of gnosis with the conceptual conversations of noetic experiences that unfold.

In many ways, this journey from before conception and across the lifespan, this blending of gnosis and noesis and weaving of inner and outer—this intraconnection of MWe—invites us to let go of the tangible certainties our narrow focus, noun-based, individualistic modern approaches have endowed us with and to embrace a wider expanse of discovery within an integrated self. If we are truly open, our conversation, in the pages of this book, will bring us to an open field of possibility—open with curiosity, open to wonder and exploration, embracing uncertainty. It is my sincere hope that this process will help us better understand and navigate the world around and within. What we felt we knew with certainty, what we thought we could control, how we filtered reality to predict actions, how we organize information into categorical divisions and concepts—each of these, embedded in the neural networks of our brains and shaped by the communications we have with one another, can change, grow, and evolve in our personal development and cultural evolution. They can even happen in the journey of this conversation.

When we embrace this emerging uncertainty, we gain freedom and the ability to reach outside the confines of our prescribed, noun-like, solo-self ways. Put simply, our efforts to strive for certainty in an uncertain world have been reinforced —pushing us to "live as nouns" rather than embrace the reality of our verb-like nature. As a noun, we can have boundaries and definitions that give us an illusion of certainty and control; as a verb, we are open and ever-changing events, deeply interlinked in an uncontrollable fabric of life. We can recognize these motivations to construct certainty and then invite this more verb-like emergence into our mindset, let the fluent nature of self arise, and perhaps even become surprised by our own becoming. As John O'Donohue once said, "I would love to live like a river flows, carried by the surprise of its own unfolding" (O'Donohue, 2000, p. 41). This is the invitation. I welcome you to the flow of whatever emerges in our unfolding conversation that lies ahead.

EMERGENCE

Who are we? How do we form our identity, the features that define who we are? And how does the world around us, the world of people and of nature, shape these features of self to resonate with the larger memberships to which we come to belong?

A Space of Being

To dive deeply into these fundamental questions linking self, identity, and belonging, perhaps it is best to start at the very beginning, to first explore some basic inquiries into the nature of reality itself. In our discussions ahead, we will explore independently discovered principles, found in a number of distinct approaches in Western science, and compare them to other ways we come to make sense of experience, such as those of Indigenous and contemplative traditions we briefly discussed earlier in our conversation. As we've seen, this effort to find a common ground among the independent ways of knowing can be called "consilience."

As an example of applying the principle of consilience, let's look at the physical reality of energy. In the fields of mathematics and physics, the pursuit of understanding the nature of the universe has resulted in a proposal that there exists a "mathematical space," known by such terms as a "quantum vacuum" and "sea of potential," a space in which all possibilities rest before they transform into actualities.

Here's an example we might use to make this abstract notion more accessible. If I think of one of the, let's say, one million English words you and I share by virtue of sharing a common language, your chance of guessing that one word out of one million is a "near-zero" quantity, as it's called. The space of possibility, that set containing all possible words, is analogous to the sea of potential, a formless source of all form, as some physicists call it. It is formless, as it contains only possibilities of what later will become a form—in this case, a spoken word. The process of transforming from the space of possibility, where all possibilities are equally likely to be chosen, to a single actuality, once the choice is made, is how some physicists define "energy." The movement from that space of possibility to the actuality of form, from possibility to actuality, can be called "energy flow."

So, when I tell you that the word I chose is "ocean," energy occurs as a flow from my mind to yours. Figure 2.1 shows what this experience might look like on a diagram: the movement from Point A, all possible words from which I could choose, to Point A-1, when I state one very specific word. The vertical y-axis ranges from all those possibilities, at the bottom, to specific certainty, at the top. When I said "ocean" and you and I were now certain of which word was spoken, that represents 100 percent. This is maximal probability, maximal certainty. The horizontal x-axis represents the time between all choices being possible and my choice of one specific word. The movement from that pool of all possibilities, each with near-zero probability and a maximal degree of uncertainty, to the highest probability— 100 percent certainty, once I state my choice—is energy flow, a sharing of that word between you and me, a movement from possibility to actuality.

Here's the range of certainties, the range of probabilities: Possibility is wide open potential, meaning both (a) lowest probability (you are most unlikely to guess the word I might say) and at the same time (b) maximal uncertainty (you are most uncertain of what I'll say when possibility is maximal). Certainty results from the movement

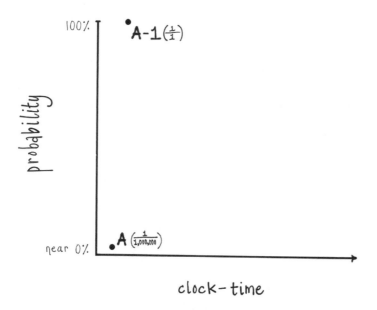

Graphing Probability from Near Zero to 100%

Figure 2.1 Energy flows from Point A—all possible words from which I could choose, each with near zero probability—to Point A-1—once I've stated my choice of a single word, thus 100 percent certainty.

from potential to actual: You are both (a) most certain of my choice of word and thus (b) most likely to "guess" or "know" that word.

Life is dancing with possibility; life is dancing as energy. The process of things changing is what we call "flow." We are inherently aware of this flow, this change, and we have named this awareness "time"—you and I can measure this flow with our clocks. At the most fundamental level, everything we experience is energy flow. Understanding the nature of energy offers us an opportunity to understand more deeply the nature of our life experience.

Sometimes we experience this energy flow as pure energy, like the sensation of a breeze on your cheek, with our consciousness as an awareness of a conduit for our experiences, letting the flow pass through us. Other times the mind acts as a constructor of meaning, such as when we label this sensation "breeze." This labeling is also an energy flow: a symbol of something other than itself, like a word, we call "information." Our experience of energy flow, then, is both as a conduit of sensory energy flow and as a constructor of symbolic energy flow. Yet despite their differences, both conduition and construction are energy flow in the mind and generate our experience of being alive.

In this view of reality, energy is the "basic stuff" of the universe, and information arises from its flow; a related perspective is that information is the basic component of the universe, and energy emerges from it. From a consilient perspective, these two notions of what the universe comprises are fundamentally energy and information flow: Both energy and information change over time—they flow.

You and I both know that there is something else we encounter every day that seems different from the conduit sensory-like energy flow and different from the constructed symbol-like information flow: matter. This book you hold in your hand or, if you are listening to an audiobook, the speakers generating the sounds that strike your ears are examples of this something we call matter. Matter has a mass; we can hold it, measure its weight, determine its spatial dimensions, and watch it change. Western science has revealed to us that all matter in the universe is composed of molecules, which are in turn comprised of atoms, which in turn consist of smaller units . . . yet all of these forms of matter relate to energy through Albert Einstein's formula: energy equals mass times the speed of light squared. The simple reality is that even mass is made of energy—very condensed energy. Scientists propose that before basic atomic particles were formed there was only potential. This might be viewed as pre-formation, in modern physics terms: that formless source of all form, a sea of potential not yet manifested into actuality.

Figure 2.2 helps illustrate this state of pre-formation by building on the previous graph: It has the same y-axis, probability of my choice of word, and it has the same x-axis, time or change in probability. But it adds a third dimension: the z-axis, going in and out of the plane of the page, which represents all the many diverse words that I could choose in a given moment, representing all this diversity of possibility and actuality. This gives the diagram a bottommost plane that represents all those diverse possibilities across time. Let's call this the "plane of possibility."

In our word example, this would be the "mathematical space" filled with all words that exist that could potentially be chosen. It is a "formless source of all form" in that it is filled with potential choices before any were chosen. This plane of possiblity on the diagram is consistent with what physicists call the quantum vaccuum, or sea of potential.

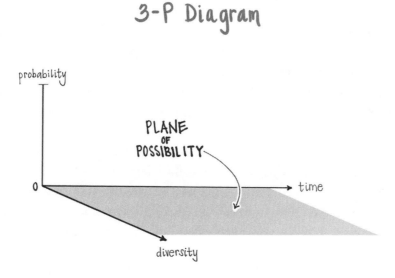

Figure 2.2 The plane of possibility represents all diverse possibilities across time.

This diagram's plane of possibility illustrates the pre-formation space of reality. Before subatomic particles formed in our universe, there existed only potential. The condensation of this energy became atoms and molecules, stars and galaxies—open possibility transformed into probability and actuality. In the diagram in Figure 2.2, this position of potentiality, this pre-formed space of reality, is illustrated as the plane of possibility.

This often-unfamiliar notion of a mathematical space of potential may at first seem odd, but for some, the notion of a space of potentiality may relate to a sense of an open field, as the poet Rumi might call it, a wide-open expanse, a peaceful sense of potential. It may be that these phrases are efforts to convey this plane of possibility, what we can call a "space of being." Being is energy, and being emerges along a range, beginning in the plane of possibility.

For some, a direct access to the subjective sense of this plane of possibility arises in experiences of meditation or walks in nature, each inviting a feeling of awe and the experience of a wide-open, receptive awareness. Open awareness and awe share an "expansion of self," a sense of subjectivity and perspective of a wider lens on identity, a broader belonging than an isolated self often entails. For some, this expansion feels empty-yet-full: empty of particular thoughts and free of an isolated sense of self—a noun-like view of identity—and full of potentiality and an experience of timelessness and connection as a verb-like unfolding of being. In our word-choice example, the moment before you knew the word I chose, "ocean," was a moment of uncertainty yet possibility, a time of freedom, an experience of the openness of the plane of possibility. At that moment, you may also have experienced that oddly worded sense, empty-yet-full, as the sensation of this plane of possibility as a formless source of potential-form filled your awareness. As we'll see, this experience may be not only something we can become aware of, it may be the source of being aware itself.

As we move forward in our exploration of the flow of energy, I hope you come to see how forms of all sorts—in the shape of matter and even of mental experiences, from emotion to memory, thought to intention—emerge from this space of potential, including how you and I come to understand what a self may be, how we form our identity, and how we come to sense our belonging in life. What's more, these manifestations of potentialities, transforming into increased probabilities and then certainties arising from the plane of possibility, not only may be the source of our mental lives, they also can be shaped by our mental experience—we can intentionally alter the flow of energy and information. You may feel the recursive, reciprocal, reinforcing nature of energy's self-organizing emergent flow as mind—as mental life both emerges from energy flow and then shapes its own becoming.

Formless Into Form, Energy Into Mind and Matter

As the formlessness of potential gives rise to form as actuality, energy moves from its lowest point, the plane of possibility, upward to higher degrees of probability. Figure 2.1 illustrates this process of becoming as the movement upward along the probability dimension (y-axis) from possibility (near-zero probability) through various probabilities toward actuality (100% probability).

Let's relate this to our daily experience by continuing with the example of choosing a word. Figure 2.3 is a simple, two-dimensional diagram like Figure 2.1, where A is all possible words I could chose, and A-1 is my final choice. Now let's say I'm thinking of all words that might begin with an "o"—let's say there were ten thousand of these. Your chance of guessing this word would be, yes, one in ten thousand. Point B in Figure 2.3 marks that location of energy on the y-axis of probability; when I say the word "ostrich," energy flows to Point B-1. Focusing this idea even further, let's say that the number of words I might choose is small, such as the number of named oceans in the world or the number of continents. Figure 2.3 also shows this movement from a restricted number of options at Point C to the actualization at Point C-1.

We shall see that if mind is an emergent property of energy flow, then mental processes may be understood as "probability positions," as visualized on our diagram. A thought or memory, for example, would be one hundred percent actualization whereas a state of mind or mood would be a lower point, one representing higher probability

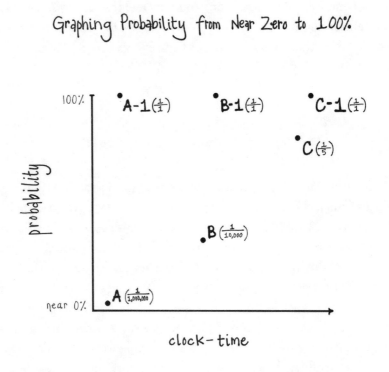

Graphing Probability from Near Zero to 100%

Figure 2.3 Energy flows from Point B, all possible words that begin with "o," to Point B-1, at which point I state my choice from the ten thousand possible words. If only five words are in the subset of possible words, energy flows from Point C, at which there is a one in five chance one will guess my word, to Point C-1, which represents the moment I select one of those five words.

than near zero, but not yet one hundred percent—like the Points B or C in our graph that signify a subset of possibilities that might be chosen, just as a state of mind or mood filters which thoughts, emotions, or memories are most likely to emerge at that moment. We'll dive deeply into this notion of mind as emerging from energy flow as we move ahead in our journey—as we develop into a being with a body and a brain that shape this flow of energy within us to influence our experience of self, identity, and belonging.

As we explore and travel a developmental trajectory and highlight specific aspects of the science of human lifespan growth that are especially relevant to understanding the self in the following chapters, we can use this diagram to picture how energy flow—the movement across these different probabilities across time—underlies the nature of mind, from consciousness to states of mood and intention, from the dynamic verb-based thinking and remembering to our experience of noun-based thought and memory.

Energy flows when we communicate with each other. When we use symbols, such as words or gestures, possibility manifests into actuality, formlessness transforms into form. Another familiar way energy manifests in this wondrous world is as the fundamental "stuff" of mass, the matter that we can see and touch and hold in our hands; the matter that makes life possible. When atomic particles form, they are condensations of energy.

If this is all energy flow, we might ask what energy itself is "made of." A basic unit of energy is called a quantum (its plural is quanta). An example of a quantum is an electron or a photon. When you see something, like these words on a page or light through a window, you are sensing quanta of photons. Now what, in fact, is a quantum of energy? In modern physics, a quantum of energy is considered a probability field. This means that probability, the way we describe different degrees of certainty—as in our Figures 2.1 through 2.3 above—actually underlies all of reality. Although in everyday life we don't usually consider this type of probability, it is, truly, beneath all of our experience, all of our energy and information flow. And consider that mass—like this book you might be holding in your hand or the floor beneath your feet—is actually very dense energy. In the world of probability, "dense energy" means a commitment, a flow, of possibility into actuality.

Our bodies are made of molecules, which are assemblies of atoms, which are comprised of subatomic particles, which are ultimately densely packed quanta. This means that even before our bodies were conceived, even before complex life forms evolved, there was the emergence of probability and certainty from possibility and uncertainty—form formed from a formless space of being, the sea of potential, into higher degrees of commitment, into form as certainty.

In my four books, *The Developing Mind, Mindsight, Mind: A Journey to the Heart of Being Human,* and *Aware,* I proposed that mind is an emergent property of embodied and relational energy flow; this flow arises—emerges—within our skin-encased body and brain (embodied flow) and within our relationships with people and the planet (relational flow). Embodied flow literally means "how energy flow occurs within the skin-encased body and its brain in various manifestations," such as the electrochemical energy flow of neural activity and a wide range of molecular processes and their chemical energy transformations, all distributed throughout our somatic systems. Relational flow indicates energy that is shared between people and between individuals and the natural environment with which they are fundamentally connected. In this way, embodied can be considered "internal" or "inner" with respect to the individual; relational can be considered "inter" or "between" as the sharing of energy and information we can call a relationship or relational connection. A center of experience—of energy flow—can have an inner and an inter spatial location that we designate as embodied and as relational. We have named the whole of the inner and inter connections of flow "intraconnected," from the perspective of the whole system of energy and information flow. In simple symbols: Me is inner; We is inter; MWe is intra.

Seeing the mind as emerging from energy flow also gives us insights into how our sense of self, our experience of identity, and the ways we come to belong—or not—can be understood from this consilient perspective. The mind emerging from energy, seen as probability, helps us understand our mind's facets of consciousness, subjective experience, and information processing. What's more, it illuminates how we come to organize our own unfolding as self in the world.

For us to deeply address who you and I are, our self, our identity, our belonging, we need to take care not to merely reinforce our own perspectives, our own sense of certainty. To try to see beyond our preconceptions, gathered through a lifetime of development, we need to think beyond the views we currently have, to consider new ways of approaching how our mind constructs a view of reality and then communicates that view via the flow of energy.

Whether as concerned individual citizens of Earth or professionals working in mental health or in the broader fields of well-being, education, social justice, environmental science, or public policy, considering these deep foundations in the science of energy can help us imagine and implement innovative and impactful solutions for the problems we now face.

If the hypothesis we are considering in this book is on the right track—that the contemporary construction of a solo-self, isolated from others in our human family and from the family of all living beings, is a significant source of our modern pandemics—then taking on an intraconnected energy flow approach to self, identity, and belonging might help us create real and lasting impacts toward a more integrative way of living together here, now, on Earth.

The Force and Matter of Life

Quanta organize into atoms, which, by assembling into molecules, enable their interactions to form self-organizing clusters of complex structures. Some of those assemblies make membranes that enfold their inner contents into what will become the basic unit of life: the cell. Cells have outer boundaries that enable their inner structures and processes to be embraced and protected, organized and directed; these membranes maintain life by determining what comes in and what stays out of the cell. As a result, inside and outside, inner and outer, are a defining feature of what Western science considers "life."

Another of the many defining features of life is replication. Cells developed the molecular machinery to reproduce themselves: nucleic acid sequences, RNA and DNA, provide a molecular library of nucleotides that form a template and map from which sequences of amino acids are constructed into the protein structures such as those that, combined with many other molecules (such as lipids), form the cytoskeleton and machinery that enable and empower the life of a cell, now and across generations.

Some of these cells organize into larger structures, realizing their potential to form organs and systems of an organism, creating bodies that we call plants, fungi, or animals. And some of these various body designs coalesce their potential to form thought, feeling, and memory and to tap into complex states of consciousness—whether a vertebrate, like us humans, or an invertebrate, such as the octopus. While some of us may be quite relational and thrive in social connections, as explored for human beings by United States Surgeon General, Vivek Murthy (2020) in his book, *Together*, all living creatures nonetheless intuitively act on, and depend on, basic experiences of separation and replication.

The challenge we have as living creatures consequently can be boiled down to this: As we take on our form of actuality as living beings, our membrane-encased cells and our skin-encased bodies become devoted to maintaining the separateness that maintains the integrity of that body or of that cell. Yet the more we have committed to the certainty of our individual composition—in this case, the form of a living entity—the less access we may have to possibility of other forms, other choices. When we envision the unit of life as the singular cell or individual organism only, we may lose the expanded possibilities that arise from that individual being a part of a larger whole system—a cell as part of a healthy body, an individual connected within a larger social and ecological system.

An Identity Lens: Inner and Outer and a Narrowing of Belonging

What is the self? Is the self our skull-encased brain? Our skin-encased body? Is who we are, the wholeness of being human, more than being an individual? Might a wider view of this center of experience, that which we call "self," possibly encompass not only the body but also the larger systems in which we are fundamentally intraconnected?

If a renegade skin- or membrane-encased living (sub)system acts as if the overall system in which it resides is not part of its self, life is threatened. In bodily terms, we experience this as an "autoimmune disorder" in which the body attacks itself; and, as we've discussed, we also call other forms of such an excessive differentiation "cancer," an out-of-control growth of one type of cell that is detrimental to the system as a whole. When we differentiate and do not live with linkages, as the intraconnected nature of a living system, the system as a whole suffers. Our mental construction of a solo-self may be analogous to a cancer in modern society, cultivating and reinforcing renegade growth of separate, disconnected selves, now running amok, out of sync within the larger system of our biosphere called Earth.

Many of us in modern cultures may think of others not like us and of nature as outside of "us"—a personal manifestation of the cellular distinction formed between inner and outer. As life forms have evolved into ever more complex organisms, this central theme of inner and outer has remained for billions of years. As human beings, this fundamental division of life into what is inside versus what is outside allows us, as living entities, to survive. Knowing what is me or not me not only keeps me alive but also influences the human constructions of categories, concepts, and symbols we use to name, identify, and shape how we belong. For example, if someone is walking along a trail with some friends and considers their body and this social group as part of their identity, they may feel a deep sense of belonging in the experience of being with this group of people. If others who walk by are of a different race, implicit racial bias may lead this someone to see those individuals as "other" and part of an out-group—and to treat them with distance if they're apparently neutral or with hostility if they are judged to be a threat. Furthermore, if the natural world in which this person is walking is not sensed as "part of them"—if they do not feel a belonging to the forest in which they are walking—then what is to deter them from leaving trash behind and treating the natural world as a garbage bin—an unfortunate but frequent consequence of this narrow sense of identity and belonging?

As we became social creatures, we relied on our connections to one another for our survival. Belonging to selected members of our species—those human beings in our personal family, those in our village whom we know and trust—involves a neural computation of determining in-group membership and distinguishing this from out-group status. In this manner, we constructed an extension of the life-protecting function of the cell's membrane by ascertaining who is in and who's out. Are you in my in-group? Or are you an outsider, someone from the out-group, apart from "me" and from the plural of me, "us"? The ascertaining of group membership has meant survival for social species for millions of years.

Yet how do we, as conceptualizing human beings, come to determine such belonging, the ways we feel connected, linking us to something more than the skin-encased body into which we are born or even the restricted social groups in which we grow and develop? How do we grow beyond individualistic and even interdependent self-construal toward a metapersonal construal of a self that embraces a membership with all of humanity—not just those like us—and within all of nature?

If we start with a cell, we might say that a cell's membrane defines what is inside or outside, what is the cell and what is not. If that cell is part of a multicellular organism, part of a body, such as a muscle cell in the heart, it is connected with other cells in organized formations functioning as systems. A system is composed of components and their interactions with one another. The constituent elements of a cloud, for example, include molecules of water and air; the components of our brain include neurons and glial cells, such as microglia and astrocytes; the parts of a cell include the molecules of its membranes, its cytoplasm, and its organelles. These are all systems and collections of systems within systems.

Systems can be sensed. You and I can sense energy flow as the five inputs to the body—hearing, sight, smell, taste, and touch. And we can sense the energy flow within the body as sensations of muscles, bones, and internal organs. We perceive these sensations within awareness in at least four dimensions: across time and the three dimensions of space—length, depth, and height. What we perceive and name as time really means change, our awareness of something being like this now, and then like that then. In this way, we can sense the parts of a system and how these parts exist in space and time, how they exist in spatial dimensions and how they change.

And we can even get a sense of a connection of the parts to each other within these systems that our eyes may not be able to see, that our intellect may not, yet, have been taught how to conceive or name. The aphorism we "need to believe it to see it" reminds us that beyond the proof of "needing to see it to believe it," if we do not have a mental model enabling us to conceive the reality of systems connections, our perceptual filters related to what we do believe—a linear view, for example—may ignore sensory patterns that actually exist. The result is that we are perceptually blind to those systems connections that are outside of our particular mental model of the how the world works. We literally are unable to see what is right in front of us. An analogy may be that of a fish being unable to perceive the water in which it lives. Some, like my colleagues Mette Boell, Peter Senge, and Otto Scharmer, might call this ability to perceive systems as "systems sensing": seeing the deeply interwoven nature of the tapestry of reality. From this sensing we are able to gain what they call "systems awareness" and engage in "systems thinking" as we now perceive the patterns of connections, and the patterns of patterns, as they emerge from the flow of systems as a whole.

When we divide and disconnect from a larger sense of identity as a system, when we perceive and believe the totality of self is the part, we lose a broader belonging that each of us is capable of experiencing—a wider sense of being intraconnected in life. When we do not sense how we belong to larger systems, when we deny the reality of this unseen, intraconnected nature of the world, we come to live a partially true life, a life of separation.

What is the system of you? What does "you" actually mean—where do you begin, where do you end? When are you? Is your self the body, or is it the larger systems in which the body called "you" lives? And are you present not only in these systems across space now but also across the unfolding of change, what we've collectively named "time," with terms like "past," "present," and "future"?

As a first step, suppose we expand this sense of the you of who you are to include identity across one dimension that we are familiar with, the dimension of time. Let's see how identity—the characteristics that identify a center of experience—looks throughout our ancestral history and across species. If we are to identify one characteristic of who you and I are across time, we might say that we are comprised of matter. This narrows us from the belonging in the whole of reality—from being a part of the process of energy transformation, formless into form, possibility into actuality. Terms such as "eternity" and "infinity" attempt to capture this wide-open expanse of possibility. In science we propose that the emergence of form as matter, the condensation of energy, has an estimated history of about 13 billion years, ever since the Big Bang or whatever process "began" existence of matter in this material world in which we live, including Earth, our solar system, our Milky Way galaxy, and all the galaxies we live within, in the totality of matter, the matter of the universe. We have moved from identifying with wide-open possibility, our origins (if we can consider that notion), to an identity as matter across space and time.

As living beings we've moved even further away from the eternal and the infinite—layers of experience that nevertheless remain with us, even beneath awareness, as part of our identity—and moved from the whole universe of matter, which was another layer, to another criterion of our identity: living. This narrows the focus of our belonging to the subgroup of energy—a subset of reality—that is a bit more modern: that collection of forms we call living matter. Now we have living ancestors—3.5 billion years of them.

If we continue up this probability axis, focusing even more narrowly and constraining our belonging, we might say that part of our identity as animals began about 800 million years ago with the emergence of sponges; and then developed further 530 million years ago, when our vertebrate ancestors arose in our evolutionary history. Somewhere around 310 million years ago, we left our fish and amphibian forebears and inhabited the land as reptiles. Then we attained fur and gave birth to our offspring as mammals about 210 million years ago. This is a rough overview of our belonging in the evolutionary journey from prelife days to living as mammals in the air-borne world of this planet.

Based on fossil evidence, it appears that somewhere around 55 million years ago, our order of primate ancestors, a grouping that includes monkeys and the great apes, appeared within the class of mammals. Our family of hominins may have begun to roam Earth sometime around 6 to 8 million years ago, coming to walk upright for most of the time and facing forward as we distributed ourselves around the globe. The genus of Homo, sometimes broadly called "humans," seems to have evolved on Earth somewhere around 5 million years ago, and some studies place the appearance of our species—what we've come to name Homo sapiens, the ones who not only know but know we know, sometimes called the "wise ones"— in

Africa sometime between 350,000 and 130,000 years ago. We and our Neanderthal cousins used tools and lived in groups.

We have evidence that around 40,000 to 30,000 years ago we began expressing our mental representations as art through drawings on cave walls and that about 15,000 years ago we began helping others who would have otherwise died from their injuries. These findings suggest that our minds had developed enough by this time to enable us to think about life and to communicate in symbols what we were perceiving and conceiving. Plus, helping others suggests we could sense another's suffering, think through what might help, and then carry out that action—fixing a broken leg, for example—in the present moment to improve a future outcome. All of this suggests the likelihood of compassion and empathy and the ability to conceive of time as past, present, and future.

All of life functions as a deeply intraconnected system of nature—connected across the dimensions of what we call space and time. This living system is our biosphere. At the broadest belonging to the living world here on Earth, we can see that we are fundamentally woven into that biosphere—we are nature. Within the magnificent biodiversity of the many species of living beings with whom we share our common home, this wondrous blue dot, planet Earth, we have a range of evolutionary lines of growth—distant from and closer to us—that includes all of life and that can be defined in narrower and narrower categories, such as the one ending in our species, human beings. In whichever ways we choose to focus on our ancestry, we can sense our connection across time, as we belong to life as an individual component within any of a range of subsystems of this larger whole of the biosphere across space, time, and species. This illustrates a fundamental point: By identifying which features we choose to highlight, we determine which group we belong to—that is, part of the infinite reality of possibility; a component of the universe of matter; or one among all living beings, all animals, all vertebrates, all mammals, all primates, all human beings; connected to people who share the immediate ancestry we name as ethnic group or race, to those in your community, to individuals in your personal family, or connected only to the person living in the skin-encased body you were born into—the individual bodily source modern culture delineates and declares as your "self."

We living beings on planet Earth all descended from common ancestors. In more recent times, we can say we are direct descendants of a mammalian line. Mammals are social creatures, but many other living beings are collaborative as well. Even single cell organisms, such as amoeba, bacteria, and fungi such as yeast, can function as colonies of massively interlinked systems. The multicellular mycelia of fungi form crucial networks in the forest soil, and trees of the forest have intricate communication channels providing ways to protect and nurture other trees in a deeply intraconnected web of life. Although the human brain may divide our experiences into categories of separation, nature functions as a profoundly interwoven system, not as separate groups in isolation. The term "intraconnected," emerging as a linguistic symbol from this human body, Dan, after being immersed in a forest, reminds us of the perspective of the whole rather than just the one, separate component isolated in its identity, even if it is interacting with the system's parts.

As we narrow our boundaries for a sense of "belonging," choosing criteria from open possibility transforming into actuality—energy flow in the universe—to densities of energy called matter, to living beings, to animals, to mammals, to primates, to the level of human beings, we can see how our concepts of membership—of belonging—begin to shift. The criteria we choose to determine our identity directly define our belonging. This capacity to shift the focus of what criteria we choose is what we will call an "identity lens," which we can adjust from a narrow focus on our body or brain alone to a wide-angle perspective, seeing who we are as fundamentally intraconnected within the whole energy system of the universe. Our belonging follows this focus of our identity lens, constricting our groups of belonging with a narrow focus and broadening our belonging with a wide-angle view.

In these fundamental ways we can see how there are many dimensions to identity and belonging. The good news about this identity lens is that we can adjust it—we don't need to choose one level of identity and belonging over another because they are each real, and each have their importance. Does focusing on being a member of all living beings mean we no longer belong to a wide-open field of possibility—or to the manifestation of that potential as inanimate matter? Does narrowing the focus of our identity lens mean the wider focus is no longer part of the reality of our self? Our identity lens can shape our center of experience as self, shifting how we feel we belong; and we can widen or narrow that focus with our intention. Taking care of our body—sleeping well, eating well, nurturing our body and caring for its needs, enjoying our body—is our identity lens focusing on the inner self, our identity within our skin-encased body that we get to keep for this personal lifetime. We can feel fully connected to our body, and within that inner sense, we feel whole. And we are also the whole system, and we can come to sense this wider identity and broaden our belonging across space and time with a wide-angle focus that is also real and is just as important.

As we move forward from the space of potential into atomic form and then form as living beings, we move into ever more committed probabilities toward actuality in the world. If our identity lens is wide-angle enough, we can see that we are the whole of this intraconnected system of reality, formless into form, across species, across time, across space. It is within our intraconnected wholeness that we most broadly belong. As we learn the skill to cultivate this wide-angle view, we are empowered to sense our collective journey from possibility to actuality, the flow of energy that is the essence of experience, the core of being.

While we may—perhaps out of necessity, perhaps out of learning—focus at times more tightly on a more narrow range of identity and belonging, let's underscore that the choice is ours: We can harness the flexibility of our identity lens to sense this broader view and learn the art of widening our perspective on who we are and with whom and within what we belong. Opening to this wider range of possibilities is our birthright. Learning to adjust the focus of this lens of identity—from narrower to wider inclusion of myriad scales and times—lets a new way of sensing the self emerge, opening our identity and broadening our belonging as we move forward, together, here on Earth, with intention and choice.

CONCEPTION AND BIRTH

We are calling the experience of reality "the flow of energy." A subset of that reality is the emergence of form from a formless space of potentiality, which is indicated on our 3-P diagram as the plane of possibility. One potential manifestation of that form from this formless open space of possibility is matter, the condensation of very dense energy; and a further subset of that form, that is, of matter, includes all living beings—life on Earth and in other locations in the Universe in which life forms may live. For human beings, our life form is contained within the somatic, skin-encased system we call a body. As we move forward in our exploration of the development of self, identity, and belonging, we should take care not to make the common "mistake" of modern times: the narrow identity lens view that who "you" are is only your body. It does matter how we define linguistic terms, these words as symbols, because they reveal and reinforce underlying concepts and categories that shape our lives directly. If the terms "you," "I," and "me" are used to indicate the inner self, then yes, "you are your body" and "I am my body." You might point to your body and say, "This is me!" Yet what we've been exploring is that the self is not just with this inner aspect of subjective experience, perspective, and agency; your self is also inter, as we've suggested in our journey, and this means that your identity, your belonging, your self, are bigger than the body alone, broader than the brain in that body; neither skin nor skull block the flow of energy and information. The wholeness of that flow, inner and inter, is what we've named the intraconnected flow of MWe. We continue our discussion here with the emergence of one aspect of your self, the individual you of your inner self. It's an important starting place in the narrative of you, but not the whole story of your identity and belonging, or even of your self.

A Body Form

Let's look at the odds of you becoming you in the body you were born into. Of the billions of eggs and the trillions of sperm that existed at the moment in what we call time, on this planet we've named Earth, one egg encountered one sperm, and the complements of nucleic acid templates, the strands of DNA of the chromosomes of each of these unique gametes, entangled themselves in their double helix molecular formations to continue your family's genetic legacy of our human heritage, a weaving of all the ancestors of your mother and all of those of your father to become a single-cell conceptus, with its membrane now encasing a united singularity of being, as two cells become one.

Along with some of those genes you've inherited came non-nucleic acid molecules, clusters known as methyl groups and histones that determine how the genes they interact with express themselves. They function as epigenetic regulators, shaping protein production and ultimately bodily form and function. These epigenetic regulators can be affected by the environment experienced by your parents, and your grandparents, and thereby directly affect the you that you become. In your own body's lifetime, experiences you have interacting with the environment or learning to shape your own inner mental processes will also directly impact how ongoing epigenetic regulation unfolds, altering things such as how you respond to challenging life events with resilience or with distress and inflammation.

Your nascent body formed in this miraculous moment of union

of all these factors. Of the nearly infinite possible matches, that one sperm and that one egg were your beginnings. Yet as we explored in the previous chapter, that single cell conceptus has the long history of all living beings embedded in the nucleic acid library passed down from your ancestors; it also has all the epigenetic regulators embedded from your parents and their parents as well as all the species known to be your ancestors and all the cosmic events known to create the conditions in which the building blocks of your ancestors could form. In this sense, you are not just your body now; you are your ancestors too.

The body serves as an inner center of sensation, perspective, and agency—this is the inner flow of energy and information, our inner self. Our genetic and epigenetic heritage confers a reality of history that will directly shape your experience of this inner self as a center of being, a center of experience that will unfold as your body grows. While your "embodied brain," the nervous system extending throughout your body, is not yet formed at conception, your genetic information carries with it a long history of ancestors and the lives they led as a type of narrative of the past, your ancestral narrative. Just as narrative links past, present, and future, this ancestral story exists, without words and mostly without our awareness, through our bodies as we live into the narrative of our current lives.

As we develop after conception, somatic systems prepare us for our life ahead, including the embodied brain that will enable us to form identity, to experience a sense of belonging, to become many versions of self in this world. Later on, as we develop in childhood, we even learn to focus a lens of identity and shape our own becoming. Before we leave the uterus and join the world out in this air realm surrounding us all, the growth of our body is influenced both by our inheritance and by the watery womb in which we are growing. The information from our ancestors—our ancestral narrative—and the experiences we have in the womb as our nervous system grows will shape how our body develops, including the brain, which has ways to remember all that is happening.

Our Embodied Brain

The origin of the cells of the nervous system reveals a surprising developmental history: The single-cell conceptus grows into many cells, soon with an inner layer and an outer layer. Just as, eons ago, atoms assembled into molecules and then coalesced into self-organizing clusters that developed membranes to encase their inner contents into the basic unit of life, this moment of differentiation—when an inner and outer layer form—represents that fundamental distinction in our lives: inner versus outer.

The outer layer, the ectoderm, is destined to become the enveloping skin, the boundary of our body's form. Part of this outer layer folds inward to create a neural tube, the origin of the nervous system. This tube will become the spinal cord and will send neurons out to connect all the major organs and to grow in complex ways inside the head. This web-like set of networks exists not just in the head but throughout the body, comprising what we are calling the embodied brain.

In fact, in our bodies we have three "brains," or parallel distributed processing (PDP) networks: one around the gut, one around the heart, and one in the head. The only PDP processor with linguistic abilities is the head brain, so later, as we grow and develop language, the head brain names itself, not surprisingly, *the* brain. As neuroscientist Antonio Damasio (2018) notes, the head brain evolved in our lives as the third brain, in service of the other two and of the whole body.

PDP processors can compute energy flow patterns into information. A parallel distributed computer, for example, can reason and learn from experience. (This is not what your serial-processing home computer is capable of doing, you might be relieved to know.) When we realize that our body has PDP network capability in more than just the head's collection of neural networks, we gain insight into how the whole body is involved in our mind's construction of information from energy flow—what we call cognition. This is the somatic origin of the statement that the mind is broader than the brain. The mind is fully embodied.

And yet the mind is also relational. As an emergent property of energy flow, mind emerges not just from within our bodies, but between the body and the world "outside"— beyond skull and skin. In later chapters we will see how this energy flow can also be shared among individuals, and with all of nature, extending beyond our skin, embedded in our relationships with one another and the larger world in which we live. Even beyond being "enskulled," our mind is not just fully embodied, it is deeply and fundamentally emerging from our relationships as well.

The ectodermal origin of the fully embodied brain suggests a fascinating implication: Just as the skin is the life-preserving barrier between inner and outer, the nervous system is always at the interface of the inner and the outer as well.

The words that the labeling, language-loving head brain constructs to name this distinction, phrases like "self versus other" and "us versus them," may parallel our primary experience of inner versus outer. With a fundamental origin of our sense of self constructed by embryologic history and by genetics—and by reinforcement in our language usage—the body's role as a defining center of experience begins early in our lives. We can see how self versus other, inner versus outer, us versus them each may have at their origins a survival stance of life versus death, cohered versus chaotic, certain versus unpredictable.

To understand the wholeness of the embodied brain as a series of systems within systems, it helps to use not linear thinking but systems thinking. Linear thinking is useful if we are working on a plumbing problem, for example, to stop a leak: There is a hole here; let's patch it and stop the loss of water. Systems thinking is needed if we are to glimpse larger systems, such as a house as a whole or a house within a neighborhood within a city within a state within a country within a continent within a global ecosystem. If we do not think beyond linear causality and come to sense, perceive, conceive, and act in systems terms, we will only be plugging metaphorical holes and never help resolve the underlying problems within our systems on this planet. We could, instead, identify factors that may be inhibiting the healthy function of our systems and then make intentional interventions at a systems level to release the self-organizing system's innate capacity to flourish. This would be using systems awareness to harness the power of what we'll call "systems intelligence": the innate capacity of complex systems to self-organize toward harmony as they adapt and learn if they are allowed to differentiate and link, enabling the interdependence of their parts to flourish.

In a biodiverse ecosystem, for example, we may find that pests are digging up the roots of trees in an orchard we've planted. We can try to kill those pests with poisons, but we may find that we've now eliminated the food source for another member of the ecosystem that was keeping other inhabitants in check. Choosing the direct linear approach—poison the pest—not only poisons the people who eat the fruit but also depletes the system of that "pest," causing another shift that can lead to the collapse of other inhabitants, and on and on. Instead, using a systems strategy, such as introducing an appropriate living organism that keeps the pest in check, helps the whole system flourish and thrive.

Studies reveal that as the soil and its surroundings become filled with living biodiversity, the system's own intelligence takes over and the biological system self-organizes to optimize its functioning. If we grow only one crop, if we let the living soil die from poisons in a linear effort to "stop a pest," we actually lose this vital, innate systems intelligence of the natural world—a system is intraconnected as a whole.

Simply Being and an Implicit Memory of Wholeness

As a fetus—a continuously fed growing body floating in a constantly body-temperature bath—there is no need to eat or breathe: Our mother's body does the vital work to meet all of our needs while we are simply being. As our nervous system grows, the connections among its basic cells, the neurons, will change the strengths of their linkages in ways we believe construct memory—an experience that has become encoded and stored and that is retrievable at some future moment. We likely remember, in what is called "an implicit level," this state of "being at one with the uterus," with nothing we need to do, only to simply be. We were a system with the uterus, at one, simply being.

The implicit memory of this state of being whole may parallel the feeling of the space of being discussed earlier, which is also in our ontological—the way we come to be—origins. We can see here our two facets of experience in which we have the birthright of existential wholeness: a sea of potential, the quantum state of wide-open possibility; and a womb state of resting at one with the uterus, in a state of wholeness.

That state of being whole, of the sea of potential (the formless source of all form), can serve as our image for how we can rest in the wide-open possibility of being before committing to any specific form or type of doing as a body of action in the world. In this perspective of the whole of being, intraconnection is being whole. With this wholeness of being, this being whole, fixed distinctions between I versus you, us versus them, self versus other have no meaning because such distinctions do not exist in the systems reality of intraconnection.

This reality that the growing fetus lives in—one reality with at least the two facets: the sea of potential and the systems wholeness of the womb—invites us to consider that perhaps a longing for a sense of wholeness, to rest in a space of being, may relate to these two facets. This sense of being whole may arise both from the quantum microstate of connection and from memories of the womb environment of just being. And once we are out of the womb, we might implicitly remember and miss this sense of wholeness. This feeling of something missing may be more than a fantasy, more than a misplaced longing; it may in fact be an implicit memory of something real, a glimpse reminding us of the womb and perhaps the less visible micro-state realm of reality, a reality that stays with us—even if beneath our everyday awareness—for the rest of our bodies' lives. And in this way, the longing we sometimes feel for wholeness and to simply be—to not feel fractured and alone, separated from the rest of reality, nor forced into the continual "doing" of survival—may be a longing to access our birthright, to return to a wholeness of being.

The nervous system remembers, before and below conscious thought, through changes in the connections among its basic cells, our neurons. This nervous system becomes activated as energy flows through its webs of interconnected cells—this is how our brain encodes experience. These activated neural linkages can store that firing pattern and, at a later time, retrieve a firing pattern similar to, though never exactly like, the pattern that fired during the encoding.

Memory can be defined as how an experience at one point leads to a change at some future point. Research suggests that early in our lives, at least in the final months in the womb, the nervous system is mature enough to encode experience, store it, and then retrieve some representation of it at a later point. The developmentally first and most fundamental layer of memory is called implicit memory. These implicit memories become available in the last months in the womb and influence us for the rest of our lifespan, enabling us to harness networks of bodily sensation, perception, emotion, and, later on, behavioral actions known as procedural memory. An important feature of this implicit layer of memory is that no particular kind of conscious attention is required to firmly establish these encodings.

When these pure implicit memories are retrieved, they activate the nervous system in a pattern similar to the time of encoding. The difference between this and explicit memory is that in pure implicit form, the memory is not labeled or tagged with a sensation of, "Oh, I am remembering something from the past." Retrieval of pure, implicit memory creates a state of neural activation similar to the original experience and without being labeled as a recollection.

For example, if a toddler was bitten by a cat, the perception of that feline, the emotion of fear, the bodily sensation of pain may all be fully encoded into implicit memory and then stored in the connections in their brain. At that early age, the development of another part of their brain, the hippocampus, has not yet occurred and therefore the experience may remain in pure implicit form. Even in older individuals, blocking the function of the hippocampus can enable implicit memory to remain in its unintegrated, pure state of storage. Later, a month or a year or decades later, in this child's life (or the life of an older individual with impaired hippocampal encoding), they might encounter another cat, perhaps of the same color or size, and this can serve as a memory trigger, and these implicitly stored memories can be automatically retrieved—and as pure implicit memory reactivations, they are not tagged as coming from the past. Thus, in the here and now, they would feel the pain as a bodily sensation, see aggression in the cat—perhaps in magnified form as a toddler might perceive the original feline attacker—and feel the fear of the encounter in the present moment; none of these sensations, perceptions, or emotions would feel like a memory being recalled, rather an experience happening now.

You may imagine how baffling this form of retrieval can be for some people, as it makes them feel they are experiencing something that is truly happening now, even though it is, in fact, an implicit recollection of something that happened in the past. This can explain flashbacks during certain painful moments of unresolved trauma, and this just may be a root source of a longing we may have for wholeness, a longing for something we seem to perceive through a foggy filter of the past, some thing or some time we cannot quite pinpoint, a sense of simply being at peace, a feeling of resonance. This feeling may be an implicit echo from our past time in the womb—and a glimpse, perhaps, into the plane of possibility that rests in the infinite present in the microstate realm of our lives.

In the womb, implicit memory encoding of just being involves sensory, bodily, and emotional memory networks that elicit a feeling of being at one with ... something—the uterus, the universe .... There would be no sense of "Oh I am remembering now," just the bodily feeling of the experience of wholeness itself. And when we sense the disparity between our busy lives, out here in this air-filled world, and this feeling of being whole, included, just being, it is only natural that our longing would intensify. Is there some way we might access the space of being, the sea of potential, and the state of being whole, at one with the uterus, that we long to return to or to find anew? Is our longing to belong arising from these facets of wholeness so that we implicitly know the peace of being fully accepted and the fullness and joy of simply being?

From Being to Doing

The transition from simply being in the uterus to needing to "do" in post uterine life is huge—the life we lead after birth stands in monumental contrast to resting in the flow of experience in the womb. While every membrane-encased cell has been on a mission to live and has been busy with its intracellular processing, the body as a whole system has never yet had to focus its energy on intentional efforts to achieve anything in particular—this is the underlying sense of our bodily self as simply being as opposed to as having somatic, body-wide systems that are driven to accomplish something, to do something to survive. This shift from being to doing is filled with a new sense of urgency, a new drive to survive.

The prebirth state of our body system likely has within its experiential memory the shift from spacious sensations and free movement during the weeks and months after conception to a restricted feeling as our body grows to fill the uterus. Then our world suddenly changes: whether by vaginal birth or by caesarian section—we experience the abrupt shift from an inner, warm, watery womb to a world filled with new sensations. Bright lights strike our retinas; breezes with various temperatures and odors flow over our skin, through our nose, and into our lungs; compressed airwaves strike our ears as sound; textures and pressures create new tactile sensations on our skin; and compounds on our tongue create tastes we've never experienced.

These are new energy patterns, reaching us from outside our skin-encased body for the first time. In the womb we had no need to distinguish our fetal form from the uterus. Our identity could include a wholeness of all—we were one with our uterus/universe, experienced and embraced without boundary. Now, suddenly, our skin membrane surrounding our somatic self is interacting with a new world, with new energy patterns, and now this distinct, physically disconnected and differentiated collection of mass, the body, begins experientially defining who it is within this new world.

With these new sensations, the body picks up energy flow from "outside" of itself and interprets it, which means that we now distinguish between internal, within the body, and external, outside the boundary of the body's skin. Every cell of our body—for eons, from the beginning of life as we define it—has made this membranous distinction; now our somatic body extends that basic inner-versus-outer contrast, using the skin as our defining "membrane."

And we also begin experiencing entirely new sensations from within our body—somatic sensations directly related to our survival. We feel an innate drive to breathe. An intense inner feeling of hunger arises, accompanied by an energetic push, a drive to eat. The pangs of needing nutrition and oxygen are new—for in the womb, all was provided via the umbilical cord. And our waste products were also filtered out, as automatic maternal processes maintained us without our having to do a thing. There was no need to eat, breathe, or eliminate—we could simply be, and all was taken care of.

In terms of an experience of self, identity, and belonging, you and I—individuals here in the world where we live and communicate among our relations—can draw only on implicit memory to imagine how the center of experience we've named "self" is now profoundly different from what we experienced in the prebirth time.

Refocusing Our Identity Lens from Linear to Systems

After birth, our body's nervous system continues to develop as it experiences, records, and links the interactions of our somatic body with the energy flows from the "outside" world. As occupants of a body with an embodied PDP-brain that is growing in a linear, narrow identity-lens-focused culture, our conscious awareness of these flows may be shaped to manifest in linear terms rather than in systems terms: My body is here; it types something now on this page. You read these words; you have a response. That is a linear sequence of cause and effect between a me here and a you there. We may interact, yes, but we are fundamentally separate in this linear worldview.

A systems perspective, in contrast, captures how we become aware of and even sense how intricate nonlinear processes of mutual influence underlie the unfolding of experience. This systems perspective is much harder to articulate with linear words, especially considering that nouns make up the majority of words in English and other modern languages. This majority is different in many Indigenous languages, such as those of the Potawatome of North America or Aboriginal dialects in Australia, in which verbs are dominant. Interdependent, multidirectional relationships are also much more difficult to measure and more challenging to illustrate in a drawing or diagram. But since the end of the twentieth century, we've developed the computational power to detect and illuminate the underlying synergy of systems-functioning using mathematical analyses that enable us to understand interactions such as how clouds move through space, how crowds interact, and how environments function as complex systems. Those insights have revealed a powerful mutuality of influence that is multidirectional, not only linear in causation, and an emergence of something greater than the sum of the system's components which are profoundly important to respect and support in the deeply connected systems in which we all live.

In the transition to life after birth, a linear view becomes part of our way of living, perhaps in all infants regardless of our cultural setting. We feel hungry, we call out, a caregiver comes to feed us, we feel satiated and good—that's all a linear sequence. It's a view that serves us well in many situations, it's just not the whole story of how the world works.

Linear thinking that views cause and effect relationships among separated parts can be a practical way to live that has survival benefits in meeting our needs from the viewpoint of the body as a center of experience—the inner self. If the individual continues to hold this linear perspective alone—if the inner self is the only self—then the larger reality of being a part of interwoven layers of systems may be lost to both perception and conception. If the embedded information messages of the family and the larger culture continue to reinforce that individuality, there may be little to challenge this survival-focused, singular view of individuality of the self; we don't even know, from this encompassing linear processing, that what we know is not all that can be known.

Our lives are really part of a larger overall set of interacting processes that affect us by affecting our caregivers: their current environment and their own life history. Learning to sense these influences helps us see in systems terms. From a linear point of view, our identity is as an entity, a noun-like thing fixed and separate from the rest. This is the origin of the solo-self. From a systems perspective, our identity is more a verb—a dynamic nodal point in a system of energy and information flow happening through us, through the body node, as part of a larger whole. As we've discussed, it may be that, for many reasons (including our survival drive for certainty and the self-reinforcing top-down constrictions of linear processing and thinking of ourselves as nouns), we are likely to take—or mis-take—the node of the body to be the totality of self rather than to identify both the inner bodily node and the inter system as comprising our true self.

Once we are born, the reality of living in a body—a large accumulation of molecules we can call a "macrostate"—becomes a dominant part of our lives. While the microstate, quantum realm never disappears, the macrostate realm may come to dominate our perception and, in modern cultural settings, to be reinforced as the only view that is real. Yet our lens of identity can shift not only from a narrow to a wide angle, from our somatic body to our connections through time and space to all aspects of the universe; we can also shift it from macro to micro.

The body is a real entity that requires action to survive: to breathe to bring in oxygen and expel carbon dioxide; to eat when hungry to bring in nutrients; to drink to maintain physiological equilibrium and hydration; to defecate and urinate to remove toxins; to sweat or shiver to maintain body temperature. But we are born helpless, and therefore, as relational organisms, as mammals, we need connection to survive as well—connections with people and connections with nature, with the planet. Each of these needs for survival entails sharing energy flow. When that flow provides for our physiological and relational needs, we thrive. Infants without physical care certainly wither and die, but so do infants without human attachment. Without connection to nature, our mental health suffers—we become distracted, depressed, and disconnected.

For these survival-rooted reasons, out in this new, post-uterine world, doing to connect—to other people, to nature—becomes a matter of life and death.

INFANCY

As we humans evolved an upright posture, as my sometimes sore lower back, especially after that horse accident can attest, our hips and spine adjusted in ways that not only put us at risk, but also resulted in a narrowing of the birth canal in females that necessitated our offspring make a relatively early departure from the womb so that the newborn's body could make the safe passage out into this new world. We enter this shockingly different, air-filled world with an immaturity that makes us very dependent on our caregivers for survival. In fact, the term during which human offspring, from infancy through childhood and adolescence, are dependent on their caregivers is one of the longest periods of any mammal. What this means for brain development is that genetic and epigenetic factors will continue to impact early neural growth at the same time as direct experiences—the flow of energy and information—contribute to shaping the function and growing structure of our immature brains. We become who we are from a starting place of essential relational connection that remains important across the lifespan.

Networks, Motivation, and Emotion

As somatic sensations stream through our body, energy flows throughout the interconnected nervous system we call our embodied brain, with its web-like tapestries woven around our intestines, enveloping our heart, and filling our head. The flow of energy through these interconnected, parallel distributed processing neural networks can be called "neural firing." This activity entails electrical energy flow as ions move in and out of membranes of the neuron. As the ionic flow of electrical charge reaches a synaptic link with a downstream neuron, neurotransmitters are released to carry the flow to the next neuron. The flow to a neuron may consist of either inhibitory or excitatory input or both from many other neurons, which links via the cell body and its many dendrites; and the neuron then sums this input and either fires an action potential (when excitatory input is greater than inhibitory)—or does not (when inhibitory input is greater than excitatory)—down its single axon to send the energy flow on to the cell body and dendrites of the next receiving-neuron's membrane.

This electrochemical energy flow emerges as patterns of neuronally distributed firing that we call "neural representations." Our embodied brain can enable us to experience bottom-up conduition—as close to a pure energy flow in the body as something can possibly be, such as hearing the breeze blowing through the trees or feeling grass between your toes. These representations also enable us to use top-down constructions to name these bottom-up sensations—we literally re-present air streaming through the forest, to ourselves and to others, as the linguistic symbol, breeze.

We are creatures living in a body, so from a certain perspective, everything our nervous system does, including bottom-up conduition as sensation, is really a translation of energy flow into information—that air blowing by the body is the air itself; once we've sensed it, even before we've perceived it or named it, it is no longer the air blowing but rather our body's experience of the air blowing.

Poets attempt to use words to name the sensation that occurs even before the top-down construction we call perception. We can try to use words and even their rhythm and patterns in an attempt to get beneath, before, or beyond the construction of words themselves. And yet, whereas the conduition of sensation is influenced by our body's anatomy, with our particular variety of senses and their capacities, our mental construction—in its many shapes and forms: perception, conception, cognition, action—is molded more by our head-brain's neural connections, many of which are constructed from prior learning. Our perceptions are shaped by our experiences—this is why we call this a top-down process. Bottom-up indicates the most direct input from our "lower" sensory organs as it moves upward; top-down means that prior events have shaped how we filter input through the "higher" neural mechanisms to influence what we experience from the "top"—from prior experience.

And from our perceptions, we construct symbolic representations, such as images, ideas, and linguistic language. These are all ways energy is in a formation that stands for something other than itself—it is information, in this case, filtered by what we've learned, molded by what we believe. This is the origin of the notion that "we see what we believe"—what we perceive is not what we sense—it is what we've come to believe is true, not necessarily a clear view of what is real. Thus, sensation is conduition, and all the rest is construction. Our experience of self—with its direct subjective experience, perception, and agency—weaves both bottom-up and top-down. Conduition is our experience of simply being; construction is doing things with that conduition, such as when we construct our memories and our mental models. Both construction and conduition are necessary—neither is better than the other; each is linked to living a full life.

Both conduition and construction shape our sense of self, identity, and belonging. When we sense energy flow in the body, we use the term "interoception." When we sense movement of the body, we use the term "proprioception." Together we can refer to these two types of sensation as body awareness, what in Western science we call our "sixth sense." The first five senses—hearing, seeing, smelling, tasting, touching—are how we take in energy streams from outside our body. The sixth sense, body awareness, is how we are conscious of energy streams inside our body. Sensing these energy streams from both outside and inside our body is vital to our well-being. In the appendices, the Wheel of Awareness and the Integrative Movement practices invite you to dive deeply into the conduition of the senses with the focus of attention and the movement of the body. One aspect of those experiences is learning to distinguish conduition from construction and then link them in the process of integration across a range of domains.

In the brain, layers of neural networks carry out and organize different roles and patterns of our conduitive and our constructive processes. With about one hundred billion neurons and an average of ten thousand connections linking a given neuron to other neurons, the head's brain—the enskulled brain—is extraordinarily complex. Its number of connections exceeds the number of stars in the sky, and the number of possible on-off firing patterns is greater than the proposed number of atoms in the universe. This organ is so complex it can even name itself: the brain.

A useful model to understand the brain's basic layering is the hand model of the brain (Figure 4.1). With your fingers enclosing your bent thumb to form a fist, your fingers represent the cortex, the outer layer of the brain. This is our mapmaking region, the one that makes neural representations of sensory input and translates them into perception, thought, memory, narrative, belief, and planning to carry out actions.

Beneath the cortex are many important regions, including the limbic and brain stem areas. In the hand model, your thumb represents the limbic area, which has a left and right side, as does the cortex above it. Though the limbic area, which comprises the hippo-campus, amygdala, and cingulate gyrus, is not a single structure, its components share similar neurochemistry and evolutionary histo-ries, so we can discuss the interrelated processes of the hippocampus and amygdala, for example. The structures within this historically named limbic region help us to assess the meaning of experience, to direct our attention, to form memories, and to mediate some aspects of emotion.

Continuing downward anatomically with the hand model of the brain, the palm of the hand symbolizes the evolutionarily older region, the brain stem, which connects to the spinal cord. The brain

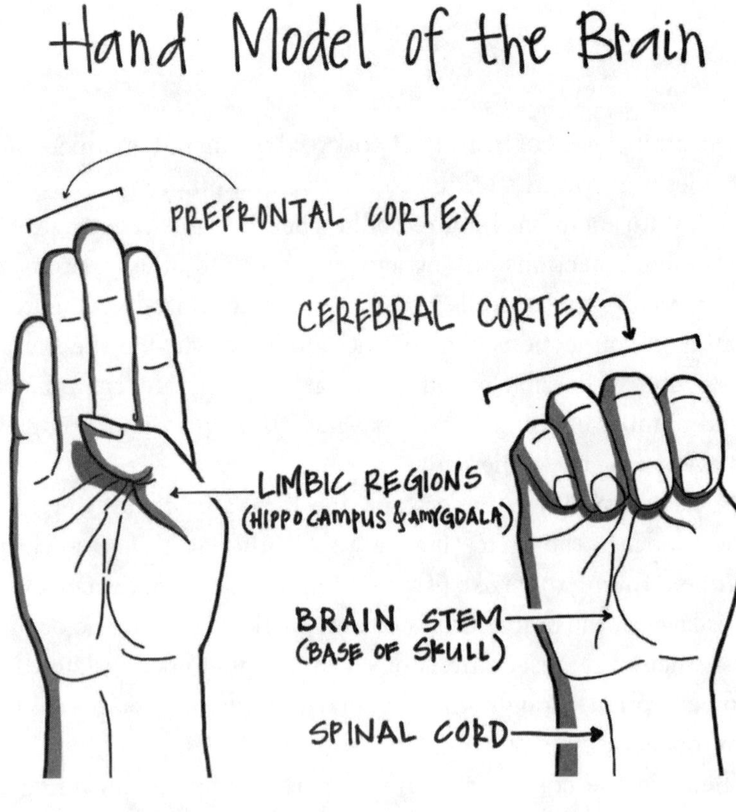

Figure 4.1 Hand model of the brain.

stem is at least three hundred million years old and is sometimes referred to as the "reptilian brain"; the two hundred-million-year-old limbic area is sometimes referred to as the "old mammalian brain," and the cortex, also known as the neocortex, is the "newer mammalian brain." The brain stem area mediates basic bodily needs, such as respiration, digestion, heart function, and the wake–sleep cycle. The brain stem also dominates how we react to threat, mediating the fight, flight, freeze, or faint reactions, or "4F" reactivity, when we face life-threatening challenges.

As you are reading or listening to these words, you are using your cortex—the outer fingers wrapping around the rest of the brain. If you are seeing these words, for example, the energy of light streaming into your eyes passes through your optical nerve and ultimately arrives in the occipital lobe at the back of your cortex. There, patterns of neural firing are coded into neural representations that enable you to visually perceive these words. If you are listening to this as an audiobook, the energy of soundwaves, as movements of air molecules, is striking your ear drum, displacing that membrane and translating kinetic energy into electrochemical energy flow in the acoustic nerve. This leads to neural firing in the side areas of your cortex, the temporal lobes, where the sensation of sound is constructed into the perception of hearing.

For language, a complex set of processes, especially centered in the temporal lobe on the left side of the cortex, enables you to decode the input from your eyes and ears into the meaning of language, empowering you to turn those visual or auditory sensations into perception, comprehension, and action as expression.

Our entire body has many energy flow patterns, sensed with proprioception and interoception—what we can collectively call bodily sensations. Some sensations emerge from the PDP networks around the heart and gut, which also convey sophisticated energy and information beyond the conduit of sensation itself— and are the source of the phrases "listen to your heart" and "tune into your gut." Our heart and gut offer insight, intuition, and even wisdom that the third brain, the enskulled brain, can act on—but may often ignore. Each of these processes is fundamental to what we mean by the term "embodied brain." Given that the heart and intestines are lower than the head brain's cortex, and that we refer to the areas in that enskulled brain that are below the cortex as subcortical, we might be wise to cultivate and integrate all of these under that broad term, "subcortical", to name and recognize these neural messages and invite them into our reasoning and decision-making processes. In this way, the reasoning that is often dominated by the head brain's cortex can become more integrative as we learn to listen deeply to this sensory, nonlinguistic inner subcortical world—to tune in to our heart and our gut feelings.

During the first days of extrauterine life, a set of subcortical networks that drives our inner experience and outer action becomes quite active. These motivational systems drive us to connect, to protect, and to correct—to make relational joining, to keep us from harm, and to right a wrong. Neuroscientist Jaak Panksepp (1998; 2009; 2010) has written extensively about what we're naming here as connect, protect, and correct and describes the subjective feeling, or emotion, of these motivational systems in these three ways: sadness and distress at separation are represented by the GRIEF system; fear as an anticipatory anxiety is represented by the FEAR system; and anger as a drive to be empowered, to have agency to right a wrong, is represented by the RAGE system.

These subcortical systems play a central role in what we can name as our "emotional life" and they help direct our cortically mediated consciousness. And our cortex also helps construct our emotional life—our subcortical inner systems and our cortically mediated top-down processes weave together to form the feeling "tone" of our ongoing experiences.

For a young child, these subcortical systems direct some of the first inner states and drives to action that arise in our awareness:

- GRIEF system: feeling forlorn → drive for connection
- FEAR system: feeling fear → drive for protection
- RAGE system: feeling fury → drive for correction

The drive to connect can have a subjective sensation ranging from mild loneliness to being sad, forlorn, or despairing. The drive for protection, to be safe, has sensations along the spectrum from feeling unsettled, anxious, or fearful to panic or terror. The drive to correct a wrong is our motivation to be empowered, to be an effective source of action; this system can give rise to feelings ranging from mild irritation to anger, fury, or rage.

In this way, the sense of a center of experience, of being and of doing—a sense of self—is shaped by these fundamental subcortically mediated motivational systems and the emotions and behaviors they enact from the very beginning of our experiences outside the womb. The subjective sensation, perspective, and agency of self are molded from the inside, in part, by these inherited subcortical motivational networks. This is a brief glimpse into the internal somatic architecture that shapes our emerging sense of experience from our earliest days. As we grow, these same mechanisms, whether we are aware of them or not, continue to influence not only what has meaning in our lives but also the focus of our attention and the interactive behaviors we have within interpersonal relationships.

Doing and the Construction of Perception

Living in a body after birth requires, in the words of my colleagues Laura Baker, David and Denise Daniels, Jack Killen, and my self— in all its inner and relational layers—that we "work for a living." We must do to survive. While this doing often involves simple linear acts of survival, such as eating when hungry and sleeping when tired, seeing the fundamental nature of life's experiences through the lens of energy flow can help us make sense of the often hidden and more complex ways we live in a systems reality.

Experience is the flow of energy. Sometimes that flow is direct, as bottom-up conduition, like water through the conduit of a hose: raw, unfiltered, without re-presenting or symbolizing something. Other times this flow of energy gets constructed based on our prior learning, as a top-down form of filtering what we sense as we build categories, concepts, and symbols. As with energy conduition, mental construction can be internal, and it can be relational. Information processing, known as cognition, is shaped by neural processes inside our body, and information sharing, the communication formed by relations we have outside our body, connect us with people and the planet. This spectrum of inner and inter ways of symbolizing energy into information fits with the cognitive science view of our mental constructions as enacted and embodied, as well as beyond the body, as they are extended and embedded in our relational worlds.

With 3.5 billion years worth of ancestors—500 million years of vertebrate evolution, 200 million as mammals, and about 50 million years as primates—we share many internal bodily structures that form how energy flows in our lives to help us survive. These networks motivate our behaviors and shape our internal sense of being alive, our feelings and sensations, and that tapestry of what we've named "meaning" and "emotion."

If we didn't have motivational systems in the body to get us to breathe, eat, drink, and connect, we would die. These somatic systems enabled our ancestors to survive and to reproduce, passing on their genetic codes—libraries of molecular information that determine how our bodies grow and develop. We share the drive to breathe, for example, with our vertebrate ancestors (including reptiles and mammals); the drive to connect, we share with our mammalian relatives. We share social hierarchies with our primate cousins, and then, as human beings, we share language use and childrearing by living as sophisticated collections of individuals that collaborate as a group. To enhance our survival, we harness a process called "alloparenting" in which we share care of our youth with a select few members of our community. You and I, together, have inherited all of this.

Alloparenting introduced to our lives the benefit of sensing the mind of another person—their intentions, emotions, mood, attention, awareness—so that we could learn to trust them, or not, with the vital care of our precious offspring. This mindsight—the capacity to sense the inner mental lives of others with empathy and compassion—then evolved, one perspective suggests, to be applied to our inner life as well, enabling us to have insight: an inner perspective on the nature of our own minds. This rich internal source of subjective textures offers us the capacity to construct an inner notion of self and identity, whether a narrow one that might come to limit us or, if we harness mindsight's power effectively, one with a wider-angle focus that actually enriches and liberates our lives. It's up to us whether our own experience of self, identity, and belonging hurts or helps the systems that we are, the systems in which we all live.

Inner and Outer: Self and Other

We need one another. When we are hungry, we call out for food; when we are lonely, we call out for connection; when we are distressed, we call out for soothing. This social connection can be seen as an exchange of energy and information: one we call communication. Besides relational needs, the body needs sustenance—food, water, warmth—to maintain physiological homeostasis, the balancing of the body's basic somatic functions. Nurturance, then, is about both material and relational needs being met by others in our lives. We are interconnected entities living in space and time. We survive by honoring the interdependent nature of our reality, not by ignoring this fundamentally connected essence of who we are. This is the reality of our lives; it is especially prominent in our early childhood years, when our dependency on others leads to life or death. As an intraconnected living system of Earth, these interwoven needs for one another remain throughout the lifespan, across time, space, and species.

From the moment we enter the womb, we need our mother, our caregiver, to enable us to survive, grow, and thrive. As mammals, we are born into the world needing a connection with our primary attachment figure, our mother. As human beings, we share this attachment with more than just the mother inside whose womb we grew—the process of alloparenting enables us to live collaboratively as a community, a collection of people whose mindsight abilities help us connect with one another's inner mental lives, from the inside, as well as through external behaviors—what we can see with our eyes, our physical sight. Our genetically shaped social brains need this interpersonal connection: Relationships provide the experiential foundations of joining that not only keep us alive but also mold how our brain grows, enabling us to thrive.

When relational connections are integrative—when we are honored for differences and when compassionate linkages are created—our brain's integration grows. Integrated brains enable optimal regulation to unfold: how we regulate our attention, how we experience our emotions and moods, how we manage our thoughts, memories, relationships, behaviors, and morality—each of these depends on neural integration. The simple intraconnected reality of energy flow and well-being, for us as human beings, is this: Relational integration stimulates the growth of neural integration, which is necessary for optimal regulation.

Neural connections emerge in two fundamental ways: experience-expectant and experience-dependent. Expectant development involves our DNA encoding the growth of our neural networks very early in life, even without outside input, such as our visual and auditory sensory systems. The growing neural systems, in every member of our species, expect that this form of input will be received. For example, our visual system expects to receive light and to, with this input, further develop our ability to see; our auditory system expects to receive sound and to further develop our hearing. These are experience-expectant neural systems.

As we experience unique events in our lives—such as learning to ride a bicycle or hearing a certain type of music—the input received will activate genes, enabling new connections to grow among neurons. The growth of neural connectivity based on novel experiences is called experience-dependent development. This growth in connectivity depends on specific experiences that are unique to each of us, experiences that our systems cannot expect to happen for every member of our species, as experience-expectant development. Learning to ride a tricycle is one example: We can develop the memory and skills to ride, build these into our synaptic connections that link neurons into networks for memory, and lay down the myelin sheaths among interconnected neurons for skill building. But not every child will have that experience. These networks, constructed from scratch, are in these ways initially stimulated by gene expression following the flow of energy into the nervous system, which are then developed and maintained by neural activity that is activated by repeated experience. This is experience-dependent neural growth.

Overall, the impact of experience—energy flow—on neural connectivity leads not only to neural firing, to neuronal activity in the moment, but also to gene activation and changes in neural connectivity in the long-run. In other words, neural firing can lead to changes in neural anatomy by changes in neural connections. This change in neural structure stimulated by experience is called neuroplasticity. The focus of our mind on energy flow patterns, originating from inside or outside the body, can harness this power to change brain structures involved in that experience of neural activation. A convenient way to remember this process is by the phrase "Where attention goes, neural firing flows, and neural connection grows."

Our relational connections, by which our brain's integration grows, manifest as our attachment patterns. Attachment—how we attach relationally to our caregivers and how they bond to us—likely involves both experience-expectant and experience-dependent aspects of our interconnecting neural systems.

As discussed extensively in the five-hundred-page textbook *The Developing Mind*, research-based findings indicate that self, identity, and belonging both reflect and impact how we, individually and collectively, create integration in our lives. Trained as an attachment researcher and working as a psychotherapist, I have found attachment science to reveal powerful, empirical ways we can understand how relationships influence us early in life as well as throughout our lifespan—and not just in our individual lives but in how we function as a human family and as a family of living beings together on Earth. How we develop a sense of self, how we experience identity, how we come to belong, each of these are shaped by attachment experiences in our personal family life; in turn, similar relational processes may be the foundation for how we experience self, identity, and belonging in our public and planetary lives.

We need our attachment figures: our caregivers. How others meet our needs influences two fundamental things: our immediate experience (e.g., how our hunger or soothing needs are met, or not) and how we adapt to that experience, to do the best we can to survive (with withdrawal, anxiety, or confidence). A way to summarize what research has found regarding these direct and indirect impacts of attachment in our lives is: safe + seen + soothed = secure. When we are safe, seen (our internal world is sensed accurately), and soothed—and when the rupture created by their absence is reliably and readily repaired—we then develop an internal sense of security.

We grow a sense of self within the relationships we have early in life. During our earliest years, we develop a sense of inner I or me and a relational we—a sense of inner and inter—that uses the body as its spatial reference point. As we develop, we come to include another category, the not-me, or "other," giving rise to the common distinctions of me versus you and us versus them.

Better Together: Relationships, Emotion, Meaning

Relationships are crucial in determining our brain's growth as well as our sense of self, a center of our experience of being alive—our sensation, perspective, and agency. But what *is* a relationship? What does it mean to have a relational self, a relational connection, to be a "we" beyond an inner "me"?

A foundational way of defining a relationship is as the sharing of energy. Our communications and connections are all about energy streaming through our lives—how energy is shared. Within these bodies we are born into, we have several ways to connect our inner world and the relational world in which we are embedded. Our actions transmit energy, as we move through our environment expressing ourselves and exchanging material things in our world, and our sensory systems receive energy from our environment—as photons, sound waves, chemical energy for taste and smell, kinetic energy for touch. When we communicate, we share energy and information flow between one another. Even the exchange of objects, of matter, is an exchange of energy, because matter is highly condensed energy. All relationships are a sharing of energy.

As bodily sensations emerge, regions of the brain that connect the body to the subcortical regions, such as the limbic and brain stem areas, move this flow of neural energy to the cortex. In many ways, what we come to call "emotion" can be defined as the integrative flow of energy from the body through the subcortical areas to cortex. Emotion can be seen as a shift in integration, embedding within its contours meaning, sensation, and relational connection: We experience emotions as directly related not only to our relationships but also to our bodies, including regions of the brain that establish value or meaning.

Studies have shown, for example, that the same region of the brain, the dorsal section of the anterior cingulate cortex, is activated with the experience of both somatic pain and social rejection. The cingulate is considered an interface between the prefrontal cortex and limbic areas—each of these regions is fundamental to weaving together emotion, meaning, and our relational worlds. In this manner, the structure and function of our brain reveal the overlap of the social with the somatic, the relational with the internal, inter with inner.

You may have noticed that relationships, emotion, and meaning in our lives are intimately interwoven within the tapestry of our subjective experience. Separating emotions from meaning, separating relationships from emotions, separating meaning from relationships—such attempts to isolate any one of these from the others, for many of us, is just not possible. These experiences are biologically woven into the fabric of who we are.

Seeing emotion as a shift in integration reveals how energy flow can be differentiated and linked. Recall that complex systems self-organize optimally by balancing differentiation on the one hand with linkage on the other. As we've seen, when differentiated components of a complex system are linked, they do not lose, in the process we are calling integration, their unique individual features. Integration is more like a fruit salad than a smoothie—it is not a homogenous, uniform blending of parts. It is from an integrative balance of differentiation and linkage that emergence arises, enabling a synergy in which the whole is greater than the sum of its parts.

When that flow of our lives as complex systems is internally integrated, we find purpose in what we are doing, we find meaning in life, we experience a sense of inner peace, of wholeness, of well-being. And when our flow of energy is integrated with our environment, within our relational lives—when we are honored as unique individuals yet are linked to others and nature without losing our inner integrity— we have an integrative relational world, an inter-self that we experience as what we might call the FACES flow of harmony (Table 4.1). And the opposite of this harmony, a nonintegrated flow, would be its reverse: IMIDU.

When energy and information flow are integrative—when there is

Table 4.1 Contrast of Integrated (FACES) to Nonintegrated (IMIDU) states

Integrated		Nonintegrated
Flexible	⟷	Inflexible
Adaptive	⟷	Maladaptive
Coherent	⟷	Incoherent
Energized	⟷	Deenergized, depleted
Stable	⟷	Unstable, unreliable

linkage and differentiation, a flow connecting differentiated parts—a sense of well-being arises. Energy flow happens inside our bodies, including the brains—the PDP processors—in our gut, heart, and head. And information flow happens between our bodily, inner self and "others," within our relational selves—the world of energy flow outside these bodies we are born into. Integration happens within and through the connections we have—within the body, with other people, and within the natural world. It's helpful to keep in mind that neither skull nor skin limit energy and information flow; this flow is who we are—and it has an inner location and an inter location. In this way, it is all our self. The question is: Can we widen our lens of identity to see this broader belonging and to embrace a subjective experience, a perspective, and agency of self that is beyond the boundaries of our skin encased bodies?

If we are excessively differentiated, without linkage—if we are disconnected, acting without awareness beyond the separation of our solo-self—then rigidity, chaos, or both are likely to arise. Yet if we are not differentiated—if we have no internal facet of our identity, no somatic center of experience, no bodily boundaries; if we are unable to find an internal integrity and instead we melt into homogeneity—then we are also in a nonintegrative state. Both differentiation and linkage are needed for integration to emerge.

With an integrative relational self, the inter flow of energy and information feels whole, feels at peace. It is a generative connection, filled with compassion, collaboration, and creativity. When we are immersed in the generative relational connections of secure attachment, our sense of self, inner and inter, is filled with harmony and becomes resilient, able to approach challenges with flexibility, adaptability, coherence, energy, and stability. This is living as an intraconnected system. These are the developmental origins of a resilient self, inside and out, inner and inter.

Developing a Core Self

Energy and information flow are the fundamental essence, or "stuff," of experience. We've discussed that, even before we were conceived, this flow can be identified as the stuff of the universe, what "reality is made of." Even before life established itself within molecular assemblies encased by cellular membranes, energy existed as the movement from possible to actual. Even before molecules were made from more basic building blocks of atoms, energy flow was the essence of reality.

Reflecting on these fundamentals of the world in which we are born reminds us of the unique experience of being a life form, of being conceived, of growing in the womb, of having a body. Yet each of these states did not entail a sense of self as separate from the rest of our reality, a self that is separate from our own surroundings. If "self" is a term we are fundamentally defining as a center of experience and if experience is energy flow, then what, exactly, constitutes "a center of experience"? What is the localization, the central source, of energy flow?

If this center is defined only by the boundaries of the skin with a narrowly focused lens of identity, our sense of belonging is restricted and our experience of self becomes a nonintegrative process. True, we have a body that serves as an important, differentiated facet of experience, yet this is not the whole of what constitutes a center of our experience. Yes, we have an inner center of energy flow, a flow centered in the body. But we also have an inter center, a self that is fully relational. Perceiving self as emerging from inner *and* inter energy flow, we can clearly see how there is both an inner and an inter facet of self.

You and I are on a journey in the universe, tracing emergence from the plane of possibility to quanta to atoms to molecules to cells of life and then to conception and development in the womb, and then to birth, when we transition into the air-filled, relational world. We are the stuff of the universe, even though we now have a body. The bodily based self is very real—it's just not the whole deal.

And this body into which we are growing, this somatic center of experience, has features that shape energy flow—this is our inner self. The inner flow of energy is one foundation for our "sense" of self. "Sense" here is a subjective feeling, a felt, sensory reality of a center of experience, comprising both a core inner self and a relational self.

The Core Self

Some, such as child psychiatrist Daniel Stern (1985), consider our experience of the inner self to be a "core self," with features of affectivity, agency, continuity, and coherence. In this developmental model, we are, beginning in the first years of life, filled with an emotional tone of the unfolding experiences with which we live that can collectively be called "affectivity." We also have a sense of being the center of action—of free will, if you will—a body that moves in the world, a self in that body that has agency. Affectivity and agency can have a continuity to them, linking events of experience across time and space. When this continuity has a wholeness and integrity to it, a sense of experience, called "coherence," emerges—a sense that experience is vibrantly held together and there is a matching of our expectations and our sensations.

This concept of coherence overlaps with Jaak Panksepp's SEEKING system that drives us to make sense of experience—to find coherence in life. Our larger sense-making, coherence-sculpting journey is likely related to the top-down constructive processes that let past experience, as a memory filter, shape current sensation into perception. This would be the inner sense of self that arises in the first years of our life outside the womb and continues to be a key part of our entire lives: we are sense-making beings. This is the core self's affectivity, agency, continuity, and the emerging sense of coherence that we construct as we seek to make sense of life. Each of these four foundational experiences influences the others.

Our attachment relationships directly impact the development of our core self—and these are remembered via neuroplastic changes that alter the structure of our brains. With security, integrative communication—in which differences are honored and compassionate connections cultivated—leads to affectivity that feels whole, agency that feels empowered, continuity that fits together across time and experience, and coherence that has a sense of harmony. When we are safe, seen, and soothed, and ruptures are repaired when they arise, we develop security. Secure attachment emerges with integration relationally and cultivates integration internally. With the various forms of insecurity in contrast—what we can name as "nonsecure" forms of attachment to avoid the misleading connotation of the term "insecure" as something being deficient in the individual, rather than a relationship being suboptimal—these foundations of the core self can each be compromised and lean instead toward chaos and rigidity. Nonsecure attachment arises with impediments to relational integration and the ensuing compromises in internal integration. Like a river, harmony is the central FACES flow, bound on each side by the IMIDU: chaos on one bank, rigidity on the other.

The foundations of a core sense of self are an important way to describe the inner experience of I or me, the inner self. While some suggest we have an "observing I" that is distinct from a bodily experience of self—for example, at times of distress we may say, "I need to get myself together"—here we will use a broader notion of "me" or "I" to indicate the inner experience of self, one that includes both this observational capacity to be aware and the sensations and mental constructions that we can be aware of. From this perspective, for us here, the core self encompasses the various internal senses of identity and belonging, our range of self-defining experiences that comprise an inner centering in the body.

The Relational Self

In subjective experience, we can feel connected to our inner life, and we can also feel connected to other people and to nature—our relational life. In this connection, our self as a center of experience shifts to include both the inner and the relational. Each are important, and each contributes to our overall experience of identity and belonging.

The inner and the relational self-experiences share the notion of self as a center of experience.

Recall that we are defining experience as energy and information flow. The following review of the features of self captures this sense of flow as both inner and relational centers of experience, the foundation of what we are naming as self, inside these bodies we are born into and centered in the relational worlds in which we live:

- Sensation or subjectivity: the felt texture of experience, the feel of energy flow
- Perspective: the perceptual direction, the point of view of that flow
- Agency: the actions that arise from that flow, a source of motion

Together, our subjective sense, perspective, and agency as we experience and interact in our physical and relational world—as our core self within our body and our relational self, initially within our family in our home and later in our community and environment—make up our center of experience, our self. As we will see as we explore further, these experiences of an inner core self and of a relational inter self are continually shaped by experience—by energy flow—that both influences and is influenced by the emergence of identity and belonging across the lifespan.

TODDLERHOOD

In our first years of life, we connect through our five senses to the world around us, the world of our caregivers. The inner sensations of our body ignite a drive to survive, and we can feel anger and rage when we don't get our way, fear and anxiety when we sense danger, sadness and forlornness if left isolated and alone. A glance, a smile, a reassuring tone of voice, a hug—each of these are the nonverbal signals of energy flow that give us the information we need to reduce our states of distress and come to feel whole again.

A World of Words

In the first years of life, the brain will take in these repeated patterns of communication that connect and redirect us—our inter-regulation—and use them to build circuitry for more autonomous soothing. This is what is often called "self"-regulation but may, for our purposes, be more accurately called "inner regulation," to avoid reinforcing the concept that self indicates the body alone and to disentangle our modern culture's narrow-lens view of what the self is. With this as our framework, we can say that inter regulation shapes our inner regulation skills.

Some writers suggest that these nonverbal relational processes are dominant in the circuitry of the right side of our two-sided brain. By differentiating the left and right sides of key areas of the brain, our ancestors achieved more complexity in function—enabling them to become more adaptive. The cortex and the limbic areas have left and right sides, and in human beings the right side dominates brain activity and growth during the first few years of life. Interestingly, not only are nonverbal signals perceived and expressed via the right hemisphere, but inner soothing is dominant on the right as well.

One way these two sides differ, as we've described earlier, is in the focus of attention. The right side of the brain mediates a broad focus of attention; the left is dominant for narrow or more tightly focused attention. Plus, somatic (bodily) input is dominant on the right, whereas language—the words we use to linguistically symbolize experiences and to communicate—is dominant on the left side for most individuals. Thus, self, identity, and belonging are shaped in part by the neural asymmetries we humans have inherited that involve both sides of the brain in somewhat distinct ways. Understanding these differences and how they can become linked into an integrated whole can support us in using these asymmetric skills and propensities in a helpful manner.

For example, emotion is present on both sides of the brain, not just in one hemisphere or the other. Creativity requires both sides of the brain. Living a full and effective life requires both sides of the brain. Left being different from right does not imply superiority of one side over the other but helps us understand, in a conservative way, how the asymmetric architecture of our brain increases our neural complexity, impacting both the conduition and construction that make up our mental experiences. The tendency to simplify these differences into broad, and at times inaccurate, generalizations in the popular literature may have led to an understandable pushback from neuroscientists, who urge us to avoid such misunderstandings. Nevertheless, the science of asymmetry can be quite illuminating, informing us of the challenges we may sometimes face in achieving what we can call bilateral integration: the honoring of the differences between the sides of the brain and facilitating links between them that do not lessen their unique contributions.

When we then apply these fundamental inner neural asymmetries to our relational lives, all sorts of previously mysterious patterns become comprehensible—and even changeable toward a more integrative way of being. (See *The Developing Mind* for a deep dive into the background science itself; here, we will simply apply that science to our understanding of self, identity, and belonging.) As the right hemisphere grows connections, enabling the core self to experience its affectivity, agency, continuity, and coherence in what we can call integrative ways, the left hemisphere is learning and growing in very important aspects as well. The left hemisphere begins to grow more and become more active after the first year or so, as it begins our lifelong journey of learning the reception and expression of language. The communication utilizing nonverbal signals—facial expression, eye contact, tone of voice, posture, gesture, the timing and intensity of response—in their receiving and sending is dominant in the right hemisphere. Studies show that the inner, reflective stance of the right side is counterbalanced by a more outward focus of the left: the left hand, controlled by the right hemisphere, tends to soothe the body, whereas the right hand, controlled by the left brain, reaches out to the world. In addition to this grasping with the hand, we also grasp with our linguistic symbols—dominant in the left side of the brain in most individuals, even for most of those who are left-handed.

Ultimately, the side of the brain doesn't really matter. Science suggests that what does matter is our specialized modes of processing information, of taking in streams of energy and, from that conduitive flow, constructing an assembly of energy patterns into information, particular forms of symbols—energy patterns with specific meaning beyond the energy flow itself. When such information processing is capable of being "dis-associated" in its anatomic and functional segregation, then its associated mental activities can also be somewhat independent in their unfolding. These modes, what we are calling a "right mode" and "left mode," are quite distinct. By honoring these differentiated modes for their unique qualities, we support their linkage to and integration with each other. Some aspects of right-brain activity may contribute to left-brain-dominant functions, so we would say this right-brain activity is a part of a left-mode function. Using the term "mode" captures the verb-like activity of the brain, helping us see the full mental and relational experience more clearly, even when each side may contribute in various ways with its constructive and conduitive activity during a given event.

Right mode is dominant for nonverbal communication, both its expression and reception; left mode is dominant for linguistic use of language. Right mode is dominant for inner reflection, including bodily awareness and autobiographical memory—recalling the self in time. Right mode also appears to be dominant for sensing context, seeing the broader relatedness of parts in a whole.

Left mode, conveniently, is dominant for the following functions that, in English, begin with the letter "L":

- Logic—syllogistic reasoning seeking cause–effect relationships
- List making—like this one we are making here
- Literal thinking—taking words at their concrete meaning rather than seeing the gist or meaning between the lines
- Language—using words to express and understand reality, helped by the left mode's more narrow focus of attention

In some ways, as we've discussed briefly before in our WELCOME chapter, the left mode seems to be dominant for a narrow focus of attention on details and in finding schemas or mental models that it can then summarize in a word. These linguistic symbols are a surface level of shared meaning, representing concepts and categories beneath the words themselves. We have the categories of animate or inanimate, for example, and the concepts that emerge from the notion of some things being alive and others not. How we interact within the world is shaped directly by these categories and concepts; and the words we use reflect those underlying mental filters as well as express them, shaping how "others" and even our "selves" view and interact with the world. If we see the world as an inanimate place that is only a space in which our animate human bodies exist, we will treat the "external environment" one way. And if we see the system of life on Earth as a living system, an animate intraconnected whole of which we are a part, then we might treat the world with more respect and care than those people in modern times who treat it as a trash can.

As a writer, I know first-hand this left-mode penchant. In some ways, the conversation we are having here is an attempt to use words in a traditional way—prose form within paragraphs composed of sentences with words and accepted punctuation—to explore and challenge the mental models imparted to us by the very linguistic left-mode language I am using. If I were writing poetry, or even composing lyrics to a musical score, we might see this message as integrating left-mode language with the contexts and textures of the right mode's broader attention and with the evoked, bodily-sensed feelings, immersing you more in the timing and tone of the nonverbal world.

Young children learn both right and left modes of conduition and construction, yet left-mode words organize so much of both our relational and our inner experiences of self. Words don't just express what we experience, they actually shape how we experience life itself. This is how the brain's top-down processes shape perception and conception. Balancing both left and right modes in our lives—both left-mode language and right-mode inner and relational experiences—can lead us toward a more integrative way of living if we can find ways, worded or not, to both experience and express this integration.

Narrative and the Stories We Learn of Self

The construction and modification of information from the flow of energy, within us and between us, follows the route from category to concept to symbol. Categories are how we divide up the energy patterns we perceive into groupings. These groupings underlie our concepts—what we conceive and believe, the fundamental filters of our conceptual minds. And words are the most common symbolic form we use to share our concepts with one another.

In our early years, words become associated with these deeper mental mechanisms, a languaging process where the linear array of linguistic symbols gives birth to our narrative self. When I was a research fellow in narrative science, I took a class with visiting professor Jerome (Jerry) Bruner, an esteemed pioneer in the field of cognitive science. Jerry taught us that a story can be considered a linear telling of a sequence of events that emerges from our relational lives. This telling includes both a landscape of action, the things you could see with your eyes that are happening in the story, and a landscape of consciousness, the things that are happening out of visual perception, within the mind—what you can perceive with mindsight. We also learned that stories were initiated by a violation of our expectations about life, such as an accident, a shift in usual behavior, or a change in environment. To make sense of such challenges to our mental models of how life is supposed to be—models generated by our top-down filters—we use our narrative processes to make sense of that violation, to place it into some sense-making relationship with our life's journey.

Years ago in my training, building on the science of memory and narrative and inspired by such researchers as Endel Tulving, Katherine Nelson, Robyn Fivush, Eric Kandel, Larry Squire, and Dan Schacter, I was deeply curious about how narrative relates to our well-being. I wondered how narrative might be a central feature not only of our development but also of how we function in the world and construct our culture, our relational world itself. Narrative combines several of the fundamental self-shaping processes we've discussed: a drive to seek coherence, to make sense through narrative; the role of mental models in shaping our lives; and the function of our "self-knowing" awareness, our autonoetic consciousness. Narrative and autonoetic consciousness, or insight into the self across space and time, are both mediated in the brain and guided by relational experiences. As a new narrative scientist in formal research training, I was deeply inspired by these wonderful researchers to try to see how all of this—memory, narrative, relationships, the brain, culture—might fit together into some coherent picture of how our mind, sense of self, identity, and belonging emerge in consciousness within our individual lives and in our collective lives.

As early as the first years of life, language, a sense of time, and other aspects of mental growth enable the narrative self to develop a self-knowing awareness that weaves representations of experience as autobiographical memory—a sense of the self in time—into a kind of foundation of self-knowledge. This self-knowing awareness, or autonoetic consciousness, is self-reinforcing both within the individual and within our relationships with family and within culture.

Over time, our narrativizing capacity develops features, described by a range of scientists, including:

- a way to organize experience within a set of mental models of the self that filter experience as it is laid down into memory;
- pathways of self-knowledge that involve a continuity of self over time, of mental time travel;
- a matching of values and goals with actions and a sense of self in the world;
- an evaluative process assessing the attributes of the self; and
- a sense of connectedness to one's inner life, to interpersonal relationships, and within nature.

Each of these aspects of the narrative self are relevant in helping our emerging life story to become more organized, to enhance self-knowledge, to match meaning with actions, to shift to more constructive evaluations of the self, and to deepen our relational connections. When I reflect on the many individuals whom I've had the privilege to work with as a psychotherapist over the last thirty eight years, I realize that, within our professional relationship as we came together to make sense of a person's life, I felt like I was integrating my own life experience too. In this way, and in many others, we can see how our narratives are co-constructed within our connections with one another.

The narrative self bridges our experience of an inner self and a relational self. And while the narrative self is not the totality of who we are, our capacity to sense and shape our sense of self in these many ways is a fundamental part of who we are and how we grow. Our narrative self can learn to weave a life story that builds on the important, core, inner self, and then widens the narrator beyond the inner to include the differentiated but linked interpersonal world as well as the natural environment that surrounds us; and even more, if we open our sense of self, we come to experience that nature, in fact, is us. Imagine if parents at home, teachers in school, peers on the playground, and, later on, in work and society were to co-construct such an integrative life narrative. If instead we only learn a narrative of separation, the self becomes constricted. If we explore our identity and expand our belonging and sense of self beyond the body being the only center of our experience, we come to feel more coherent and connected as we differentiate and link our inner and relational selves into an integrative, intraconnected narrative of who we are.

The neural correlates of this self-knowing awareness, this mental time travel that connects a self across past, present, and future, include aspects of the prefrontal cortex and posterior cingulate cortex—part of what we call the "default mode network," or DMN. This is that set of interconnected regions that we discussed earlier as possibly having been temporarily knocked out of commission following my horse accident in Mexico. The neural connections of these mostly midline areas of the DMN are considered the brain's way of constructing a sense of narrative self, embedding top-down memory and emotions into a repeating, self-reinforcing pattern of sensation, perspective, and agency that we come to call "I" or "me." Studies reveal that our narrative self is sculpted from the interpersonal communications we have—exchanges of energy and information with our caregivers, friends, teachers, and the larger culture in which we live. In these ways, we learn the story of who we come to narrate our self to be.

In other words, if we are taught that we are separate, we will encode, store, and retrieve memory representations of a self that is, for all intents and purposes, a separate entity. Then, using this self, we build a story of who we are—the summed narratives of our lives that we use to make sense of our memory of experiences. And this story reinforces this view of separation. Sometimes we experience "violations," unexpected departures from that learned mental model of self as separate, and then we try to make sense of these ruptures within our existing narrative self's perspective. We thus are vulnerable to closing our minds with these narratives of separation, to explaining away potential, new ways of living until they conform to our prior expectations.

With a learned model of separation, our DMN is driven to attain certainty, the certainty of self-as-noun, and it inserts its own, self-reinforcing way of living into the narrative we are telling ourselves about who we are. We then re-store and re-encode this reinforced narrative into our memory, which then influences our own reflections in those sense-making mental models that form the structure and shape the content of our narratives. But what we are encoding is not random behavior—we are encoding how we interact with ourselves, with others, and with the natural world in ways that are themselves shaped by our narrative. Often without realizing it, we convince ourselves we are who we think we are.

I recently had an internet-based dialogue with neuroscientist and psychiatrist Judson (Jud) Brewer. Jud had discovered that when meditation helps quiet the excessively activated DMN of individuals who are anxious or depressed—who feel disconnected and despairing—these individuals feel a shift to being filled with a sense of kindness, connection, and curiosity. The DMN appears to be an important circuit needed for these healthy qualities. Yet when the DMN is excessively differentiated—not linked and therefore not integrated with other regions of the brain—the result is impaired integration, which makes us prone to chaos and rigidity.

Being open—having an open awareness or a beginner's mind— lets us be curious about the world as we embrace the mystery of life's uncertainties. Being and feeling connected, the subjective sense of being at ease, at ease in one's inner life and relationships with others and the larger world of nature, correlates with well-being. And being kind—filled with a sense of universal positive regard, honoring one another's vulnerability, having the vital force of love suffuse our inner and interactive ways of being—is an integrative outcome of well-being.

If these states of being connected, curious, and kind are natural ways to be happy and healthy, why aren't we integrative merely as a natural state of being alive? If integration is the natural emergent way we optimize self-organization, why wouldn't linking differentiated parts, in the complex systems that are our relationships and our embodied brain, just naturally happen? What gets in the way? One reason is the push for certainty. In modern culture, even before our earliest school days when we write our name on a piece of paper to identify "who we are," we are rewarded for the top-down certainty of our narrative self's capacity to construct a noun-like identity.

What would happen if that narrative self was instead more fluid than a clearly defined, constructed noun-like entity, more like an open, flowing sensory experience of the bottom-up? If we were born into such an open awareness, we could embrace the curiosity of identity that opens us up to a more verb-like unfolding of events—we could let go of expectation and embrace uncertainty. I was a newcomer to formal mindfulness training when I wrote *The Mindful Brain*, a work in which I wondered if that state of receptivity and wonder might be expressed with the acronym, COAL, as we were curious, open, accepting, and loving. COAL may be the attributes of what the space of being is comprised of, a state of wonder and receptivity.

Upon leaving the womb, certainty becomes equated with safety and survival. With our anticipation-machine brains, we seek patterns of energy and extract information from them in order to make life predictable and, what we might later call, understandable. Predictability means we can anticipate what will happen next with at least some degree of certainty. And if we can be certain, we can be safe because we can predict and prepare—we can survive. In these ways, certainty can become a life-or-death matter.

How might we balance these two trends—the push for certainty as noun and the reality of uncertainty in life as verb?

Our need for certainty reverberates with the continuing messages of separation—me or you, us or them—that we receive in our relationships, at home, at school, in the media, and then even in our own reflections. Each of these processes can go on automatic pilot, outside of reflective awareness, and we come to believe separation as a self is true. In these modern times, we may rarely question the validity of the definition of self as existing only in the body. This is the developmental and relational origin of the contemporary, fast-paced, disconnected-life narrative of the solo-self, which may be at the root of many of our inner and relational challenges to well-being. We may long for the wholeness of that space of being beneath the surface of our awareness, yet outwardly, even to our own consciousness, we may be living out the narrative of a macrostate, matter-based story of a separate, solo-self.

When language limits us, our narratives constrain us. And yet we can use language to liberate us as well, to create narratives that free us. One simple strategy is to realize that a linear narrative of self as a noun-like entity says the self lives in the body only. Yet when we expand this limited narrative to include relational, verb-like, unfolding events as also the self, we can have an integrative narrative that includes both realms of reality of life, both as noun and as verb—we do not need to choose one over the other; MWe are both.

Our challenge, as we try to make sense of our world and try to use words to communicate with one another—in childhood and beyond—can be seen as follows: How do we keep a "beginner's mind" like that of toddlerhood, one that is free from expectations, an open state of awareness not constrained by that "flimsy fantasy of certainty" that keeps us from the fullness of being?

We can keep a childlike, innate curiosity, kindness, and connection alive as we develop past the early years of life—and as adults we can recapture it. We can nurture our fundamental capacity for open awareness; the love of caring, positive regard, and compassion; and that sense of inner and relational connection which underlies a thriving life. We can intentionally strive to take on the categories, concepts, and symbols of separation that may pin us down as noun-like things in our modern culture. These mental constructions, in the form of top-down filters, mental models, and narratives we live our lives into, can severely limit how we experience life, keeping us far from the rich rainbow of color that is our bottom-up birthright as ever-changing, verb-like living beings. As Louise Glück (2012) wrote, "I was once more a child in the presence of riches and I didn't know what the riches were made of" (p. 366).

Play, Presence, and Possibility

We have been exploring how experience is energy flow. That flow happens inside our body, and it happens between our body and our surrounding environment, connecting us—our bodily me—with people and with the planet. As we grow in the early years of life, our brain learns, developing top-down filters that make it increasingly challenging to see what is truly in front of us—in front of our eyes, yes, and in front of our lives. This also means that energy flow patterns streaming through our embodied brain—in our head and in our whole body, including our heart and intestines—influence the parallel distributing processor of this extensive, weblike, interconnected neural system as we learn. Some of the things the PDP learns are mental models, or schemas. These are basically how the pattern-detecting PDP system summarizes across events and identifies a repeating feature of experience, and then generalizes that detected pattern across experiences. This is how we learn.

In the first five years of life, we learn, paradoxically, how to move from being at one with the uterus—from a life without separation and only connection—to a life alone in a body. How sad it sometimes feels; at other moments, how filled with opportunity to find connection, with the excitement of discovery and joining. We find that our body needs other bodies within nature to survive and thrive. We discover ways to connect not only with our life-affirming caregivers but also with friends. A separate "me" becomes joined as a "we" in widening circles of connection—close friends, playmates, acquaintances. And we learn to join in play, discovering the joy of laughter and creation as we collaborate and lose ourselves, or lose our separate selves, in this flow as a spirited, intraconnected whole.

Notice how learning is not just acquiring input and storing it as information, like putting more books in a library. Learning entails molding how we organize this information, where and how we place the books. From those categories, we extract concepts; and with these categories and concepts, we create symbols—we write more books based on the books we've acquired in our library of knowledge. And what we learn shapes how we learn—a self-reinforcing self-construction process.

Let's consider this view of how we learn—not just in the early years but throughout life—in light of our physics perspective of energy as the movement from possibility to actuality and relate this to our drive for certainty and even to our experience of awareness itself. You may recall the probability diagram from the chapter EMERGENCE, wherein degrees of probability are degrees of certainty—different wording for the same process: Wide-open possibility means low probability and low certainty; high probability, the same as high certainty, means lower possibility.

On the diagram in Figure 5.1, the position with lowest certainty, the lowest probability, is in the plane of possibility. In discussing this diagram with physicists, as mentioned earlier, this point on the graph corresponds to what they describe as the quantum vacuum, or sea of potential. In the example in EMERGENCE, before I chose my word from all possible words, we were in the plane of possibility; as I chose narrower and narrower subsets of all words, probability rose on the

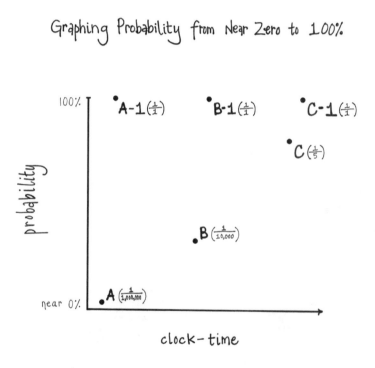

Figure 5.1 Energy flows from Point A, all possible words from which I could choose, to Point A-1 when I choose a single word; or from Point B, all possible words that begin with "o," to the choice at Point B-1; or from C, all possible named oceans, to the choice at Point C-1.

y-axis, the probability distribution, until I stated my choice and achieved the highest probability: 100 percent certainty. This corresponds to the physics definition of energy as the movement from possibility to actuality.

We can now name these positions on the probability distribution spectrum (the y-axis; Figure 5.2): Open possibility is in the plane of possibility; higher degrees of probability are plateaus—greater likelihoods, but not complete certainty, like Points B and C in Figure 5.1; maximal certainty, that is, 100% probability, is represented as a peak.

The 3-P diagram, and this 3-P framework, so named because of the words peaks, plateaus, and plane, set up a vocabulary that you and I can now use to communicate these ideas, a language we can share in the story of this framework, to explore how bottom-up processes get filtered by top-down mental models and how they restrict which further energy flow patterns we will manifest as actualities. In other words, experience is energy flow, and this flow is transformed into

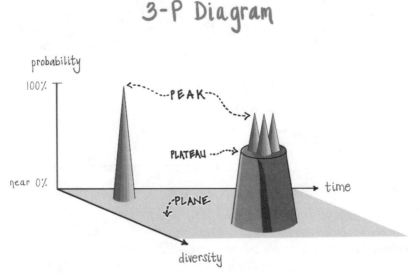

Figure 5.2 The 3-P diagram.

narrowed conduition or constructed information by filters that we here are calling plateaus, and these filters determine which particular peaks, or actualities, arise.

Figure 5.3 shows how we can use the 3-P diagram to illustrate energy flow. The x-, y-, and z-axes represent all energy that is free to move from the plane of possibility to a peak. Some peaks arise directly from the plane of possibility, without any filtering by plateaus. Other peaks arise from a given filtering plateau. Peaks that arise directly from the plane, from infinite possibilities, are how we might envision a beginner's mind: free of filtering plateaus, capable of bottom-up emergence into actuality—an openness of mind not constrained by prior learning. In contrast, only a limited number of peaks can emerge from a given plateau: Ironically, learning filters, or limits, what can arise into actuality. Such actualizations, such plateaus and peaks, are constrained subsets of what is possible, filtered by prior learning. The more we know, the less we may see.

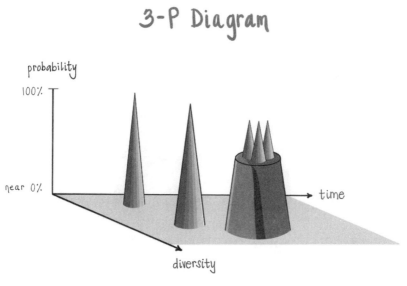

Figure 5.3 Using the 3-P diagram to illustrate energy flow.

We have many types of plateaus, many forms of filters, that give rise to particular peaks. Some are things we've learned, such as how to throw a ball or how to play catch. Some are distinct states of mind that shape the sense of self we experience in that particular moment, what some might call "self-states." A propensity toward sadness—an example of a factor molding an individual's ongoing subjective experience, perspective, and even agency—may construct an enduring "state of mind" we would label as a "self-state" that, as a pattern over time, we might use to characterize their "personality" or their proclivities that define "who they are." Another illustration of a self-state might be a set of skills, such as the ability to dance or play tennis, that would be filtered through a plateau to enable the felt sense, the perspective, and the agency of action for such activities. Each of these can be represented by a plateau, each with its particular subset of filtered peaks manifesting as actualities in how we feel, perceive, and act in the world (Figure 5.4).

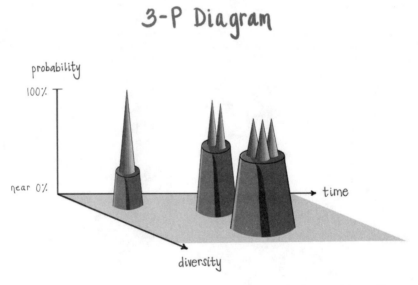

Figure 5.4 Examples of plateaus we learn, which enable a filtered, and therefore necessarily constrained, set of possible peaks to manifest.

Figure 5.5 is another example of how the 3-P diagram can help us envision categories, concepts, and symbols and how they serve as top-down filters. In this example, our learning that the self is separate is illustrated as a lower, foundational plateau—a mental model we use to build other schemas of reality, shown here as smaller plateaus arising from it, from which limited sets of peaks, filtered initially by the lower plateau, can arise. Each layer of a plateau constrains our experience of life—for better (as in protection and efficiency) or for worse (as too limiting or imprisoning)—and attempts to provide a sense of predictability and certainty in our lives.

A low-lying plateau over the plane of possibility can be seen as a category our mind constructs, such as the division of self versus nonself. This division of the world into "like-me or not like-me" and "us or them" can be observed in humans as young as a year and a half. In one

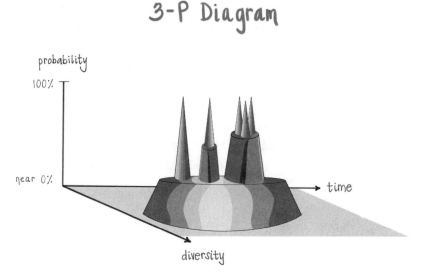

Figure 5.5 Categories form foundational plateaus, from which conceptual plateaus arise.

study by Karen Wynn and colleagues (2012, 2013), for example, fourteen-month-old children were asked which cereal they prefer, oatmeal or cornflakes. The children were then presented with puppets who preferred either the favored cereal or cereal the child disliked. The puppets then left, and after an interval, each puppet returned in different settings to evoke the child's emotional and behavioral reaction to the puppets. The children clearly treated one puppet kindly and with affection, and they showed signs of dislike to the other puppet and treated it harshly. Which puppet do you think these subjects treated kindly?

If the issue were about resource allocation and not wanting someone to take the cereal one prefers, you might imagine this competitive drive would cause the young subjects to mistreat the puppet who enjoyed the same cereal as they. That would make sense from a purely survival perspective, one based on limited material resources. But that is not what the researchers found. Instead, the children treated the puppet that liked the same cereal as they more kindly. Even at this early age, we seem to ask the question, "Who is like me and who is not?" We treat those who are like-me, those who share similar mental models as expressed as preferences and proclivities, with more kindness and care. And we do not want to be friends with those who are not like-me.

Even the term "like," at least in English, has a dual meaning: to be similar (one thing is like another), its antonym being unlike, or dissimilar; and to find agreeable, enjoyable, to favor, to be pleased by, its antonym being to dislike or hate. In this way, we see, built into the English language, the notion that we favor what is similar to us, that we like those who are like us. The root of this term from old English is the Germanic term "lician," meaning "to be pleasing." Words convey deep meanings even when we aren't initially aware of the symbolic messages in their underlying concepts and categories.

In this way, we can see that our experience of plateaus of self-identity, features that define "who we are," shape our sense of belonging: those individuals don't belong to my in-group because they don't like the same cereal as me, but you are in my in-group because we like the same things—or, later on, because we believe the same things, or look the same way, or make any of myriad other choices the same way that I do. These preferences can be embedded within the states of mind represented by the plateaus on the 3-P diagram.

The 3-P diagram can also be applied to other aspects of our mental life. This next proposal comes from an extensive survey of more than fifty thousand people who have now engaged in a practice called the Wheel of Awareness, which you may have been practicing from the appendix, and which we'll explore in more depth later on. This reflective exercise enables us to differentiate the knowing of being aware, represented by the hub of a metaphoric wheel, from that which can be known, illustrated by points along the rim. Then, when we apply our attention to these points on the rim, symbolized by a spoke on the wheel, the knowns become both differentiated and linked to one another—they become integrated. In an advanced step, attention is turned inward to the hub itself, to focus on pure awareness, sometimes experienced as the letting go of attention, as dropping into open awareness.

Some fascinating outcomes from the experience of becoming aware of being aware—the awareness of awareness or, more simply, resting in pure awareness—have been described by participants in the Wheel practice (for more detail, see my books *Mind: A Journey to the Heart of Being Human* and *Aware*). Reports of mental experience seem to correlate well with this visual portrayal of how the mind might function along degrees of probability in the 3-P model. In Figure 5.6, mental experiences, like a thought, an emotion, or a memory, are represented as peaks. The processes of thinking, emoting, and remembering are illustrated as cones beneath the peaks. A plateau represents various mental processes, such as a state of mind, mood, or intention. These states contain mental models that are activated in that moment, in that situation or context, and that filter which peaks arise from that state. After practicing the Wheel of Awareness, individuals reported their experiences of being in the hub—the awareness of awareness—using terms like "empty yet full," "wide-open expanse," "connected to everything and everyone," "bliss," "joy," "God," "timeless," "infinite," "peaceful," "home," and "love."

Here is a simple hypothesis: The experience of being aware emerges when the energy probability position is in the plane of possibility. This idea might be wrong, it might be partially correct, or it might be accurate. This hypothesis fits with the descriptive terms people use to describe the wordless experience and the science-based notions of the characteristics of the microstate, or quantum realm of reality. And it fits with aspects of the wisdom teachings from a wide range of spiritual, religious, contemplative, and Indigenous traditions as well, including those we discussed in the Wisdom Traditions section of the WELCOME chapter, from Buddhist practices to the experience of being a part of nature that Indigenous cultures around our planet, from North America to Australia, have taught for thousands of years. In many ways, as discussed earlier, the consilience underlying this hypothesis weaves recent perspectives of Western, modern

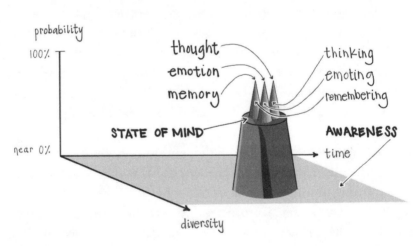

Figure 5.6 3-P diagram of mental experiences reported by people practicing the Wheel of Awareness. See text for description of the probability position and its associated mental experience.

science in a way that matches ancient wisdom. Consilience does not prove this or any hypothesis to be true; it simply supports its potential truth and encourages future explorations and applications to be developed to see if the proposed framework is both accurate and useful. Over these decades so far, as I explore in *The Developing Mind*, there is much support for this framework to be both valid and of practical benefit. We can see the common ground of this 3-P framework: It fits with a wide array of disciplined approaches to understanding our reality, it is consilient, and it allows us to then build a common conceptual foundation that welcomes many ways of knowing into a collaborative conversation. One approach is not better than another; each is different, and each has something to offer us in finding this common ground to move our selves, our ways of literally constructing selves, forward in a generative, integrative direction that promotes well-being on Earth.

When we speak of "beginner's mind" and "dropping beneath the filters" of our top-down mental models that define and confine how we construct and experience self, we can envision this as accessing the plane of possibility. When we see this plane as the portal through which integration naturally arises, we can envision how the release of energy from the learned filters enables integrative differentiation and linkage to emerge, to permit the natural drive of self-organization to arise, instead of being blocked by potentially restrictive and rigid plateaus. The plane of possibility can thus help us understand how connection is cultivated with an open, loving awareness, with what we can call "presence."

When we pay attention to something, it can enter consciousness; and when it does, it has the potential to attain longer-lasting stability as it activates neuroplasticity, growing new neuronal connections, sometimes making new neurons and laying down more myelin sheath to strengthen connections, and sometimes changing our epigenetics, all regulating how we learn in the future. Recall the adage, "Where attention goes, neural firing flows, and neural connection grows."

In our discussion of identity, then, this means that the more a life story—a plateau, in our 3-P diagram, shaping and restricting which peaks can be filtered into being—restricts which thoughts and attitudes arise, the more that narrative reinforces its own beliefs. If we are trapped within such limiting plateaus, the peaks that can arise in our lives are severely constrained, as what can arise from the freedom of the plane of possibility is now restricted by this tightly woven filter of a narrative of a fixed, noun-like entity identity. In day-to-day life, we may never even be aware of this limitation, nor question the notion that our sense of self and our boundaries of belonging are being constricted, not conscious that our own, learned, constructive mental process has created a limiting life story, perpetually self-reinforcing and self-affirming.

From a mind point of view, our drive for certainty may have us cling to these plateaus and their peaks. Yet the freedom to live more fluidly as a self that is evolving more as a verb-like emergence would arise directly from the plane of possibility.

Even this hypothesized 3-P framework itself could initiate a self-reinforcing process, so we should keep a doubting mind active while we try out new ideas and see how they fit with our experience of reality. That's a powerful challenge, to be open and question any absolute sense of certainty, any yet-unquestioned confidence in the accuracy of our beliefs and convictions. We might need to access the plane of possibility to become more comfortable with uncertainty—whose synonyms are freedom and possibility. These are all the mechanisms beneath the "flimsy fantasy of certainty," the longing to know for sure how things are, that commonly limits our identity and narrows our belonging. To avoid such a constriction in identity and belonging, we may need to become open to uncertainty and to not try to control outcomes but let experience come—we can decide to wander.

Energy flows in patterns. These patterns have at least five features that include their contour, location, intensity, frequency, and form. For example, a high-pitched sound has more cycles per second—a higher frequency—than a low-pitched sound. In the brain, waves of electrical energy sweep through the neural networks in ways we can measure with electroencephalogram technology and its more recent computer analyzed rhythms, detecting oscillating patterns of waves in what are known as harmonics. From the perspective of the harmonic modes of the brain, we might say we need to shift our harmonic repertoire to retain the diversity that childhood offers in maintaining a beginner's mind in life. As children, our brain is wide open to enable a range of harmonic waves to sweep through us, much like a conduit of energy flow. As we grow, as we gain more experience, as we learn more, we come to see less, to be less open, to do more, and be less. Now our brain has limited harmonic patterns and it actively constructs its own reality. This is illustrated in our 3-P diagram as how a set of learned plateaus limits which peaks can arise—in the brain, this translates to which harmonic waves are possible. This is our common challenge as we grow through childhood as human beings: to embrace the freedom of uncertainty without collapsing under the pressure to know with certainty—we need to live more from the plane of possibility. This does not mean living in the plane only; it means living from the plane—finding a way to keep that open state of harmonic diversity— the flows of waves of energy that are diverse, a wide-open energy field—available to us as the formless source of all form as we move through our lives.

Part of a poem by Louise Glück (2012) may speak to this challenge, as the world shifts, changes, and no longer exists, "It has become present: unending and without form" (p. 428).

Many States, Many Identities

The mind becomes organized within a given moment in something we can call a "state of mind." From a harmonics perspective, this sweeping process recruits particular intensities, localizations, and frequencies into a spatiotemporally—space and time—distributed set of energy flow patterns. These spatially diverse, anatomically distinct regions of the brain become active within harmonic waves during a brief time span that we will call a "moment of now," clustering together these activated neural nets into a repeatable pattern of neuronal activity.

Dan Stern (2004) has argued that this "moment of now" is about five to eight seconds; other scientists suggest briefer periods of clock time, depending on the harmonic firing patterns and which regions they recruit. This harmonic can be considered a neural correlate of what we are calling a state of mind. The subjective side of this state is a sense of something holding together, of being cohesive, in that moment. After many episodes of similar activation—multiple repetitions of matching harmonic sweeps—these energy patterns, comprising "moments of now," may promote a sense of continuity. If the state holds together in harmony, in the moment and across moments—if it is both cohesive and has continuity, as well as having an integrative wholeness—we say that state of mind has coherence.

We can use the acronym COHERENCE to remember and describe this synergetic, integrative state:

- Connected: a subjective term often used to describe the feeling of joining, of being a part of something, of belonging.
- Open: the expansive sense of inclusion, of feeling receptive to whatever arises, moment by moment.
- Harmonious: literally, the quality of synergy emerging from the linking of differentiated parts—being integrative.
- Emergent: the sense of being a verb, not fixed like a noun, of arising, moment by moment, in fresh ways, perhaps difficult to control or predict.
- Resonant: the quality of being influenced by something but not becoming that thing—we can resonate with the parts of a group yet not lose our uniqueness, just as strings on a guitar resonate with one another without becoming each other.

- Engaged: the sense of meaning and purpose, the sense of life energy driving us to be a part of the whole.
- Noetic: that sense of knowing as conceptual wholeness—things making sense, fitting together, being consilient, and having common ground across ways of knowing.
- Compassionate: the state of mind in which we are open to and can feel suffering—within our own body or that of another being—and then consider ways we might help reduce that suffering and take steps to alleviate it.
- Empathic: the gateway for compassion, which includes empathic resonance as we feel another's feelings, empathic understanding as we cognitively imagine what it might be like to be the other person, perspective-taking as we see from another's point of view, empathic joy enabling us to rejoice in another's success and happiness, and empathic concern—the caring about another's suffering as the doorway for compassion to be engaged.

States of mind can have cohesion, continuity, and coherence, but they don't always. In some states, all three of these features are well developed; in others, one or another feature may be developed to some level but the others not. When a state repeatedly emerges in our lives—what we can call a "self-state"—it directly influences our sense of self not only in that moment but across time, influencing our identity and belonging.

When we come to appreciate the many self-states of mind we enter throughout our lifetime, we come to understand that we also have many identities that define our diverse boundaries of belonging. These persistent and impactful states directly shape our sense of self—or selves or self-states—as these repeating patterns of harmonic sweeps directly mold our center of experience with cohesion and continuity, determining our subjective sensation, perspective, and agency within each of our diverse states of mind.

States go way beyond the boundaries of the skull, involving many systems in the body, such as our gut, our heart, and our muscles. This is why we use the term "embodied brain": to remind us of this whole-body feature of our mental lives. And states of mind even extend beyond the boundary of the skin, recruiting activity from the world around us, especially other people. This is how we interpersonally resonate with others. You might sense this yourself in ways a certain feeling arises when you meet a friend or return home to family. These "relational fields" that you sense can be coherent or incoherent, depending on the circumstances and the people involved—a single person's presence can shape a relational field in powerful and often hidden ways. You might also feel this relational field when you enter a room with a group of people and suddenly your inner state of mind shifts in response to what you feel is going on in the interpersonal communications in the room. Some people call this specific form of relational field a "social field"; others call this the vibe in the room.

We also have a state that resonates not just with people but with the whole of nature—plants, fungi, animals, our natural environment—so that we feel joined within the intraconnected world in which we live. Studies reveal that when we take time to be in nature, to stroll through a forest or walk along the beach, we increase our sense of well-being. When we feel connected within nature, we are happier and healthier. With the "self-expanding" emotions, traditionally called "self-transcendent," we experience this broader belonging as we feel gratitude, compassion, and awe. These states transcend the solo-self view and allow our center of experience, our self, to be broader than the brain, bigger than the body.

Each of these self-expanding emotions, generated from shifts in integration, increases both our differentiation and our linkage. Awe, gratitude, and compassion generate an emerging sense of integrative synergy—we can feel that resonance, be that resonance, in which the whole is greater than the sum of its parts. We become the whole.

Who we are is the whole; the system in which we live is the self; and the inner facet of self is but one aspect of the intraconnected whole. We feel connected and we feel coherent. We are interconnected from the view of the bodily self, and we are intraconnected from the sensation, perspective, and agency of the whole. MWe might call this our "intraconnected state."

States allow us to function in an organized, efficient, and resourceful manner. If I am getting ready to hike a rainy hillside on a blustery day, my state of mind will enable me to prepare for muddy slips along the trail. If the weather is sunny and dry instead, I take the same hike but do not need such a vigilant state of mind—I can be more relaxed and let my mind wander without risking injury. States enable us to be in the world and adapt in the most energy efficient and functionally effective manner we can. This is one reason we have many states: there are many conditions of life for us to engage with. This is also why we need to have the vital capacity to intentionally adjust our identity lens and shift our sense of belonging to fit our conditions as needed. Today, facing the challenges of modern times in our world of disconnection, we have a deep and pressing need to intentionally expand the limited and limiting view of the solo-self in order to widen our lens of identity, broaden our belonging, and, in these ways, increase the synergy of integrative living on our intra-connected planet.

Security, Epistemic Trust, and Our Relational Self

In the early years of our lives, our relationships of attachment shape our sense of self as we grow, and they continue to mold our many facets of self across the lifespan. With the elements of secure attachment, in which we feel safe, seen, and soothed, the core self emerges with a sense of wholeness in its affectivity, agency, continuity, and coherence. With this integrative security, our narrative self expands its way of making sense of life's events as we construct a coherent story of who we are in the world. With security, a relational self grows the capacity to connect, to belong within a "we" without losing the integrity of a "me"—our inner, core self. If our lens of identity is flexible, we can move among these facets of self and embrace the layers of our belonging as we connect within our inner bodily self and as our relational selves, which have interpersonal connection and connection within the whole of nature. We come to feel connected within and between.

One process that is woven with security of attachment—as we develop resilience in each of these three aspects of self-experience: the inner core, the narrative, and the relational inter self—is something researchers call "epistemic trust." When people in authority share with us information and perspectives that correspond with our experience of the true nature of reality, we develop epistemic trust: we can trust that what they say is true. Within attachment relationships, this communicative authenticity conveys to us a sense that we can relax into an ease of well-being, that there is a shared sense of reality that is accurate and can be relied on to interact with the world in predictable, trustworthy ways. This is epistemic trust.

Relationships that engender epistemic trust enable us to build a relational self that feels safe, a narrative self that can accurately make sense of life, and a core inner self that feels whole and coherent. Violations to epistemic trust in foundational attachment relationships early in life—when a young child is presented a view of reality by their caregiver that is inaccurate and does not soothe and comfort—generate an unsettling feeling of dis-ease. The core self feels incoherent, and the narrative self is unable to make sense of life, yet the relational self may try its best to fit into the unsettling view presented by the attachment figure. In this setting, joining-as-a-we sacrifices the internal integrity and coherence of our core and narrative selves. Coherence involves the experience of being connected; with violations of epistemic trust, we come to feel disconnected and incoherent.

As we grow, authorities beyond our parents, such as teachers, organizational leaders, and public figures, can also present to us versions of reality that are not accurate. As we live with the modern culture view that the self is separate, that who we are is a separate entity living in isolation, might this also generate a form of epistemic mistrust? Could such distorted views of reality and the ensuing mistrust, even beneath the surface of awareness, lead to vigilance for danger, an unsettled feeling that something just isn't quite right? While we might strive to fit in, to act as if what we are being told is accurate and true, when the message is inaccurate and false, then this method of contorting our lives to fit in will manifest incoherence and dis-ease.

When we don't feel whole, we may come to feel activated in our subcortical motivational networks. With anger, we can feel empowered with agency to right a wrong: our drive to correct. With fear, we can feel the need to defend ourselves from danger: our drive to protect. With sadness, we can feel the need to reach out to others: our drive to connect. Yet if we are told that the self is only separate—if we experience this break in epistemic trust—our three subcortical circuits of distress may become repeatedly activated to various degrees, and, unique to each of us, often a particular circuit is activated more than the others. Without knowing why, we may be prone to anger, fear, or sadness. These survival drives, if activated with enough intensity, may shift us from being in a brain state of receptivity, with trust and safety, to one of reactivity, with mistrust and a sense of danger. On high alert for threats to our survival, we then continually enter the reactive states of fight, flight, freeze, or faint, hindering our ability to connect—within our inner bodily self and with our relational selves of interpersonal relationships and the whole of nature.

If society can experience a collective parallel to our individual development and attachment, we may gain insights into both our own personal experience from our family of origin and our sense of belonging within our community and culture. How might attachment patterns be relevant for us as a modern society—if we were to see everyone as siblings of our human family?

As a quick review, parents or other caregivers interact with their children, and that relationship, that connection, is called attachment. Attachment is not a feature of the child nor of the caregiver—it is a feature of the relationship between the child and the attachment figure. This relationship can be broadly categorized as one of four recognizable forms, three nonsecure and one secure:

- Avoidant results from shutting down and becoming disconnected and arises when our attachment figures do not provide us
  with the experience of being seen and soothed.
- Ambivalent results from the revving up and being flooded by
  our attachment needs when our caregivers are inconsistent and
  intrusive; we learn that we can't rely on them to meet our needs
  on a reliable basis—sometimes they do, sometimes they don't.
- Disorganized results from being terrified and becoming fragmented—a dissociation that arises when our attachment figures
  are the source of fear and we have two incompatible circuits
  simultaneously activated: one drives us toward our attachment
  figure to seek protection, and the other drives us away from our
  attachment figure, the source of terror.
- Secure results from being seen, soothed, and safe. When our
  caregivers offer these qualities on a relatively consistent basis,
  and ruptures to any of them are readily and reliably repaired, we
  develop an internal mental model of security.

Attachment research has long shown that these mental models of
adaptation, these patterns of attachment, are changeable across the
lifespan. As an attachment researcher who has applied these scientific
findings to the practice of psychotherapy for over thirty-five years, I
find it exciting and deeply rewarding to consider using the same principles of healing—of becoming whole—to address our larger cultural
challenges, expanding on these lessons of individual growth. We can
move toward the integrative healing of security at any point in our
lives—within the attachment of our personal family and, perhaps, in
our attachment within our larger human family as well.

If we see our larger world, our human cultures, as versions of family life, perhaps the ways we feel safe, seen, and soothed and have the
experience of epistemic trust and coherence can illuminate how com-
munity-belonging may offer a deep sense of relational security and
wholeness. Perhaps this is what a broader belonging emerges from.
If 1) we recognize tendencies from these attachment patterns; 2) this
recognition leads us toward a coherent, secure sense of self, identity,

and belonging—for ourselves and our culture; 3) we learn, together, to offer ways of being safe, seen, soothed, and secure; and 4) we acknowledge ruptures and make repairs as life unfolds, then perhaps we can move beyond the reactions and adaptations we acquire in our nonsecure attachments, not only in our family of origin but also in our cultures. Parenting toward security is not about perfection, it is about being present. Perhaps the lessons from the science of foundational familial relational connections can guide us as a larger human family, and family of all living beings, to move toward the vibrancy of connection and collaboration of authentic belonging within trusting, secure relational attachments throughout our intraconnected living world.

SCHOOL YEARS

For the next dozen or so years of our lives, we leave our family homes to join peers and teachers in a system of experiences we call education. Whether in the setting of community school, of an apprenticeship in the community, or of a home-guided learning journey, the systematic imparting of knowledge, skills, values, beliefs, ethics, morality, and habits of behavior and thought shapes the self we experience, the identities we develop, and the senses of belonging we come to embrace.

The Tree of Knowledge, the Knowledge of Trees

When we consider mind as a fully embodied and fully relational process—an emergent property of energy flow arising from a system—we can see how the mind emerges in a synergetic way from energy flows, both within our body and between our body and the world in which we are embedded. "Synergy" refers to how the whole is greater than the sum of its individual parts. In recent studies of forests, we've come to learn how the synergy of trees involves deeply interwoven care in a tapestry of what Janine Benyus describes as mutualisms: "Now we know that it's not just one plant helping another; mutualisms—complex exchanges of goodness—are playing out above- and belowground in extraordinary ways" (Hawken, 2017, p. 213). As we link differentiated components of a system, we integrate that system, and synergy is the natural emergence that arises as the components interact with one another in creating the system as a whole. What we learn about integration from the wisdom of the forest may be just the mutualisms that will help us identify what has gone wrong and how we can now course-correct in our human journey on this planet.

A proposal from interpersonal neurobiology is that the human mind has four facets (Figure 6.1), each of which may be a synergetic outcome emerging from the embodied and relational flow of energy:

- subjective experience, or the felt texture of existence;
- consciousness, which allows us to be aware of that felt sense of being;
- information processing, in which energy flow symbolizes something; and
- self-organization, a property of complex systems.

This fourth facet, self-organization, is the source of the proposal of integration as health.

You may recall the FACES flow—being flexible, adaptive, coherent, energized, and stable—from the chapter INFANCY. This is the flow of harmony. The FACES flow is the manifestation of optimal self-organization. While mathematicians suggest that this is how the complex system maximizes complexity, we can get an everyday feeling for this flow with the simple example of walking down a path. We differentiate our left leg from our right leg as each carries out its special roles; yet each is linked in the overall experience of walking as we step forward, carry the weight of the body, and release as we bring the leg forward again. Imagine if instead each leg functioned without being linked—or if each functioned without differentiation. Instead of walking harmoniously down the path, we'd be stumbling along as if we were intoxicated or hopping down the path

FOUR FACETS of MIND

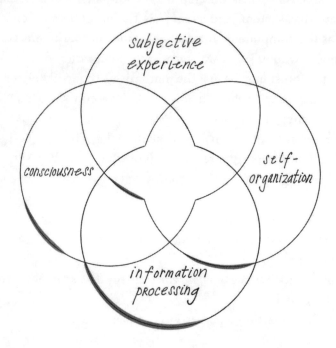

Figure 6.1 The four facets of the mind, each proposed to emerge from the embodied and relational flow of energy.

like a pogo stick, up and down. Differentiation and linkage enable a complex system to achieve this flow of harmony—how the system optimizes its capacity to adapt and even to learn. The term "integration" we are using here refers to a very specific balance between differentiation of components as individual elements and their linkage into a synergetic whole. As we've discussed, integration entails the integrity of the individual components even as they are linked to one another; integration is not blending or making homogenous—

it is a very special way we create a whole that is more than the sum of its parts, more than the addition of different things together into one. Integration enables that "something more" to emerge in an optimal FACES flow.

Many, if not most, contemporary schools emphasize the achievement of designated milestones, evaluated by standardized measures, rather than the encouragement of curiosity, individual creativity, and collaborative learning. In many ways, each of these three—being creative, curious, and collaborative—are each created by and facilitate the synergy of integration. Being creative entails weaving differentiated ways of approaching challenges. Being curious involves a fascination with the many differentiated knowns of life and seeing their linkages. Being collaborative comprises optimal relational flow with the linking of many differentiated viewpoints and that creates something more than any single participant might be able to offer. Sadly, the love a young child has for connecting internally and interpersonally, for integrating in life by exploring new ideas and discovering how the world works, may be squashed beneath the pressure to achieve the certainty of predetermined outcomes of success. Is modern education promoting the fiery spark of integration's curiosity, creativity, and collaboration, or the drive for certainty in the accumulation of an isolated learner? In conforming to such cultural norms and expectations, curiosity, collaboration, and the courage to be wrong can collapse.

We each learn in our own way, yet a standardized approach to education does not accommodate the inherent individual proclivities of learning that each of us carry. Such an approach offers little room for identifying a child's unique propensities to build on those strengths or to help each of us develop differentiated ways of contributing to the collaboration of the whole. Often, this approach does not develop our natural systems intelligence.

One of the constricted ways we learn is the common approach of teaching about the world in a simple, linear fashion: A leads to B leads to C. Reality comprises not only these linear sequences of causation but also a larger mutuality, one we can perceive with a systems lens: reality is made of systems with deep interconnectivity and interdependence of their many layered components, ones that, when seen through the lens of the whole, are intraconnected—knowing this is natural systems intelligence.

What gets in the way of harnessing this natural systems intelligence? I propose that our mind's vulnerability to striving for predictability and certainty, revealed in our modern history of categorizing, classifying, and symbolizing the solo-self as our unquestioned yet nonintegrated identity—our restricted belonging, getting fixed in a narrow lens of identity—is what gets in the way of letting our thriving nature blossom.

In other terminology, we attain an illusion of certainty with a noun-like construction of a solo-self; we free our self and ourselves from this vulnerability by welcoming the reality of self in its verb-like emergence. The related experiences of identity and belonging can then either become constricted, as ones of a fixed, noun-like separation—me here, you there—or they can become free to be integrated as the inner and inter nature of subjective sensation, perspective, and agency widen and emerge across a lifespan of joining in the synergy of self, within and between.

But if the mind, as shaped by our immersion within the messages of modern culture, is indeed getting in the way of life thriving on this precious planet because of these understandable susceptibilities to clinging to certainty, then with the mind's own intention and awareness, we can directly name and then reframe these vulnerabilities as opportunities for growth. We can learn to let our natural systems' intelligence blossom and let our innate capacity to live an intraconnected life on Earth be fully realized. This is a possibility, and perhaps a promise, of what an integrative education and an intentional, integrative cultural evolution might do for all of us in our shared world.

Comparison and Competition, Connection and Collaboration

"Comparison is the thief of joy," President Theodore Roosevelt once said. For author and humorist Mark Twain, comparison is "the death of joy." You might think, "Isn't it natural to compare oneself to others?" Recall the study where children preferred the puppet that liked the same cereal as they did? These children were assessing who is like-me and who is not, liking the former and disliking the latter.

Comparison to others often begins when siblings enter a household. Once we are in a school setting, the ways we fit in shape our experience of self, as do the expectations of our peers, our teachers, and the curricular demands. We come to evaluate the goodness or badness of who we are based on how we measure up to others, how we achieve our class milestones, how we function on the athletic field. Sadly, these comparisons with other selves can lead to a loss of the joy-in-discovery that we call curiosity, the love of learning; and this can seriously hamper a child's natural drive to explore. In this way, the linear construction of individuality, its accompanying comparison—competition, and sense of something lacking, something being wrong, can curtail our natural systems intelligence, the systems-knowing of how to live with ease within a complex mutuality of beneficence.

Activist and author Lynne Twist (2017) has noted three toxic myths of modern society, views that are widely held, yet not just inaccurate—but lethally so: 1) scarcity: there is not enough; 2) more is better; and 3) that's just the way it is. The unconscious and false thinking of this combined unexamined mindset, she proposes, is a prescription for the troubles we now face on our planet. As Twist explains, "Scarcity is the mindset of separateness" (Twist, January 19, 2022, Costa Rica). As I heard those words she spoke during a wellness seminar where we were both teaching in Costa Rica, the lessons from another citizen of that courageous and innovative country, Christina Figueres, along with her colleague, Tom Rivet-Carnac, reverberated in my mind. Their experiences as architects of the 2015 Paris Agreement for climate mediation are described in their book, *The Future We Choose*. Three mental attitudes or mindsets, in their view, are needed to help humanity achieve the needed practical steps to reverse climate change: 1) optimism; 2) abundance; and 3) regeneration. Finding the consilience between their two approaches, we can see that: a) with optimism we can see options that were not initially in view and regain a sense of hope and a practical path with purpose; b) with the mindset that the world, with reciprocal ways of being with nature, can be both sufficient and filled with abundance; we can then c) release our approach from sustaining a growth-at-all-costs goal to one of regeneration, and then liberate a built-in reciprocity of how we consume and produce on our planet.

If we come to realize these three dimensions of our overall mindset (which I couldn't help placing into the acronym, OAR), we can row our boat with optimism, abundance, and regeneration down the river of integration; the flow of harmony in the world. In this perspective, we become grateful for life. Life echoes in these reverberant, consilient ways when we open to its mysteries and the reality of the often-invisible threads that weave us together in our intraconnected wholeness. As an example, the documentary filmmaker, Louie Schwartzberg, sent me the new, full-length film on being grateful before its finalization. In that beautiful artistic demonstration of our deep connections was Lynne Twist being interviewed by Louie, who states this (Schwartzberg, Gratitude Revealed, 2022, February 15, minute 30, used with permission): "When you're in touch with enough, it overflows into natural abundance, not excess, not waste, but natural abundance out of which generosity is a normal, flowing way of being because you feel totally interconnected with everyone else." In that same film, teacher, dancer, and storyteller Luisah Teish states: "We have a lot to be grateful for. I just wish that we had enough gratitude to overcome greed and selfishness." Gratitude, compassion, and awe are considered transcendent emotional states, ones that help us transcend the solo-self and that may bring us to the plane of possibility; that space of being aware where new options are waiting for us—and where we find our deep connections with one another. As Twist continues: "When you are in touch with generosity, you are in touch with the eternal. Every time we tap into the eternal, to the sacred, it's timeless, time actually stops. Don't insult Creation with your human arrogance, be grateful for the miracle that is your life. That's the source of generosity, of prosperity, of gratitude, and of fulfilment. It's one of those places where we express love. And there's nothing quite like love because that's what it is all about."

We can be hopeful and realistically optimistic that there is the potential for natural abundance—not a scarcity— in our world, and we can aim toward the reciprocity of regeneration. With these proposed OAR aspects of our minds set toward integration, we can cultivate a new way for modern humanity to live among all living beings on Earth, transforming from a mindset of separateness and comparison to one of connection and collaboration.

Culture involves patterns of communication within a community, and communication is the sharing of energy and information. A generative learning culture, one that promotes the integrative sharing of energy and information, helps us develop both differentiation and linkage. Such a generative learning culture taps into our natural systems intelligence and integrative learning, promoting what Boell, Senge, and Scharmer (2019) call systems sensing, systems awareness, and systems thinking. Harnessing systems intelligence empowers the principles of integration at the heart of an intraconnected synergetic whole.

We can cultivate integrative communities that build an integrated identity in which an embodied "me" is differentiated and linked within a relational "we." When we access nature's innate systems intelligence, we embrace the mutual belonging of living as intraconnected, expressed within the linguistic symbol of our integrative self as MWe.

Inner and Outer: Private and Public

Attachment relationships begin at home. We turn to our caregivers to achieve the four S's: being safe, seen, soothed, and thus secure. The ways we adapt at home are then carried into our school experience. Studies suggest that we will bring to school the attachment pattern we adopt with our primary caregiver, and we evoke from our teachers a similar pattern of response. If our needs are met at home and we have an inner model of security, we are more likely to ask for help at school when we need our teacher's support. If we have avoidance at home and our needs are not met, we are more likely to act in independent ways, not asking for help when we need it. And if we have ambivalence in our attachment—if our needs are inconsistently met, and sometimes others' emotions intrude on our own state of mind—then we may seem excessively needy with our teachers, unable to find a balance between trying on our own and seeking help when we need it.

Our sense of belonging in interpersonal fields of connection can range from tightly knit to wider concentric circles, perhaps beginning with our caregivers at the center, then our closest friends, and then to social friendships, peers, and acquaintances. Our belonging ranges broadly, from our most intimate relationships to those that feel more distant. Certain close circles of connection can also reflect our patterns of attachment, as we transfer our need for caregiving attachment figures as we leave childhood to close friends and to romantic partners, those to whom we turn when we are distressed. Our identity is shaped by these important attachment relationships throughout our life, which form but one set of circles of connection that create our sense of belonging in the world. These fields of connection may be formed by our identity lens as it ranges from up-close and narrow to more distant and wide-angled. We can see then how the experience of self as sensation, perspective, and agency is shaped by both our identity-lens focus and the ensuing circles of belonging in which the "I" of our individual, inner self becomes woven within the "We" of our relational self. When the fields of connection include an ever-widening embrace encompassing all living beings, we come to an identity as a fundamental part of nature and belong to the intra-connected whole of our living planet.

If our genetically evolved brain, immersed in family and societal messages of separation, leads us to the false belief and inaccurate perception of the solo-self, the self only embedded in the skin-encased body, then our circles of connection and compassion will include only those nearest us, only those similar to us who we identify as "like-me." We will then express intense in-group identification and out-group exclusion, with the consequent social inequities, racism, and genocide and with the whole of our natural environment seeming to be "outside" of who we are. Sound familiar? A narrow lens of identity constricts our circles of belonging. We know from research that when we place an individual into the out-group category, even when distinguished by what seem to be the most subtle signals of separation, we shut off our circuits of compassion. This neural vulnerability contributes to the construction of the solo-self, both as singular "self" or as plural "in-group."

Yet our species evolved in cooperative groups, immersed in the collaboration of alloparenting and community life, not isolated as solo-selves. If in education we direct the growth of the minds of our youth to embrace a wider focus in our lens of identity, widening their circles of compassion based on a broadening of our belonging, we might bring such shifts in identity and belonging into the larger culture, beyond the pages of this book, beyond the curriculum in schools. The challenge is to develop a growth mind-set, that state of mind Carol Dweck (2006) has suggested can empower us to see the opportunities for growth in the face of difficulties, and not collapse as we might with a fixed mindset in which we see challenges as revealing our weakness. With a growth mindset, these contemporary challenges can be experienced as an opportunity to learn and grow in our collective efforts to change. But change how? In the conversation of this journey that you and I are on, we are considering the notion that integration is what is missing in modern times and that finding a way to integrate identity—to differentiate and link our experience of self and belonging—may be a path to consider taking, together. While genetic evolution takes time, cultural evolution is much more rapid—and it can be intentionally directed.

What might be our shared intention? To focus on how human development, shaped in homes, schools, work, and our larger society, can be guided toward a systems-intelligent way of living.

The Stories of Our Lives, the Lives of Our Stories

You may recall from the chapter TODDLERHOOD that narrative is initiated when there is a violation to expectation, what scientists call a "canonical violation." A "canon" is a general law or principle by which something is judged—it sets our minds in a certain stance about what to expect in life. The stories of our lives are how we wrestle with expectations and how the world conforms, or not, to these filters of experience. When something doesn't go the way we've learned life "should" be, we tell a story about what happened and the mental experiences of those involved, in an attempt to make sense of what happened and why within our understanding of how life works. This helps us learn from experience and convey that learning to others, sharing our knowledge and lessons of life for the betterment of the whole.

While narrative is useful, we've also seen how it can imprison. Expectations act as top-down filters that funnel experience into mental constructions based on what happened before. This is how a tightly woven plateau in our 3-P framework filters the peaks that might arise in a limited and limiting manner. These mental models then shape how we think the world actually is, determining which peaks emerge and become the "stuff" of which we are aware. Because we come to perceive what we believe, this adds a sense that it is accurate, that it is true—just the "way things are." Having a narrative self that constructs stories means that after initial sensory input—the initial conduition—the more experience we have in life, the less we will actually truly see: We get lost in our own beliefs, caught up in our own life story. Narrative and belief shape perception.

The mind's own self-reinforcing processes make understanding our narrative-self crucial in freeing us to approach unlearning ways of living in the world that have been, even unknowingly, limiting and unhelpful, and then freeing our narrating minds to find new stories for us, new ways of making sense, individually as well as collectively as a family of humanity living within our shared natural world. These autobiographical narratives, or stories of our self, are literally the stories we tell, to ourselves and to others, of who we are. Such narratives, as studied by attachment researchers, can be viewed as cohesive (i.e., stick tightly together) and as coherent (i.e., resilient and flexible, recognizing reality's pleasant and unpleasant components). A cohesive yet incoherent narrative may be somewhat logical, yet often deny or restrict aspects of reality in order to hold itself together. Our innate drive to make sense by linking differentiated elements of our own life history can be restricted by a strictly cohesive yet noncoherent life narrative.

Neuroscience has identified a network within the brain that violates a previously established belief of that field: The canon that divided anatomical regions of the brain have clear and distinct functions, such as perception here, motor action there. This canon-violating network comprises what have been named "mirror neurons," which have both perceptual and motor properties and are activated when we watch another creature's actions. For example, in one study if a researcher or another monkey ate a peanut, the same motor neurons of a monkey watching or hearing this action became activated as if they were eating the peanut. A single neuron was involved in both perception and motor action, hence the name, "mirror neuron"—because there is a mirroring of perception and action in one cell. Later research revealed that groupings of this type of cellular function, "mirror neuron systems," are distributed widely throughout the human brain. While this finding is still controversial, the implications of the mirror neuron system are relevant for our discussion of self, identity, belonging, and the stories we tell internally and collectively.

We imitate others' behavior and feel their feelings as a natural part of our relational selves. With behavioral imitation, we prepare, or prime, our motor system to imitate an action we are perceiving, and then we can enact a similar motion. With state simulation, we shift our own internal state, including bodily physiology and emotional processes, to resemble that of the individual we are perceiving. Mirror neuron functions offer us one way to understand how we resonate with one another in both subjectively felt experience and agency—they directly link our experience of self beyond the skull and skin. And if we are unaware that we have made this shift in priming and in feeling, if we don't come to realize that our current internal state is due to the input from another and not solely from our internal source of self, we may become confused, perhaps akin to being fused as a "self" and an "other." The role of the mirror neuron system in enabling us to join without becoming the other, to differentiate and to link, may be an important way we distinguish between individualism at one extreme and collectivism at the other. If we keep our "self" totally distinct, if we don't soak up the inner states of others in our emerging experience, we may be on autopilot as separated; if we lose the distinction of a bodily self from others' experiences, then the perception of the other individual may flood us with state simulation and behavioral imitation and we become fused rather than integrated. Perhaps the fear that drives individuality in modern times is this dread of losing one's own differentiated being. The idea and practical implication of the two components of integration—differentiation and linkage—may support an integrative path forward, avoiding the extremes of both disconnection and fusion as individualistic and collectivistic polarities of identity.

These findings also suggest that our embodied nervous system uses the overall body, with its physiology and brain states, to resonate with others, and then that resonance of the body acts like an antenna and amplifier—often beneath awareness. We sense another individual; those sensations soak into our perceptual processing. And if we interpret another's state as having organization, an intention, we have a way to predict what is likely to happen, and we prime ourselves to initiate action as imitation or to simulate state as emotional resonance. This is how we can join as a we without losing a me.

If you dance with a partner, you may feel the music linking you with your partner; the continuing flow of a slight tilt of the head or pressure on the arm allows two to become one, with a synergy linking you. If you play music in a group, you may feel that resonance in your differentiation as you play your instrument and yet linkage in the overall piece. If you sing in a choir, you may feel the harmony arise as the differentiated voices become connected with melody and rhythm. These are states of joining, moments when we (perhaps engaging our mirror neurons) temporarily and willingly suspend our sense of an individual self to allow us to expand our self-experience and let go of separation. We share the subjective sensation, join in perception, and have agency on behalf of the synergetic whole. This capacity enables us to choose to be in the flow of joining within the intraconnected wholeness of the relationship.

When we perceive another person as having a subjective experience, we make our own mindsight map of that individual's inner state. Mirror neurons may be a part of that process, enabling us to sense the mental state, the intention, the mood, the meaning of an organized state of being within another, and then to map that state onto our own physiology and mental states.

Mindsight maps come in at least three fundamental forms: a "me-map," our own inner state; a "you-map," the inner state of another;

and a "we-map," the state of the collective. A me-map lets us know how we are feeling internally, what our individual intentions are, what our emotional meaning is in that moment. A you-map lets me infer from my me-map what is going on inside of you. These are maps of the internal state with the body as the spatial reference point. A we-map plots the system that is us, a relational identity, and our intentions, sensations, and emotional meaning as a collective unit.

A we-map is how we represent the relational we, referred to as a "relational field." This is the relationship as a center of experience—the source, the location, of energy and information flow. We-maps help us use systems-sensing and systems-thinking to become aware of the interdependent, interactive, interconnected, interlaced connections of parts—to sense the intraconnected whole.

When we are under threat, we increase our in-group versus out-group evaluative process, and we treat those in the in-group with more kindness and those in the out-group with more hostility. If we deem an individual to be not like-me, the circuits of empathy and of compassion are shut off—they literally become inactive. We stop resonating with that person, shutting off connection. In mindsight terms, this means we do not make mindsight maps of that person and we do not perceive that person as having a mind. In relational terms, we dehumanize them—they stop being human and they are no longer a part of our we-map. In this way, we constrict our own lens of identity and restrict our own belonging. This may be one means by which the threat of scarcity creates the mindset of separation.

By becoming aware of and naming this vulnerability, perhaps we can reframe it and widen our lens, broaden our belonging. We could use our mindsight maps to see all people, not just those like-us, and we could see the self in all species, not just in humans. This may be how we move from a mindset of scarcity to that of optimism, abundance, and regeneration—the OAR we need to row our biodiverse boat from disconnection and disaster toward connection and thriving. Perhaps we can use these mindsight maps to create a sense of self—a center of experience—within the system as a whole, a living, breathing ecosystem of life on Earth. While this vulnerability that constricts our lens of identity is part of our human history, does it need to control our destiny?

Our awareness of the inner and inter processes shaping the continual emergence of our experience of self, identity, and belonging can offer the opportunity to cultivate more internal and relational well-being, if we choose. What is this choice we face? Automatic mechanisms, built into the tendencies of the human embodied brain, can push us toward a restricted set of "like-me" criteria when determining "in-group" versus "out-group" membership. Without awareness, teachings of a noun-dominant culture—as conveyed at home, in school, in society, through ways we communicate with one another on the street, at work, on the internet—can restrict our self, limit our identity, confine our belonging.

To live more fully and freely, to address the major pandemics of our times effectively, we can choose instead to cultivate an awareness, to intentionally become conscious of these current forces at play in our lives, so that we can have the capacity to override these inherited ways of dividing and the learned messages of separation we take on as true.

What does awareness permit us to do? The human brain has neural networks that enable identity to be constructed using a narrow or a wide-angle lens, to constrict or broaden our belonging, to limit or expand the defining experiences of what we call our "self." Awareness permits choice and empowers change. If the message of modern times is one of the solo-self, a belonging confined to only those "like-us," with "us" narrowly defined, then we will construct a life of isolation and division. Awareness enables us to move past these contemporary constructions of separation, an excessively differentiated life, toward an integrative way of living, honoring the gifts of each individual while at the same time linking as a collective whole.

Who we are with such awareness can be freed as a dynamic verb-like emergence, liberated from the stagnant, stifling limits of a linear, noun-like construction of self. Fear of fusion, of becoming lost in the experience of joining, or dread of disconnection and being completely isolated and alone, may be the pendular emotional extremes that push us toward that flimsy fantasy of certainty, the longing to know, noun-like, who we really are. Yet embracing uncertainty may be what "becoming aware" is truly about, accessing that plane of possibility in which we can realize that the synonyms for uncertainty are openness, freedom, and possibility. Choice emerges from that plane of possibility from which consciousness arises.

And so, our choice begins with opening awareness. But what comes next? To move beyond a construal of self as separate, we can learn from the millennia old wisdom of Indigenous teachings and contemplative practices, which are supported by more recent explorations in modern science, that a systems view of reality illuminates a world of deeply interwoven parts—a reality of interconnection of components that, seen from the whole, is intraconnected. When we think in linear terms, our focus of reality is primarily on its parts. A systems view enables us to sense the subjective experience, take on the perspective, and have the agency of a verb-like me and we, a dynamic unfolding of an interacting whole. As MWe've seen, integrating the inner me with the inter we creates the intraconnection that is MWe.

In this awareness and its systems sensing, it becomes possible to let go of the illusion of solidity and certainty, to let go of vulnerability that drives us to cling to linear and noun-like notions of self, and to instead open to the freedom of verb-like becoming. That's a shift that can feel disorienting at first, yet ultimately grounding as we come to live the truth of how things actually are. With this shift in sensation, perspective, and agency, with this shift in self, what arise are the inner, the inter, and the intra as an ever-changing emergence in the flow of energy and information. Instead of constructing an appearance of separation, we feel the reality of intraconnection. Instead of viewing the nodal body as the self-alone, we come to see the body as a rich conduit, or part, of that whole—the inner part; and we add to that internal reality not only the interconnections with other parts, but the intraconnection as we come to embrace the system-as-a-whole from the experience of self, identity, and belonging. Me is the inner; We are the between, the inter; and MWe are the intraconnected whole.

The body and its brain may construct a sense of self as separate, that, in our school years, may continually be reinforced by messages we receive in the process of education. But if we realize how neuroplasticity enables the brain to change at any age, then we can see how our mindsight maps can also change as we widen the angle of our identity lens. Consilient in many ways with Robert Kegan's theory of an "evolving self" (1982, 1994), and with the movement through stages of ever more complex capacities to sense the mental states of self and others, here we are exploring not stages but a continuum of mindsight-map making abilities that build across development from the inner mapping of self-experience as "me-maps" to the representations of the inner states of others as "you-maps" and of the relational whole as "we-maps." The interpersonal neurobiology framework of development we are exploring suggests that integration is the heart of the drive to ever-more complex states of a system's flow. Self-organization naturally emerges toward harmony with the FACES flow of being flexible, adaptive, coherent, energized, and stable. How we learn to adapt to our family of origin with acquired attachment patterns, to attempt to fit in to school life, and later to cultivate a role in society will each become the top-down ways we've learned to be and behave in the world. We soak in the inner world of others by way of the social brain's various networks, including mirror neurons and our mindsight map-making circuits that are continually shaped by our experiential immersions, especially in the social world. In these ways, we come to focus our identity lens on sensations, mold our perceptions, and enact our agency by what we've learned in self-reinforcing ways. When modern messages of isolation and the need to be certain repeatedly shape our experience of self as separate, the self-organizing flow toward the harmony of a FACES life may be compromised with such impediments to integration, and unsettling experiences of chaos and rigidity may emerge within our personal, public, and planetary lives. This may be the unfortunate—but changeable—outcome of the solo-self in modern times.

With respect, intention, and purpose, we can learn to recognize our vulnerability to living separately as noun-like solo-selves throughout our lives; beginning in our homes, extending to our schools, and then moving out into society. We can rise above that vulnerability and move to a healthier, fuller, integrative identity honoring the inner body and the inter relationships and the reality of the whole. We can, together, acknowledge where we've come to now, and then, with intention, move our shared construction of self to a more integrative way of living.

ADOLESCENCE

During our first dozen years of life, we tend to have a brain that soaks in all the lessons we are exposed to, growing new synaptic connections that help us remember our experiences, learn social skills to adapt and cope, and take on the worldview we are taught. But as we move toward our second dozen years, our brain begins to take on a new growth strategy: As we leave primary school age and prepare for middle school and beyond, our brain growth will enter a stage of remodeling.

Adolescence is a time when identity and belonging will be a primary focus of our growth. We begin to experience quite distinct ways of being—our public personas—that reveal the different roles we play in various settings within the different social groupings we find ourselves drawn to, such as the classroom and out on the streets. Our membership within those groups will in turn alter how we experience our identity. Identity shapes belonging; belonging shapes identity.

One of the deep challenges of shifting from preadolescence into adolescence is the movement away from our birth parents as we start to turn to our peers for comfort and connection. Our inner sense of life's order, the image of the world as we were told it was supposed to be, will become shaky as we begin to question the nature of reality and even the meaning of life itself. Why are we here? What if what we've been told about the world is not true?

In adolescence, a new awareness of the major pandemics confronting us may emerge—the challenges of a virus, of social injustice, of polarization, of attention-addiction, and of environmental destruction—and we can come to feel inspired to make a difference or overwhelmed and driven to avoid such knowledge. Yet during this tender time—this transition from the dependency of childhood to the responsibility of adulthood—we may have few resources that encourage us to consider that the inherent validity of what we've been taught, what we've been told about the self being separate, is even something to question. The sixth and underlying pandemic, that of the solo-self, may not even come into view.

The ESSENCE of Adolescence

Seen in many species besides our own, adolescence involves fundamental challenges and opportunities as well as a core set of features that shape our individual experience across the lifespan. The essence of adolescence, and perhaps even health throughout our lives as well, as I suggest in *Brainstorm*, can be symbolized with the term "ESSENCE" itself:

Emotional Spark—the passion to fully feel a wide range of emotions
Social Engagement—the connection to join and collaborate interpersonally
Novelty-seeking—the courage to try new and sometimes risky things
Creative Exploration—the imagination to envision and innovate in new ways

The ESSENCE of the adolescent period is to cultivate this passion, connection, courage, and imagination in ways that support our growth and the greater good. During adolescence, the brain prunes down some connections and strengthens others. This important brain remodeling creates these ESSENCE features, which can last a lifetime through which they continue to support our health and resilience as we create integration inside and out.

During adulthood we may let go of our imagination and live a life focused primarily on what is, rather than creatively exploring what might be or even considering what could or should be. Yet keeping imagination alive in our adult lives lets us free our brains to become active in many ways that support our health. When we are imaginative, we open to new possibilities, we reflect on our values, keeping what has meaning for us, we find purpose, and we rethink habits that are unhelpful or based on inaccurate information and beliefs. These creative explorations even include you reading this book and considering these components of your own ESSENCE and how they might be nurtured, or rekindled if they have dwindled, so that passion, connection, courage, and imagination can help support your journey from this moment forward.

If you find that some of the features of this ESSENCE are missing in your life, the great news is that you can reclaim your ESSENCE at any time—I once worked with a person in his nineties who was able to do just that. Thanks to neuroplasticity, our brain can continue to grow throughout our life: Where attention goes, neural firing flows, and neural connection grows. The neural correlates of living a life with ESSENCE is a more integrated and integrative brain—and that neural integration, research reveals, is the best predictor of our well-being. It's a win–win situation: Integration empowers our ESSENCE, and our ESSENCE builds integration, throughout our lifespan.

When we approach adolescence, something starts happening in our brain that will make the sense of who we are—our identity—begin to change from what we knew in our early years. To whom and to what we belong also begin to shift. We feel one way with some friends, another way with peers in school, and even another way with kids on an athletic team. Studies in the setting of the United States show that in the beginning of these second dozen years of life, we have these different self-states but are not very aware of them. In the middle of these years, around ages fourteen and fifteen or so, we start to become aware of these distinct states, but we are still not clear about how to handle them. And then in our later teens, in the middle part of adolescence (our brain continues remodeling deep into our twenties), we may be faced with leaving home.

But for those of us in households that are more comfortable than the "outside" world, why in the world would we want to leave? Yet nature needs us to leave, needs us to mix with other nonfamily members, for the benefit of our potential offspring and our species. What has nature done to get us ready for that transition?

Adolescents who have tapped into the four components of their ESSENCE—emotional spark, social engagement, novelty-seeking, and creative exploration—are more likely to be ready to leave. Emotional spark can be thought of as the passion that serves as fuel for evoking motion—that's one way to think of the term "e-motion": evokes motion. The downside of this spark is intense waves of emotions, and the meanings that are woven with them, which can feel overwhelming at times—unpredictable moods and waves of feelings that are hard to understand or contain. But the upside is the reward of a meaningful and exuberant life. How we learn to ride those waves of emotion is essential for harnessing our emotional spark.

We are also driven toward social engagement. In the wild, an isolated adolescent is more likely to become a predator's lunch—social engagement means survival. Connection to peers helps us get ready to leave home and face the adult struggles awaiting us. The downside of this need for social connection and belonging is that we may cave in to peer pressure, sometimes letting go of morality to gain membership. The upside is that, during the adolescent period, we learn the life-affirming, health-promoting social skills we'll need for a lifetime.

Another way nature readies us to leave home is by increasing our drive for novelty. Nature gives adolescents an inner drive to seek out, or at least tolerate, conditions that are unfamiliar, risky and unsafe at times, and filled with uncertainty by shifting our remodeling brain to change the reward circuitry that uses the neurotransmitter dopamine. This vertically distributed group of networks is an interconnected set of neurons that extends from our cortex down into our limbic area and our brain stem. When dopamine is secreted, we feel satisfied; when dopamine is depleted, we may feel a drive to do something that releases it again. During adolescence, nature shifts these dopamine levels. Some findings suggest that the levels of dopamine release are higher during adolescence so that we are rewarded even more for trying new things—novelty is one of the best activators of the reward system. Other studies suggest that our baseline levels of dopamine may be lower during adolescence, inducing us to feel restless, like something is missing, and like we need to do something, try something new—like leaving home!

Another shift nature has created is centered more in the limbic and cortical areas that assess risk and reward, a process called "hyperrational thinking." This change creates more focus on the positive aspects of an activity and minimizes our focus on any downsides of actions we consider. When an unfamiliar and uncertain world presents us with the unknown, the dopamine drive for novelty and the hyperrational thoughts emphasizing potential positive outcomes each help us overcome hesitation.

During adolescence we also experience a drive to move beyond what adults have told us about the world, to experience creative exploration, to help us use this tolerance for uncertainty to explore our possibilities and use our imagination. But is there a downside to this imagination? Perhaps a sense of disillusionment that the world we are handed is not what we imagined it could be, or a feeling of disappointment, despair, discouragement, and disconnection? How we move through these feelings into realistic optimism and practical idealism—how we come to see that the cracks in our systems are in fact where the light may come in and guide us forward—is how our imagination and our sense of creative exploration can empower us. This is the upside of creative exploration: to reach for the stars while our feet are firmly planted on the ground.

Romance, Relationships, Identity

An important, emerging set of experiences shaping our identity and belonging involve gender and sex: gender role, gender expression, gender identity, and sexual orientation.

"Gender role" is a phrase used, especially in the past, to indicate what is expected of us by our culture based on the sex we were assigned at birth. For example, if you have an X and a Y chromosome, like me, you likely have external sexual features—your genitalia—that made the delivery clinician and your parents call you a "boy"; and if you have two X chromosomes, you likely were born with genitals that made these people call you a "girl." Some individuals are born with what are called "ambiguous" genitalia, which make it unclear which gender they should be assigned at birth; the term "intersex" is sometimes used for this situation. Other individuals have extra chromosomes, such as XXY, or genetically induced effects on hormones that create an inconsistency between their genetic makeup and how they look (their phenotype). These and other factors in our physiology affect our "assigned sex."

"Gender expression" is a term for our outward manifestations of gender. The Human Rights Campaign offers a glossary of important, carefully articulated wording for these issues of identity and belonging, including gender expression: "External appearance of one's gender identity, usually expressed through behavior, clothing, haircut or voice, and which may or may not conform to socially defined behaviors and characteristics typically associated with being either masculine or feminine" (Human Rights Campaign, 2022).

Gender expression is often generated and judged by cultural expectations. When I was young, people around me expected me to like trucks, which I did, and sports, which I did not. People expected me to enjoy being competitive on the baseball diamond, which I generally was not, but I loved dance—which meant I was one of only two males in a high school dance class with fifty adolescent females. That was a great situation as far as I was concerned, even though the males in my grade thought I was odd. We can say that I did not conform to their expectation of my gender expression.

As we can see, the gender expression that others expect of us and the gender role others assign us don't always match with our own proclivities, often because of something quite distinct happening within us. Inside, a distinct feature of our identity is our gender identity—how we identify ourselves in terms of gender. When I was an adolescent—in the United States in the second half of the twentieth century—there seemed to be only two gender identity choices: male or female. Since then, there has been a cultural shift toward recognizing that this binary set of male or female is actually a mental and social construction, an artificial division of gender category that is not consistent with the reality of a spectrum of gender values that we can and do experience. The Human Rights Campaign states this succinctly in its definition of gender identity: "One's innermost concept of self as male, female, a blend of both or neither—how individuals perceive themselves and what they call themselves. One's gender identity can be the same or different from their sex assigned at birth" (Human Rights Campaign, 2022).

A gender identity at odds with one's assigned sex can happen for several reasons. A brief review of sexual development in the womb is illuminating. Typically, all fetuses begin with a female brain. Fetuses with XY chromosomes develop testicles, which secrete the hormone testosterone, which enters the bloodstream and reaches the head, where it "masculinizes" the brain. The result is that certain proclivities can be created by subtle shifts in brain connectivity—invisible to a scanner—shaped by hormone exposure in the womb. In other words, a radiologist or researcher looking at a structural brain scan won't be able to ascertain the gender identity, assigned sex, or other gender features of that individual. For example, if a young fetus with two X chromosomes is exposed to excessive androgens (e.g., testosterone)—such as from the mother's adrenal glands and/or due to certain medical conditions—that fetus's initially female brain often becomes masculinized. Alternatively, if for some reason testosterone in an XY fetus does not cross the blood brain barrier, even if this hormone is secreted by the testicles, that brain may remain more or completely in its original, female state. In other words, these changes in brain structure and function are not all-or-nothing—they range across a spectrum from no masculinization to a huge amount. For these reasons, unlike the usual binary states of the appearance of the genitalia, the brain develops along a remarkably broad spectrum and can be something other than only male or female.

My own assigned sex is male, and my internally determined gender identity—shaped in utero, we believe, by my masculinized brain—is male. In this way, some might call me "cisgender," as the Human Rights Campaign defines it, "a term used to describe a person whose gender identity aligns with those typically associated with the sex assigned to them at birth." You might say that my identity as male enabled me to belong to the group called "males," but that story is much more complex, as you'll see shortly.

Even in my youth, I knew individuals who felt that their inner sense of who they were, their inner identity, did not conform to this division—this forced choice—of male or female. The Human Rights Campaign offers a term that would have been welcome by those friends back then: "nonbinary," which they define as

An adjective describing a person who does not identify exclusively as a man or a woman. Non-binary [sic] people may identify as being both a man and a woman, somewhere in between, or as falling completely outside these categories. While many also identify as transgender, not all non-binary [sic] people do. Non-binary [sic] can also be used as an umbrella term encompassing identities such as agender, bigender, genderqueer or gender-fluid. (Human Rights Campaign, 2022)

As you can see, our gender identity, along with our gender role and gender expression, greatly influences our overall sense of identity. And we have a fourth facet to our experience of self, belonging, and identity: sexual orientation. Here is the Human Rights Campaign's definition for sexual orientation: "An inherent or immutable enduring emotional, romantic or sexual attraction to other people" (Human Rights Campaign, 2022). Our attraction is oriented to certain types of people—the "type" might be those of a different gender or those of the same gender. To describe a range of orientations, the Human Rights Campaign suggests such terms as "bisexual," "gay," "lesbian," "same-gender-loving," "pansexual," "straight," and, for those who experience no sexual attraction, "asexual."

When we use the adolescent experience of growth and change to illuminate these important facets of identity, we come to respect how challenging it can be for a range of individuals. First, these new sexual and romantic feelings can be so intense that they overwhelm us. Second, since adolescents are typically deeply relational, engagement with others to explore the romantic attraction and sexual interactions can make us feel very vulnerable. Third, as we learned in the chapter INFANCY, because social rejection is mediated by the same brain region as physical pain—the dorsal anterior cingulate cortex—this vulnerability and the inevitable misunderstandings, miscommunications, and rejections that may happen can feel very painful. Fourth, as our culture's messages of gender role match or don't match our gender expression, there may be a sense of being accepted or rejected by the larger social group called society. Finding membership—the experience of belonging and being fully accepted as an authentic you, wherein the inner you and the outer you can match and are seen and respected by others—can be tricky and risky for any of us. Fifth, while we are growing as an adolescent and trying to sense how we feel, these distinct facets of our life—including assigned sex, gender role in the larger culture, gender expression, gender identity, and sexual orientation—each play an important part in our sense of belonging.

Timeless Wisdom, Timely Action

Consider your own positionality in this life: How do your various facets of self-experience shape your identity and how you belong within the cultural contexts in which you live now or where you've lived before? Have you found that you can, with intention, focus your lens of identity to see close-up and then widen it to sense a larger identity, a broader belonging, beyond your body or beyond those whose bodies look like yours? How has sensing your identity, from both its internal sources and the external constructs from community and culture, felt to you? How has having an awareness of this inner and inter aspect of what shapes your experience of self—your sensation, perspective, and agency—influenced your life?

If you've known for a long time or are just now realizing for the first time that you've been in a state of mismatch between your inner sense of identity and your inter sense of belonging, in what ways have you compromised your behavior? How have you acted, what of your authentic self have you hidden, to protect your life from rejection? Have there been moments when you've experienced confusion about who you are from trying to fit in with what the world expected you to be? Has that adaptation stayed with you in your public life? How has it influenced your private life?

While these issues may first present themselves in intense ways during adolescence, they stay with us for the rest of our lives. If we've been marginalized, if our external identifying features have caused us to be mistreated, dehumanized, disrespected, or rejected, how have we handled that? For some this feature would be a sex assignment of female in a male-dominated world; for some, this feature would be skin that has color in a white-majority society. These impacts can be direct—the pain of that social rejection—and can also include how we've tried to adapt: what we've done, in the best ways we know how, in our attempts to survive and thrive. As the documentary film *High*

on the Hog reveals, we carry the journey of painful marginalization and dehumanization forward across generations while adapting as best we can.

In a culture that implicitly values white skin over dark complexions, male sexual assignment over female, and heterosexual attraction over other sexual orientations, a huge percentage of our population may be experiencing significant marginalization. For those of us in privileged, nondehumanized positions in our culture, it is our duty, our moral responsibility, to be an active participant in bringing protection and empowerment into the world—to live with absolute integrity. One meaning of this integrity would be, essentially, to aspire to bring integration, in all its forms, into the world.

Integration has this simple foundation: We honor differences, and we cultivate compassionate linkages. This means that we attempt to wake up to and move beyond any automatic, autopilot racial and/or gender biases and learned, top-down filters, and toward a more inclusive way of living, of being aware, of behaving, of inviting a mutuality of belonging and participation. This means not just tolerating differences but learning to thrive because of differences. In a prime example of consilience, a broad range of sciences, with a wide array of perspectives, agree that when we have more diversity, we have a richer, more complex, more adaptive system. In our diversity, we can achieve more, solve more, flourish more.

Integration reveals how optimal self-organization, creativity, and well-being are founded on thriving with diversity. But it goes further than only having space for lots of differences: integration is the linkage of those differentiated components. We link with compassionate communication. We link by being interested in the experiences, perspective, and empowerment—the self—of all members of our system.

Our experience of adolescence directly engages our subjective sensation, perspective, and agency—our emerging self—in examining the internal and relational foundations of identity and belonging. Gender, race, sexual orientation, religious beliefs, and many more features of our unfolding selves each impact who we see our self to be and to whom and to what we belong during this important period of brain remodeling. When integrated, we emerge from our adolescence feeling whole and ready to take on adult responsibility, to participate and to bring to the world a full sense of who we are. With such integration, our identity and belonging weave the authentic differentiation of our inner sense of self that is fully accepted with our inter sense of who we are. We are both a "me" and a "we."

MWe, as an integrated identity, brings a sense of broader belonging, expanding beyond the individual alone to also embrace the cultural relational field that is MWe. MWe seek a way to have both the broad belonging and the integrated identity that allow for the wide focus of attention on our overall world, while at the same time honoring the importance of our individual, narrow focus on our inner, personal experience. MWe invites both the integrative linkage of connection and the differentiation of individuality.

As discussed in the WELCOME chapter sections "Wisdom Traditions" and "An Ancient Invitation for Modern Times," for thousands of years the teachings of Indigenous cultures and of contemplative practices have focused on the importance of seeing our place in life as woven within a larger whole—what we, in contemporary science terms, would call a systems perspective. The susceptibility of the human brain to mistaking the body—a part of the whole—as the sole center of self is not only an old proclivity of our human lives, it is a dangerous mistaken identity if we lose the larger systems view of our wholeness. Yes, our self, identity, and belonging are shaped by the inner bodily experience of this manifestation into actuality, this flow of energy that gets about one hundred years to live on Earth. We are descendants and ancestors of a long line of animals, a family member of all living beings; we are fundamentally interwoven with all life: here, now, there, and then. We are also the emergence of energy as it flows from possibility to actuality, manifesting in this bodily lifetime with our personal identity, and at the same time a part of the intraconnected whole of not only all of life, but all of reality.

As discussed at the beginning of our journey, most Indigenous traditions—from the Tayuna of South America to the Aboriginal peoples of Australia—emphasize the importance of the individual belonging to community. One's identity, in these wise teachings, is bigger than the boundary defined by the body and is a part of all humanity. Our human belonging, Indigenous knowledge suggests, is even broader than our connections within humanity—it extends to embrace all of nature. We are siblings of the family of all living beings on Earth. Regaining that balance, individually and as a society, will bring connection back into our lives while retaining the equally important ways we thrive with our diversity.

The fundamental mechanism of integration potentially underlies how systems function well in our world to promote harmony and health. By delineating the differentiation and linkage components of integration, we gain a practical way to identify sources of chaos and rigidity in our lives—individually, socially, and ecologically—and to take action to liberate the various levels of impaired integration at the root of these forms of suffering. Our contemporary cultures may mold our modern minds toward linear thinking and away from systems wisdom across the lifespan —which can become set in adolescence, creating lifetime patterns—yet whatever our place in life, our positionality, our developmental stage, we can participate in this move toward integration.

Preparation for Separation and Change

Adolescence helps us prepare to separate from the familiarity of home, to move out into the world, to widen our lens of identity so that we can embrace a larger set of experiences that will define us, expanding our circles of connection, broadening our belonging. This preparation draws on our ESSENCE so that our passion fuels our emotional spark, our drive for connections establishes social engagement to support us as we venture off, our courage enables us to seek novelty and take on new experiences, and our imagination empowers us to creatively explore the world. There are downsides to each of these four foundations: feeling overwhelmed by our emotions, feeling pressured to conform in order to belong, being harmed by risky behavior, and experiencing disillusionment upon seeing the world as different from what we imagined. Yet we can hold on to this ESSENCE to enrich us for the rest of our lives—and to help us dispel the myth of the solo-self in modern society.

As adults we carry the view that we've worked hard to find our niche in life, we've settled into the world we've adapted to and are now trying to maintain, and we may feel threatened by the ESSENCE of adolescents, the next generations, who challenge the status quo. While our adult brain may long for things to remain the same, evolution has programmed adolescents—teenagers and individuals in their twenties—to have passion, to crave collaborative connection, to express courage and imagination, which can make us feel uneasy. If we, as adults, have forgotten our ESSENCE, whose core features help us live a vital and integrative life, we eschew these characteristics when we see them in others, adolescent or adult, who challenge business as usual.

Yet, drawing on the three deep subcortical pathways to correct, connect, and protect, described in the INFANCY chapter, we are also empowered to move beyond the deeper survival reactions of fight, flight, freeze, and faint. Yes, the world's pandemics—and adolescents' intense desire to feel their ESSENCE in response to them—can make us feel threatened. And this threat is about issues of life and death. Our challenge ahead is to move beyond this sense of threat, to support one another in liberating ourselves from the automatic pilot states of reactivity, and cultivate a receptive state of mind that enables us to find solutions, working together—to enable our collective ESSENCE to address these existential threats to all life on Earth.

As adolescents ready themselves to leave home, they take these foundations of development into their lives and effectively take Louis Pasteur's advice: "Chance favors the prepared mind." Knowing these facts can help us find a way forward, away from the comfort of our set-tled, established world, beyond the business-as-usual fixation in our modern culture. As we relearn important skills of connection, as we become more aware of our inner mental lives and learn to live beyond automatic responses in thought and behavior, we can intentionally tap into our capacity to bring integration into the world. MWe all need to support each other's ways of finding and maintaining our ESSENCE and to empower each other in the collective journey of both our human family and the family of all living beings as an intra-connected system of Earth.

LEAVING HOME

At home and during our early years of education, we build the foundation for a shared mental construction of reality as our brains are molded by the messages we receive about the nature of the world. This "home life" may also be a metaphorical business as usual (BAU) developmental phase for our current state of cultural evolution. BAU is home base for both children and adults. Adolescence may be that window of opportunity for letting go of the familiarity of home, for us individually, and of the familiarity of BAU, for us collectively. In our first dozen or so years of life, we learn how the world is and what knowledge and skills we need to survive. Adolescence, in preparing us to leave the familiarity of home, offers us a chance to rethink what has meaning in life and to imagine how the world can be and how we think it should be.

Then we leave home. This moment in life—leaving home—presents us with a deep challenge: to try to survive based on skills learned from home life, yet on our own, away from home base, but with our peers—a world that may require much more than our homegrown learnings. For humanity, the metaphoric notion of leaving home might require a similar set of skills beyond BAU, a new way to perceive that may invite us both to unlearn our home-base learnings of BAU and to learn anew with a wider lens on reality.

If this proposal of seeing the transformation of adolescence as

Figure 8.1 Mindsight lens.

truly parallel to what is now challenging us as a species is useful, what can we do to remodel our selves to handle these contemporary challenges well and cultivate not only resilience but also a regenerative way of living? Can we harness the ESSENCE—as a developing human family—to have the emotional spark and passion, the social engagement and connection, the novelty-seeking and courage, and the creative exploration and imagination to move beyond BAU and create the world our intuition and wisdom deeply know we need?

A Mindsight Lens

To begin the journey of leaving home, we need to stabilize a lens through which we take in experience. A simple visual metaphor is that of a camera to imagine how we sense the energy flow of experience—a "mindsight lens" (Figure 8.1). Just as a camera lens focuses the energy of light from the surrounding world, the mindsight lens focuses our attention and takes in the energy flow from what we focus on inside, in our mental lives. If the lens is unstable, what we sense will be blurry—unfocused, lacking detail, unclear, and indecipherable. If we stabilize the lens, we can focus what we see and take in details with depth and breadth, the images are clear for us to perceive.

How do we stabilize the mindsight lens? Continuing the analogy of the camera, we can use a tripod (Figure 8.1), comprised of three legs:

1. Openness—being receptive to what is
2. Objectivity—sensing input as objects of the mind
3. Observation—knowing there is an agent of sensing

Openness is a state of receptivity to taking in whatever arises with minimal filtration of what emerges; letting go of expectation and prior learning as best we can. Objectivity is the capacity to perceive that what we are taking in is a product of the mind—an object—that we can then see from a bit of distance rather than becoming lost in it with fusion or confusion. Observation empowers us to have layers of attention. One layer might be on the energy flow being shared with our inter-self, the relationships we have in our connections with people and the planet; another layer would keep in direct touch with our inner-self, our internal flow of energy and information within the body. This observational capacity lets us choose where we focus our attention, lets us adjust our lens of identity, to use the contents of this awareness in integrative ways and then to select, moment by moment, adaptive and flexible behaviors in response to our rapidly changing world.

When we stabilize our mindsight lens with openness, objectivity, and observation, we can work directly with our own vulnerabilities, including a proclivity to be on autopilot with such issues as implicit racial bias and with our reactive states of fight, flight, freeze, or faint. We can also become aware of the automatic tendency to be taken over by the three subcortical networks of distress, creating anger, sadness, and fear, that drive us to correct, connect, or protect. With a stabilized mindsight lens of openness, objectivity, and observation, we can more clearly see maladaptive attachment strategies of survival that may activate when we are under stress.

In many ways, stabilizing or strengthening our mindsight lens is the fundamental skill we all need: individually, to be ready for the world when we leave the familiarity of home, and as a human family, to transform our BAU cultural habits and to collectively address the pandemics we face today.

How do we stabilize and strengthen our mindsight lens? What challenges do we face in learning these core capacities? How might we learn how our individual minds—our own sense of self, identity, and belonging—support or hinder how we work collectively to see the world clearly and to move it in a positive, integrative direction?

If we are holding on to a fixed mind-set, we may feel—individually and perhaps communally—as if these conditions we face, these challenges in modern life, reveal our failure. While we may cling to what is familiar and convenient, deep inside, beneath awareness, we may have a sense of hopelessness and despondency. A fixed mind-set can bring up the helplessness and despair of what is called a "shame state."

This feeling of shame, which many of us hold deep inside, carries with it a belief that we are fundamentally inadequate as we are, flawed in some essential way, perhaps defective in our core. Shame can be so painful that it often persists beneath our awareness, yet the mental model—the plateau of a shame state of mind in our 3-P framework—continues to filter our thoughts, emotions, narratives, and behaviors, limiting which peaks of actuality are allowed to emerge.

A state of mind is depicted in our 3-P diagram as a plateau, with its specific emotions, thoughts, memories, beliefs, attitudes, and behaviors represented as those peaks arising directly from it. In this dia-

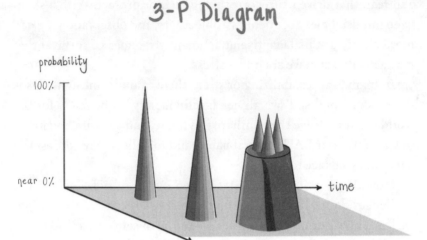

Figure 8.2 The plateau of shame.

gram, a "state of shame" can be seen as a filter that selectively engages negative mental activities—from thinking to actions—that reflect this state of mind in which the inner self is viewed as defective. Plateaus—our states of mind—can often be beneath awareness, yet their outcomes—the peaks of emotion and memory—can preoccupy the mental life of the individual.

Those of us who have a sense of shame may also have a sense of helplessness. Unlike with guilt, when we've actually performed a wrong act—a past behavior that we can correct in the future—with shame we feel and believe that we are inherently inadequate or fundamentally flawed and that there is nothing we can do about it. For those of us who experience this, an intense conviction that such beliefs are accurate makes even simple conversations like this one painful and for this reason often avoided.

Whatever fixed plateaus we've developed from our experiences and whatever ways to best adapt to life's challenges we've learned, if these states of mind are too rigid, if they do not permit access to the many other ways of being that arise from the plane of possibility, then we may feel imprisoned by the past and stuck, prevented from moving forward. Even the BAU of how we've learned to be and act in the world, including the business as usual of the solo-self of modern culture, may be an underlying plateau that constricts our ability to move ahead in our individual and in our collective lives on Earth. Finding access to the plane of possibility—the hub of our metaphoric Wheel of Awareness—offers one way of visualizing how we might approach the challenges ahead in a more effective and enduring manner. For those who practice the Wheel, as perhaps you have been exploring from the Appendix, learning how to access the hub offers a practical tool for building resilience as we, individually and collectively, work to bring more integrative growth to our world and confront the many pandemics that challenge us in these modern times.

From Grief to Growth

Leaving home invites us to reimagine who we are and who we might become. Sometimes that reflective process gives rise to a deep sense of sadness that what we thought we had—security, certainty, solidity—was just an illusion our minds created in an effort to do the best we could. In the awareness of the plane of possibility, we may come to sense the plateaus of expectation and the specific peaks of thought and emotion we planned to have in our life. Yet for us as a human family, moving forward may involve sensing what environmental philosophers Glenn Albrecht and colleagues (2007) have named the "Earth emotions"—including that of solastalgia, the feeling of longing we sense in our bones for a biodiverse planet that now is dying away: "distress that is produced by environmental change impacting people while they are directly connected to their home environment" (Albrecht et al., 2007, p.S95).

Grief is necessary for us to grow in the face of loss, and we must make time for grief. For example, activist and systems scholar Joanna Macy, in her approach called the "Work That Reconnects," first invites participants to grieve the loss of the world they thought they once had to become fully open to the world as it is. This first step of grief is necessary for growth and for us, as individuals, to be present for the world and to have openness, objectivity, and observation. And this grief enables us to work together to see the world's challenges, the many pandemics we face, and to find solutions to social injustice, misinformation and polarization, attention-addiction, environmental destruction, and even a rapidly spreading virus, which all compromise our well-being as siblings in the family of life on Earth as "planet people" (Macy and Johnstone, 2022).

To permit us to feel all that is emerging, we can envision the capacity of the hub of the Wheel of Awareness being strengthened as we build resilience by expanding our awareness. Recall that the hub of the metaphoric wheel symbolizes the knowing of consciousness, of being aware. If we have a limited size container of consciousness, then a life stressor will make our awareness overwhelmed, just as a tablespoon of salt in a cup of water is too salty to drink. If we had a much greater size container for our awareness (if instead of a thimble- or espresso-cup-size container, which many of us may have, our awareness was expanded to be one hundred gallons in size), we would have the capacity to manage that stressor, just as one hundred gallons of water with a tablespoon of salt mixed into it is drinkable—the salt is undetectable. For us to resiliently and creatively approach the challenges our world now faces, we need to become receptive to the emotional experiences that arise. We can begin to do this using practices that open our awareness, letting us feel fully the grief of what we've lost and thence become available to embrace the possibilities of what can become. This is how we "train the mind" to prepare us for the work ahead—to build stress resilience by "expecting the unexpected" (Epel, 2022).

Keeping our inner mind healthy to take on the challenges of contributing to a vibrant inter-mind is essential. Research reveals that doing "three-pillar" mind training (Figure 8.3) can build our well-being in empirically demonstrated ways. Doing such a practice on a regular basis, for a minimum of about 12 minutes a day—a daily dozen—has positive effects on our well-being, increasing integrative function and structure in the head's brain, including helpful growth of (1) the corpus callosum (linking the two cortical halves); (2) the hippocampus (linking dispersed memory systems); (3) the prefrontal cortex (linking the anatomically distinct regions of the cortex, limbic areas, brain stem, and body and interlinking these with input from other people—the social world of other embodied brains); and (4) the interconnections of the connectome (interlinking, in function and structure, distinct and anatomically separate areas of the

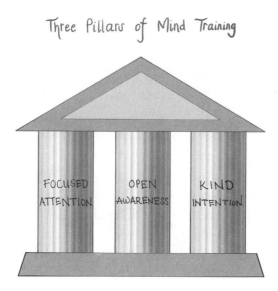

Figure 8.3 Three pillars of mind training.

brain). These are four ways we structurally and functionally develop neural integration—the linking of differentiated parts of our embodied brain. Studies by Smith and colleagues (2015) suggest that a more integrated brain, as evidenced by a more interconnected connectome, robustly predicts many measures of well-being. In addition, as summarized by Villamil and colleagues (2019), studies of practices involving the various components of three pillar mind practice result in improvements in several measures of physiological well-being, including: 1) decrease in the stress hormone cortisol; 2) enhanced immune system functioning; 3) improved cardiovascular health; 4) diminished systemic inflammation via modulations in epigenetic regulation of the inflammatory response; and 5) optimization of telomerase, the enzyme that repairs and maintains the vital ends of the chromosomes, our telomeres. Overall, these improvements (especially the last one) show that what we do with our mind's attention and awareness can slow the aging process and enhance medical well-being.

One way to get in your daily three pillars is with the Wheel of Awareness practice I describe in the TODDLERHOOD chapter (and explore in more detail in the WHEEL appendix). Perhaps you've been trying out the Wheel practice during your journey with this book. If you haven't, you can get a sense from the description that this practice includes strengthening the focus of attention, opening awareness, and building kind intention toward the inner, inter, and integrated self. While the research has generally been done on different, separate practices for each of the pillars, the Wheel of Awareness combines all three in one flowing experience. If you try this or any practice that integrates the three pillars, you may come to see this as a practical way to open your awareness to intraconnection, to feel your relational sense more fully, and to access the wisdom of systems-intelligence in your life.

Lessons from the Wheel of Awareness

The Wheel of Awareness practice has several steps. Briefly (see the WHEEL Appendix), in this reflective exercise one envisions the center of consciousness—the knowing of awareness, of being aware—as a hub of a metaphoric wheel, surrounded by a rim that represents a wide range of what we can become aware of (the knowns), which are linked to the hub by a singular wheel spoke, representing the connection between the knowing and the known. In the practice, attention is systematically focused and directed along the rim; with practice, this strengthens our awareness, our sense of connection, and our ability to focus our lens of attention across a wide range of experiences.

When I began teaching the Wheel of Awareness outside my therapy suite—with students, therapists, and workshop participants—something very powerful emerged: Existential angst began to melt away. Feelings of being whole, of feeling at ease, began to fill participants' lives. While I knew from clinical practice that the Wheel of Awareness was helpful for specific impairments to integration, which took the form of trauma or anxiety, I didn't know what to expect from a broader, nonclinical group using this integration-of-consciousness practice.

To share these observations and their implications for our discussion of self, identity, and belonging with you, let me walk you through an advanced step of the practice (see Figure 8.4): After focusing attention on each of the first three segments of the rim, we now bend the spoke around and aim it at the hub itself, at our knowing. For some, the visual image of turning the spoke was helpful, and for others it was helpful to visualize the spoke reaching out to the rim and then pulling back to the center. These images guided their experience toward becoming aware of awareness, dropping into open awareness itself.

Each morning when I do the Wheel practice, I experience a shift of various sensations—each day is different from the last, yet all involve the experience of subjective sense (felt texture of experience, the feel of energy flow), perspective (the perceptual direction,

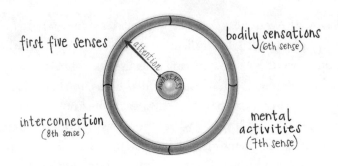

Figure 8.4 The Wheel of Awareness: The standard practice (top) shifts attention, emanating from the hub, along a range of locations to various categories of knowns, represented along the rim. An advanced step (bottom) turns the spoke back onto the hub for the experience of open awareness, of being receptively aware and of being aware of awareness.

the point of view of that flow), and agency (the intention and action arising from that flow, a source of motion—even if just in moving the spoke around the rim or back to the hub). Immersion in the hub has a sense of openness, timelessness, connectedness; a perspective from wholeness; an agency that feels not of action but of a center of possibility, of potential action without motion. In these ways, each of the three aspects of "self"-experience we've been exploring shift during the practice of the Wheel—sensation, perspective, and agency unfold in new ways each day and in emerging ways throughout the elements of the practice. Practicing the Wheel of Awareness enables a fixed, noun-like self-experience to expand and transform toward a more verb-like emergence.

As I described in the TODDLERHOOD chapter, this practice may be permitting the mind to experience the plane of possibility in pure form—not aware of something, just aware. And in this state, there are no entities, only verb-like events, unfoldings that are massively interconnected from the perspective of each event and intraconnected from the perspective of the unity of the diversity of the whole. The experience has a feeling that the Wheel practitioners' commonly reported phrase, "empty-yet-full," attempts to capture. This directly felt experience has been shared by so many people that I began to explore research findings beyond brain studies to determine if there might be a scientific view that is consistent with this subjectively felt sense of fullness; this open, connected, timeless state. The discoveries of physics and the notion of the sea of potential—the "formless source of all form" as a mathematical space known as the "quantum vacuum"—might help us understand what the energy state, the probability position, of pure awareness may be arising from, embedded in, or inherent to. Odd as it feels to write this, the findings suggest that the knowing of consciousness, the experience of being aware, may be an emergent aspect of the quantum state of maximal uncertainty— the plane of possibility in our 3-P diagram—the generator of diversity from which all manifestations emerge.

If we empower ourselves to live life from the plane of possibility and to intentionally cultivate our relational sense, we can liberate ourselves from the often-constricted vision of persistent plateaus and their limited definitions of various versions of the solo-self, singular or plural. We can let peaks arise directly from the plane, unfiltered by those innate or learned plateaus of separation that segregate and constrict our potential. We can thus liberate ourselves to participate freely and fully in the integrative flow of a compassionate and kind world, the birthright of us all.

Science, Spirituality, Subjectivity

How do we come by the experience of being mindful, of opening our awareness to a wider sense of who we are? Not long ago, my friend Jack Kornfield asked me this question when we first met, and for reasons I did not understand at the time, I brought up the horse accident I shared with you early in our journey. A few hours later he called me, and during our conversation he said something like, "Do you realize that people try for decades to achieve what you got by accident?" That made no sense to me, I told Jack. "People meditate to loosen the grip of their sense of self as separate. Meditation frees you from an illusion of separation—that is a basic teaching of Buddhist practice." I hadn't spoken much about the accident in the decades since turning twenty, but I had always wondered about the feeling of freedom I had felt—whether it might be from a brain injury or existential awakening or something else. It felt energizing, and somehow relieving, I told Jack, to share this experience with him. "Welcome to the family" he said.

Over the years I've learned, partly through my relationship and teaching with Jack Kornfield, about the contemplative tradition of Buddhism, and as I've mentioned, I've had the opportunity to teach alongside his Holiness, the Dalai Lama. The insights I've gained from these and so many other individuals from various Western, Eastern, and Indigenous traditions as well as what I've learned directly from immersion in meditative reflection have opened the door for me to find consilience—a common ground—beneath a range of religious traditions. What strikes me so deeply in the wide-ranging and fascinating conversations I've had among the broad array of religious, spiritual, Indigenous, and contemplative thinkers is how the consilience among these various ways of living and thinking, ways of being in this life, illuminate how we can discuss identity and belonging.

Yet collaborative conversations across these traditions, according to those I've had the opportunity to share these ideas with, seem to be rare. I've even encountered the notion that any narrative we have is false: Everything is everything, all is one, and to divide it in any way in a story you come to believe is true is an error—a form of "dualistic thinking" that keeps one from discovering the truth of the whole. Others—such as some within the Buddhist tradition (e.g., the Dalai Lama and Zen master Thich Nhat Hahn), where nondualism is sometimes discussed—express a view that we have what might be called a "relative," "conventional," or "close-up" perspective and we also have a broader, "ultimate" or absolute perspective. They believe each is valid, both are important: The close-up view corresponds to our narrow focus of self-experience, and the broader view, to our wide-angle focus as a part of the universal whole.

An integrative view embraces the differentiation of elements and their linkages in a synergistic whole as the way in which complex systems optimally self-organize to achieve the most adaptive, flexible, coherent, energized, and stable states—to flow in harmony. Self, identity, and belonging have an inner facet, an inter facet, and an intra facet. Each are important, each with a role in our lives. We sense these facets through adjusting our identity lens from narrow—within—and broad—between and among—opening to the integration of self and belonging as an intraconnected whole.

Is this a story of our inner self, the preoccupations perhaps of a head-brain that is driven by a compulsion to make sense, to construct a narrative we hope will coherently embrace reality? Yes, perhaps it is. Yet this is our legacy, as human beings, as a narrative species: We are born into a body, an animal body, a somatic reality with a long, long ancestral history. Denying that reality, as Melanie Challenger (2021) suggests, is a denial of our "being animal" that has dire consequences for us individually and collectively. The head-brain's susceptibility to construct an identity as separate when reinforced by linear thinking and cultural messages of individuality can make us prone to limiting our belonging, to disconnecting from other members of our human family, to believing we are separate from not only other species of animals, but from all of nature. Believing we are separate is a limiting story—a narrative we on this journey are naming as a violation of epistemic trust—a story that, if taken as the whole truth, can explain the suffering we are living in, the suffering we are creating from the false narrative of self-as-separate.

As a story-telling species, then, we can reflect on where we are and even come to recognize—to re-think—how our own modern narrative of self, identity, and belonging have led us astray from living a life of health. We can intentionally course-correct; it is not too late. Awakening to our mistaken identity as a solo-self, we can now construct anew what the term "self" really indicates: inner, inter and intra facets of sensation, perspective, and agency. We can cocreate this awakened story as we move ourselves, with intention, openness, care, and collaboration, into a future that is not something we passively report about but that we can live into and create with purpose and meaning.

Stories do not have to limit us or deceive us; it is through the co-construction of narratives that we create culture. And culture can evolve. Narrative itself is neither good nor bad—stories are the way we remember and construct our lives; it is the nature of those stories, not the narrative process, that will determine our present and our futures. What will be the new story of our human family emerging in these challenging times? What integrative narrative of our lives as a family of nature—beyond members of our personal family and even of our human family, as an intraconnected family of all life on Earth—can we feel and live into?

Sometimes our narrative propensities, imbued as they often are with a drive for the safety of certainty and predictability, can get in the way of co-constructing a coherent story of our identity and who we are capable of collectively and individually becoming. When we investigate the stories about mindfulness from neuroscience, we glean clues as to what might be challenging us, as a species, to take on the necessary developmental changes to face our contemporary conditions. The positive impact of mindfulness meditation—learning to focus attention, to open awareness, and (part of this definition, for some) to cultivate kind intention—can be correlated with quieting an overactive DMN, that default mode network we discussed earlier as a mostly midline set of cortical regions in the brain. Since an overactive, highly differentiated DMN is associated with anxiety, depression, and preoccupation with the solo-self, when we free our self from that prison, we come to feel connected within and connected between. An integrative, well-balanced DMN plays a critical role in our well-being, contributing to our insight and our empathy as a gateway for compassion. When the DMN's pathways are excessively differentiated and not linked well with the overall networks of the brain, this contributes to the chaos and rigidity of nonintegrative living, a source of disconnection and suffering in our lives.

Mindfulness training that includes focusing attention as well as opening awareness and cultivating kindness—what we've named "three pillar mind training"—can help reduce our stress levels and has been shown to increase compassion. These findings suggest that training the mind in more integrative ways than only focusing attention for a brief period of practice helps us embrace the wider sense of self we need to support prosocial shifts in behavior. Some preliminary studies in need of further elaboration suggest that our self-construal may directly impact how these trainings influence our development of prosocial behavior. If we have an individualistic stance compared to an interdependent self-construal, as Michael Poulin and colleagues (2021) suggest, we may not be as likely to reach out to help others even if our attention is briefly trained to be more focused. If further research verifies this observation, then aiming to construct a wider self-construal, combined with mind strengthening practices, may be helpful as we strive to cultivate a more collaborative and compassionate world.

In the seemingly distinct field that studies how we respond to exposure to nature, researcher Dacher Keltner and colleagues (2003, 2016) have found that feeling awe leads to an increased sense of belonging and connection—and to prosocial behaviors. In my discussions with Keltner, we explored how the historical term "self-transcendent emotions" for the grouping of awe along with gratitude and compassion might be more appropriately named "self-expanding" emotions. Collective findings in the study of awe and the impact of self-construal on prosocial behavior suggest that a key may be not to lose, to go beyond, or "transcend" the self, but to expand the self— dissolve the domination of the solo-self and integrate our identity by opening to the many layers of self-experience, close-up and wide-angle, as we broaden our belonging and move from being a noun only to living life also as a verb.

Sometimes we want to figure out what we should be doing to help. This makes sense in our body-oriented world—let's take action in this world of things. Yet we can begin not with the doing but with being. Accessing a sense of integrative identity, a MWe that emerges beneath plateaus of separation from the deeper plane of possibility, we tap into a way of being beneath and before even compassionate activities. What is this state of being that may help us explore more integrative ways of acting, of doing in the world—of "being mindful doing"? In current research language on self-construal, a separate individual constructs an independent self while an interdependent self-construal involves both relational or group identity as interpersonal or collectivistic. As Hazel Markus and Shinobu Kitayma (1991) initially proposed:

> People in different cultures have strikingly different construals of the self, of others, and of the interdependence of the 2 [sic]. These construals can influence, and in many cases determine,

the very nature of individual experience, including cognition, emotion, and motivation. Many Asian cultures have distinct conceptions of individuality that insist on the fundamental relatedness of individuals to each other. The emphasis is on attending to others, fitting in, and harmonious interdependence with them. American culture neither assumes nor values such an overt connectedness among individuals. In contrast, individuals seek to maintain their independence from others by attending to the self and by discovering and expressing their unique inner attributes. (p. 224)

In developing the research assessment of self-construal, Theodore Singelis (1994) elaborated these ideas, stating:

Following concepts introduced by Markus and Kitayama, this study describes the theoretical and empirical development of a scale to measure the strength of an individual's interdependent and independent self-construals. These two images of self are conceptualized as reflecting the emphasis on connectedness and relations often found in non-Western cultures (interdependent) and the separateness and uniqueness of the individual (independent) stressed in the West. It is argued that these two images of self can and do coexist in individuals and that they can be measured. (p. 580)

As we've discussed, the notion of a metapersonal self-construal has also been proposed by Teresa DeCicco and Mirella Stroink (2007), one that views self as belonging to all of humanity and to the universe. Experiences we have—at home, in school, in our larger culture— shape which forms of self-construal are active in our lives. Researchers might discover, as Singelis suggested, that a given individual can hold aspects of each of these self-construals. Future studies may show how we can differentiate and link—how we can integrate—an individualistic self-construal with both a relational and collective interdependent one and, even further, how we might weave into our lives a sense of self, identity, and belonging to the whole of nature, not just to other human beings—a metapersonal self-construal. What would it feel like to hold all three forms of self-construal in our lives as individuals? Maintaining a differentiated inner "me" while also cultivating a relational "we," in its widest expanse from interdependent to metapersonal, would combine the differentiated and the linked aspects of self-construction—of adjusting our lens from narrow to wide, embracing our various circles of belonging. Yes, who we are is the totality of our belongings in our connections, our we—and who we are is our inner bodily experience, our me. Perhaps we might call such an integrated way of living into our range of centers of experience an "intraconnected self-construal."

From a developmental perspective, adolescence is a time when we leave home and, ideally, cultivate the skills to move beyond our personal and cultural business as usual—which in modern times is a life of an individualistic, solo-self—to wise, integrative action in the world that we can call "being mindful doing." In dropping into the plane of possibility, that space of being that is our origin in the journey of life, we reconnect with a way of living that enables us to do from an open, spacious place of connection—one in which the linguistic terms denoting self or other, me or you, inner and outer, begin to lose the solidity of their implied entity-like meanings. When we come to life directly from the plane of possibility, filled with connection, open awareness, and love, we are doing actions from the integrative space of being, of being whole.

TRAVELS

Once we leave home, we find ourselves invited to travel out into the world, focusing on doing to survive and attempting to thrive. How well our skills help us move beyond our personal and cultural business as usual and foster wise, integrative action in the world determines in large part the nature and extent of our travels ahead.

Selfing as Noun and as Verb

The travels we are invited to take in life can expand our boundaries, guide us back to that beginner's mind, encourage us to let go of what we conceptually know and then perceive more clearly all that is around us and within us. Yet throughout our development we have collected information filters that serve as cognitive boundaries—categories, concepts, and symbols—illusions of certainty that we must overcome to attain a broader systems perspective beyond the linear view that modern life so often emphasizes.

Even our given names can convey unnecessary boundaries of certainty, of in and out, of separation rather than wholeness and connection. What general word would you use for who you are, besides such terms as your name or "I" and "me"? When the COVID-19 pandemic first began and many of us found ourselves in virtual gatherings, I first typed my name, the one that appears at the bottom of our rectangular video images on the screen, in online meetings as "Dan Siegel"; then after a few months I changed it to all lower case letters, "dan siegel," to de-emphasize some solidity of that noun; then I simplified it to "dan." But even that one linguistic term seemed too noun-like, too specific, too concrete. As the viral pandemic went on and the virtual meetings continued to be a major way we tried to stay connected, I then tried an abbreviation that felt to me a little bit closer to what you and I have been exploring—beneath my image on the screen now appeared "abcd"— an acronym for the simplest phrase to express what that image was por- traying: a body called dan. Who I am is more than this body; yet on the screen, what is visible is this body—real, but as we have explored, not the whole deal. As Zen master Thich Nhat Hanh's powerful poem, "Contemplation on No-Coming, No-Going", states (2007, p. 262), "I am life without boundaries." What ways might you choose to describe the center of your identity other than the simple word "self"? How do you construe the self of you? In English, adding "-ing" to the end of "self"—"selfing"—changes the noun notion of self into a verb-like word: I am selfing. Can you feel a selfing with the somatic source of sensation, perspective, and agency as your individual, independent self-construal? Can you broaden that SPA of self to extend beyond the body to include the inter of your relationships with other people—your interdependent self-construal with people you know in relationships and people with whom you share common ground as in your collective identity? And even further, can you widen your identity lens, beyond these human relationships, to embrace the belonging within the whole of nature—and the entire universe—as your metapersonal self-con- strual? What does that mean to the you that is you-ing? How do you experience and express the who of you from inner to inter to intra?

One day I found myself wandering along the beach and reflecting on the physics of energy. When we see a wave that is far out at sea, then one hundred yards away, then fifty, twenty, ten yards offshore, then crashing at our feet, what did we just see? Water molecules moving toward us? No. It seems that way, yes. Yet although the waves appear to be separate things moving toward us, that surface appearance is an illusion: The water itself is not traveling toward us. What arrives at our feet is energy from far away, traveling as a wave through time and the space of water, not specific molecules in the process of traveling from there to here.

In a similar way, we are energy—oscillating waves of energy inside these bodies in which we are born, and within the whole of life in which we will always exist. Gabrielle Roth (1998), the creator of the Five Rhythms dance technique, suggests that we are energy in motion, composed of patterns, waves, and rhythms. This ability to sense that who we are is energy enables us to move away from a fixed, noun-like entity view, an ability also recognized by the anthropologist Gregory Bateson. He realized that life arose in patterned flows, offering the notion of a metapattern this way:

> The pattern which connects. . . . It is a pattern of patterns . . . think of it as primarily a dance of interacting parts only secondarily pegged down by various sorts of physical limits . . . a world of something not being separate from something else." (Bateson, 1972, p. 425)

Energy is ever unfolding, ever flowing from possibility into probability into actuality and back into possibility. All things must pass—we do not need to lock on to a fear of uncertainty. When we let go of the drive to control, we open to the freedom of that expansive formless source of all form, that plane of possibility. Yes, we live in a Newtonian body with all the noun-like experiences of being a somatic entity, one with separation across time and space. And yes, we also live with a mind that emerges from energy flow; and energy, empirical studies have affirmed, can move in the quantum realm in which there are no nouns, only verb-like unfoldings without separation, without even the Newtonian dimensions of time and space. One of the most striking things about the 3-P diagram is its visual representation that maximal uncertainty, the plane of possibility, is actually freedom and potentiality. As physicists suggest, a "formless source of all form" is the sea of potential from which actualities emerge from a wide-open space of possibility. We can access that verb-like "dance of interacting parts" that has the freedom of the intraconnected whole.

Fitting with Indigenous and contemplative wisdom and consilient across science and spirituality, these perspectives of self emerging as energy flow in our inner and relational worlds free us to live both as noun and as verb, in both the macro- and microstate realms of our one reality. We can walk upright on land and dive deeply into the waves of the watery ocean world. We can ride the infinitely unfolding metapatterns and dance the rhythms that connect us across time and space.

Who we are is a noun-like and a verb-like self with patterns emerging through a center of body-based energy flow that is grounded, in part, in the realm of space and time in its entity-based realm. And who we are is also apparent in a more verb-like mode, the selfing of an inner bodily "me" as well as the dynamic, ever-changing "we" in the hugely connected emergence that includes as well as transcends the classical physics distinctions of space and time, riding the meta-patterns that connect us all. In an integrative life, we do not need to choose—we dance in both of the seeming poles of the wide range of experience: noun and verb, the macro of the classical and the micro of the quantum realms, inner and inter, me and we.

MWe can remind us of this consilient truth. MWe can learn to widen our lens of identity, to broaden our belonging and come to embrace the wholeness of who, together, MWe can be and who, deep within, beneath those constructed concepts and categories of separation, MWe already are.

Diversity and Possibility

The documentary film *The Biggest Little Farm* chronicles a couple's journey, with guidance of a mentor, to transform arid farmland into a thriving ecological community over several years. The couple moves to a piece of land where monoculture (growing just one type of crop at a time) and tillage (ripping up the ground in destructive ways) contributed to what often results from modern mega-farms throughout the world: loss of biodiversity and depletion of the soil.

The secret to the couple's success in transforming the land into a highly productive farm is revealed as the biodiversity of the ecosystem serves as the source of wide open potential. The now diverse farm, unlike the neighboring monocrop farms, had the resilience to maintain its ground coverings and its variety of flora and fauna and to soak into its aquafer millions of gallons of precious water during a massive storm. The other lands nearby, without biodiversity, saw their topsoil washed away to the sea.

The mathematics of complex systems gives us insight into how and why diversity is the gateway to possibility. Within the discipline of math is the field of probability studies, and within probability studies is the subfield of collections of components called "systems." One type of system we've been exploring is that of a complex system, which has the features of being open to influences from outside itself, of being capable of being chaotic, and of being nonlinear—the latter meaning that a small input can lead to a relatively large and difficult-to-predict outcome. The study of complex systems is sometimes called complexity theory, or nonlinear dynamics. Dynamical systems have a diversity of components, connections among these system elements, and influences on one another that are interdependent—meaning the direction of influence is not only one-way. This linkage of diverse and interdependent parts enables the system to be adaptive and to learn—to self-organize. We might say that each of us, being open, chaos-capable, and nonlinear, is part of a complex system.

A general principle of complex systems, simply put, is that the more things that are going on in the system, the more possibilities there are for things to happen; with less diversity, less potential and fewer choice points. Yet there is also a flow between completely unpredictable and changing unfoldings, or what can be called "chaos," and completely rigid unfoldings, or what can be called "order" or "rigidity."

If the many components of a system act independently of one another, the system moves to a very chaotic state—imagine a dozen choir members each singing a different song at the same time. But at the other extreme, if those dozen singers sang the same note in the same way at the same time, the result would be total predictability, rigidity, and uniformity. Now imagine those same singers choosing a song together. The linking of their distinct voices in harmony can produce a goose-bump-raising magnificence of a song, filled with vitality, with joy—harmony is the natural outcome of optimal self-organization that emerges with the linkage of differentiated parts of a complex system.

On the biodiverse farm, the farmers had to figure out, day to day, how to enable their emerging biodiversity and balance. Though complex systems do not need a conductor, sometimes their self-organizational flow needs nurturing to support the differentiation and linkage needed to release the natural harmony that arises with optimal self-organization. From finding ways for dogs to protect chickens from coyotes while enabling coyotes to keep the gopher population low so it does not destroy the peach trees, to keeping the potentially excessive snail population in check by the ducks who could safely be transported out of their protected pond zone to the orchards—each step of the way, this documentary demonstrates how biodiversity gives rise to the ultimate sense of harmony, which we can feel as we watch the farm grow.

Biodiversity reveals an integrative ecosystem, a generative living world. We've named this balance of diverse yet connected components, "integration," the mechanism beneath harmony. Integration is the mechanism of health, of being whole, of being resilient, of thriving.

Figure 9.1 illustrates how integration—a flow on the "edge of

Figure 9.1 Integration is the flow between rigidity and chaos.

chaos" as it moves between rigid predictability and chaotic unpredictability—emerges between order and randomness, blending the
familiar and the unfamiliar in an ever-evolving flow of differentiation
and linkage. Integration reminds us that diversity is not something
we merely come to tolerate—we thrive with diversity. When we nurture both diversity and linkage, we can reach our infinite potential in
the ever-changing emergence of a dynamic, harmonious life.

Zen master Thich Nhat Hanh (2017) proposes the term "interbeing" to capture this sense of our interdependence:

> The view of "being" is one extreme view, and the view of non-
> being is another extreme view. We need to transcend both these
> notions. The term "interbeing" can help. By adding the prefix
> "inter" to the word "being" we have a term that is no longer the
> opposite of non-being. Interbeing has no opposite, so we can

make use of it to avoid falling into the trap of dualistic thinking. (p. 58)

In contemplative experience, this effort to find the linkages across seeming polarities may be akin to the experience of integration. Thich Nhat Hanh (2017) notes that

> interbeing means you cannot be by yourself alone; you can only inter-be. Interbeing can connect the conventional truth to the ultimate truth, the true nature of reality. On this level, there is no beginning and there is no end. There is no birth and there is no death. And the notions of being and nonbeing are removed. . . . You are empty of a separate self, but you are full of the cosmos. So "emptiness" is an expression that we could say is equivalent to "God." God is the ultimate, and emptiness is the ultimate. (p. 58)

He elaborates further (p. 56): "At the level of conventional truth, there is discrimination and separation. Things are outside of each other. One thing is not another," yet in "the realm of the ultimate, where everything is in everything else—everything interpenetrates, so the notions of inside and outside do not apply."

From a consilience view, conventional truth can be seen as our Newtonian, classical physics, macrostate realm, and ultimate truth as our quantum, microstate realm. Thich Nhat Hanh (2017) proposes that

> not only the human body, but all phenomena are empty of a permanent, separate self. . . . The insight of interbeing is that nothing can exist by itself alone, that each thing exists only in relation to everything else. The insight of impermanence is that nothing is static, nothing stays the same. Interbeing means emptiness of a separate self, however impermanence also means emptiness of a separate self. Looking from the perspective of space we call emp-

tiness "interbeing"; looking from the perspective of time we call it "impermanence." (p. 45)

Might the emptiness here be the formless source of all form—empty of form, yet full of possibility? And might this notion of God be the generator of diversity, the plane of possibility, the portal through which integration arises, this vital source of love, awareness, and connection?

Who we are is both potential and actual, both the plane of possibility and the positions above that plane, as plateaus of increased probability and peaks of actualization. Who we are is the flow of energy, ever emerging verb-like events in the timeless microstate realm in which physical separation does not impede our relational connections; and we are also the macrostate realm with the experience and appearance of spatiotemporal boundaries that distinguish one from the other as noun-like entities. We are both noun and verb, time-bound and timeless.

We see the consilience between the contemplative teachings and our journey into the physics realms of the macro and the micro, weaving these with our exploration of self, identity, and belonging and the glorious exuberance, the joyful way of living, the freedom, as Thich Nhat Hanh states, that arises with this realization that "everything is empty of a separate self" (Hanh, 2017, p. 45). We can live this reality in our daily lives with one another as a human family, and we can live with this in our family of all living beings: "When we are able to see that the nature of all things is our own true nature, we become free." (Hanh, 2017, p. 101)

Letting Go of Certainty

If love and connection are truly the "natural threads" of the tapestry of life, why don't they naturally just emerge in our individual and collective lives? If integration is the innate drive of a complex system to optimize its self-organization toward harmony and the FACES—flexible, adaptive, coherent, energized, and stable—features of that flow, what gets in the way of this natural emergent process of self-organization?

In our journey together, we have seen that the vulnerabilities of the human mind, the inner mind within and the inter mind between, can—often without conscious choice or awareness—make us prone to inhibit differentiation and linkage. When integration is blocked, IMIDU—inflexible, maladaptive, incoherent, de-energized, and unstable (the opposite of FACES)—unfolds with chaos and rigidity, shaping our lives internally and relationally.

We have explored how, throughout the lifespan, from our childhood to our adult life, so much of our home life, our school life, and our adult life push us to be certain. It is a rare teacher who invites us to embrace nonknowing as a way to respond on a test. Once we construct this understandably predictive stance, we internally and relationally tend to reinforce that drive to know, the drive toward certainty.

This drive for certainty may be at the root of "nounifying" our selves so that we have the appearance of predictability when we construct a view of our self as an entity. This survival drive, especially in the face of scarcity, may create a need to be special, to be unique, to be separate and better than others. And this same push to be certain and survive may be at the root of our species' excessive differentiation from the rest of the natural world in viewing our species—and our selves—as exceptional; as different from the rest. As history researcher and writer Melanie Challenger (2021) suggests:

> On the one hand it's obvious to most of us that we are animals. When asked, people are convinced this must be true. Yet we're still told society must be approached as if we're not. For millen-

nia we've viewed ourselves as separate from all other creatures. The thought that we belong to the same physical world as the rest of life on Earth is one that successive generations of people have found impossible to accept. (p. 201)

We live with a paradox of having an animal body with an animal history of evolution and ancestors, sharing much of our DNA with our animal siblings, and we have a mind capable of reflecting on its own life, creating a map bridging past, present, and future. This mental time travel capacity not only helps us plan and create civilization, but it also enables us, and burdens us, with the awareness of our mortality. Challenger (2021) addresses the central relevance of this existential dilemma this way:

> As we became self-conscious, our personal view floodlit what can be a danger to our bodies and laid bare the inescapable danger of death. We've become the conundrum of an animal that doesn't want an animal's body. What was survival has re-emerged, by a long, curious path, as psychological imperative . . . . If we don't belong to the rest of nature, its dangers can't reach us" (p. 203). But rather than reassure us, this strategy has left us reliant on a falsehood. The myth of human exceptionalism is as unsettling as it is irrational . . . . And so our lives are spent quietly haunted by the truth of a connection to nature we can barely admit. (p. 204)

In short, we have excessively differentiated our sense of self as an identity and belonging apart from nature as an example of a modern culture's violation of epistemic trust. In truth, we are not only a part of nature, interconnected with all living beings, we are nature, intraconnected as a whole of the system of life on Earth. This fear of linking in the face of an existential push for differentiation, for "exceptionalism"—of being apart from others, as Challenger notes—is driving humanity and the natural world toward the non-integrative states of chaos and rigidity. In reflecting on our current state of affairs, Challenger (2021) postulates:

Our intelligence made a discovery that doesn't belong only to us . . . . We discovered that life, for all its hurt and predation, bears in its onward journey the kernel of generosity. We can even think into what the wants, if we wish to call them this, of an ecosystem might be. When our minds generated insights, love escaped the bounds of self, of kin, of neighbour, and spread outwards . . . . It's possible that when we see the world as alive with intelligence, it doesn't seem such a threatening place." (p. 217)

Systems intelligence suggests that the natural emergence of diversity and linkage—of integration—enables optimal self-organization to emerge. Such a letting go of control requires letting go of certainty as we venture into uncertainty, and this may be what gets in the way of harmony in our modern human lives. The drive for certainty acts as a veil, preventing us from seeing fully, freely, and clearly. This perspective of integration as a possible direction forward helps us see how we may need to go through this curtain of certainty, intentionally opening to uncertainty, to let the light of reality shine in our lives and illuminate a clear path toward liberating integration.

Another difference to consider as we move through our adult travels is the distinction between making something happen and letting something arise. By dropping into the maximal uncertainty of the plane of possibility—a source of "being at peace"—by letting the mind move into this space of being, of being present, of not forcing one thing or another to happen, we join in the natural flow of integration as it unfolds, moment by moment. We are free of the planning and focus on the future, which was driven by our need for certainty, and instead we can experience the free flow of energy as it emerges.

We may find that we need to go through a grieving process, to let go of the drive for certainty and mourn the loss of the noun-like identity of our modern times—our solo-self. The potential released from such a grieving process is the liberation of possibility—of connec-tion, open awareness, love—that no longer needs certainty, that can fully embrace the freedom of being.

As literary and cultural writer Maria Popova states, "This is how the world changes: We loosen the stranglehold of our givens, bend and stretch our minds to imagine what was once unimaginable, test our theories against reality, and emerge with vision expanded into new dimensions of truth" (Popova, 2017, para. 1). Letting go of fixed definitions of the self may be "falling to pieces," yet the peace arising from this space of being lets a new experience of selfing unfold.

Transcending the Solo-Self with Awe

Could awe be a state of dropping beneath fixed plateaus and their limited peaks as we access the plane of possibility? Such an opening of our conscious experience from this generator of diversity and the free emergence of peaks that might arise unfiltered by prior learn-ing would be our 3-P framework way of visualizing what awe might involve. How is the experience of self changed with awe? Our top-down plateaus of learned experience would be loosened or dis-banded, giving us a subjective felt sense of wide-open possibility and vastness beyond what we already have learned. Our perspective would expand to embrace a sense of the connectedness that may have been hidden from view. Awe might also include a feeling that at first resembled overwhelm and paralysis, but would then open to a sense of empowerment to act—to have agency—on behalf of a belonging that extends beyond the private self. In these ways, awe transforms our experience of the SPA of self from narrow to wide, from alone to all-one. As Keltner (2016) describes:

> we have found that awe—more so than emotions like pride or amusement—leads people to cooperate, share resources, and sacrifice for others, all of which are requirements for our collec-tive life. And still other studies have explained the awe–altruism

link: being in the presence of vast things calls forth a more mod-est, less narcissistic self, which enables greater kindness toward others. (para. 10)

Keltner explores the ways in which our modern cultural pat-terns of isolation and individualism have created great suffering in our lives. Given these ways in which we have constructed our disconnected living in contemporary times, he offers these wise suggestions:

> In the face of these big cultural trends, our own individual actions may seem meaningless. Yet the research on awe suggests that modest steps can have a major impact on our well-being. So don't underestimate the power of goosebumps—actively seek out the experiences that nurture your own hunger for awe, be it through appreciating the trees in your neighborhood, a complex piece of music, patterns of wind on water, the person who presses on against all odds, or the everyday nobility of others. Take the time to pause and open your mind to those things which you do not fully understand. You will be the better for it—and, as your feelings of awe ripple out through acts of kindness, so will the rest of us. (Keltner, 2016, paras. 17, 18)

These findings of health and an expansion of selfing may be at the heart of what inspired Keltner to suggest we take "awe-walks" and enhance our experience of this healing—making whole—emotional state. The Wheel of Awareness practice (see WHEEL Appendix) offers one reflective exercise to access what I am suggesting may be the underlying mechanism of awe: the plane of possibility. When Keltner and I taught together in a workshop, he gave questions from a mystical experiences scale to the participants following the Wheel of Awareness practice and found high degrees of the sensation of awe. But walking through daily life outside of such awe-inducing mental practices can also involve many moments of opportunities to experi-ence awe. As sociologist Emma Stone (2017) suggests:

Many of us traditionally associate awe with rare transcendental or extraordinary events, such as religious ecstasy or near-death experiences, but awe also occurs in everyday contexts . . . . Opportunities to experience awe are ever-present in the quotidian, but we must be open to and mindful of these more subtle moments that can easily evade us. Keltner suggests live music, art galleries, theater, museums, spending time outdoors and allowing unstructured time for exploration to invite more awe into our everyday lives. The potential awe holds in our lives for providing meaning and transforming our experience of the world was perhaps most eloquently expressed by Albert Einstein, who was once quoted as saying, "The most beautiful thing we can experience is the mysterious. It is the source of all true art and science. He to whom this emotion is a stranger, who can no longer stand rapt in awe, is as good as dead: his eyes are closed." (paras. 4, 5)

If we take this perspective from the science of awe and consider the notion of "transcendent" experiences as transcending the limited lens of the solo-self, might we then call these "self-expanding" instead of "self-transcending"? When I asked Keltner this question at that workshop, I found his enthusiastic, positive response "awe-some."

Awe evokes a sense of something that is initially difficult to comprehend and a sense of being a part of something larger than our individual self—we transcend what we usually know to become, perhaps, initially overwhelmed and uncertain. In our 3-P framework, we would say that instead of living from the plateaus of prior learning, we open to the new possibilities arising from the plane. As our subjective experience, perspective, and agency shift, the experience of selfing expands—as does our identity and our belonging in the world.

With states of awe, when accessing the plane, we can open this experience of selfing to include a relational belonging to something broader than our body, our family, or our immediate circle of friends. We now "transcend" these more confined boundaries of belonging and expand the self to include a wider, expanded state of being connected to our whole human family, all of nature, all of the universe.

Inner and relational become woven as one. We move from being connected within small confines to interconnected across time and space, expanding with universal compassion and an extended identity and broader belonging. Even if only a glimpse within a brief window of experience, we come to sense the wholeness of intraconnection.

Longing for Certainty in an Uncertain World

The mindset to control leads to disconnection, not joining. In the drive of survival reactions in the setting of scarcity and threat, separation from those we deem "not like-us" is the instinctual push away from a wider connection, a broader belonging. This is the challenge confronting us in our modern world. Often, we try to control in an attempt to predict in the face of a confusing world, the chaotic, messy reality of life. In many ways, this prediction compulsion makes us vulnerable to using mind-numbing substances or behaviors to distract ourselves from the loneliness or fear that accompany the disconnection we dread. What's more, sadly, this addictive prediction and control cycle itself reinforces and deepens disconnection.

Adding to these vulnerabilities are our mental constructions, which drive us to keep our vision of things as we think they should be, a push to maintain our constructed reality despite any input to the contrary. Even with cognitive dissonance, the psychological resistance we may feel, we may continue to attempt to avoid conflict, to keep our longed-for sense of control at least somewhat tempered, even if we are not fully satisfied. This describes a profound and potentially lethal mental state of denial. An addiction is a maladaptive yet rewarding behavior that is compulsively repeated despite its detrimental consequences. Whether the addiction is to alcohol or to business as usual, this ultimate construction of denial—to not see, to not think about these sometimes devastating consequences, to not receive the information—is a persistent and pervasive mental move that keeps us going back for more despite its disastrous consequences.

From a 3-P perspective, the addiction is a constructed, tenacious, and restrictive plateau that allows only a very limited set of peaks that fit its prescribed boundaries to arise. Energy flow from actual experience in the world can be filtered out, blocking our awareness—what is going on in the world is literally blocked from our internal experience of awareness. Is our being lost, as individuals and as a contemporary society, in the modern narrative of a solo-self such an addiction?

As we look back at modern human culture over the last century—from the first reports of the impact of carbon emissions on our natural world to the civil rights movement in the 1960s and the efforts to shed light on social injustice that has existed for centuries to the increased realization of the potential for viral pandemics to the increase in polarization and misinformation to the more recent invention of attention-addictive digital devices and platforms—we might come to see a similar parallel of denial within the 3-P diagram for our contemporary human family.

We live in VUCA times—that is, volatile, uncertain, complex, and ambiguous. These conditions drive us to try, as best we can, to feel at ease as our prediction-seeking brains struggle to make sense, to anticipate, and to control what is going on in the world. And so we naturally pull back, we shrink our self, limit our identity with a close-up, narrowed lens, focusing tightly on the body as the sole source of our identity and now restricted belonging. We restrict our connections to other people, restrict our connections to other species. Under states of threat, too, we more intensely discern who is a member of the in-group, who is in the out-group—caring for the former, dehumanizing the latter. Brain studies reveal, for example, that the networks of empathy and compassion are activated for those we deem members of our group, and those same networks are turned off for those who we perceive as "not belonging to us."

These are unfortunate, though understandable, evolutionary adaptations to a VUCA world of modern humanity; yet with our solo-self defensive stance, we are actually intensifying the very qualities we are reacting to. Much of this process of denial is a mental construction—the human mind, perhaps in large part, has created this degenerative mess. That's the sad "bad news." But the good news is that if our minds created it, then together the human mind of MWe can help us develop beyond this troubled phase, to be the source of generative solutions. It really is possible to stop our path of a flawed system, to stop business as usual, and reimagine and then recreate the world as it could be. As Aldous Huxley once suggested, the habit we humans have of not taking the time to reflect on what went wrong to learn from the mistakes we've made in the past is one of the biggest mistakes we continue to make. Might we instead awaken from this addiction and change this habit? Could we learn from business as usual and its addictions of the solo-self, to learn from this mis-taken identity, of mis-taking the body as the sole source of identity, to now culturally evolve to see our way to a more integrative approach of living that we can choose to cultivate?

The travels we are on now can take us far from home, far from the development and reinforcement of these now all-too-familiar mental constructions, and instead toward a possible pathway forward, beyond this longing for certainty and the fear of losing control to liberating our innate capacity for courage, creativity, connection, and collaboration.

Let Go and Let G.O.D.: Generator of Diversity

The bridge between the spiritual—a life of meaning beyond survival and connection beyond the body—and activism, meaning action on behalf of the greater good, no longer needs to be an exhaustive shuttle back and forth between two seemingly separate lives of meaning. When we sense and perceive the whole as the relational web of life within which MWe are intraconnected, a synergetic self-experience where MWe belong, integration of the inner and the relational leads to actions that support and reinforce the optimal self-organization of the whole.

In theistic belief systems of religion, God is evoked in the narrative of creation; in other belief systems, a "life force" may be seen as a source of all that is, the wisdom of nature, rhythm of the universe greater than human comprehension—each may be held as the origin story of how we've come to be. The 3-P framework of the plane of possibility, based in quantum potential, offers a conceptual map of a generator of diversity, a g.o.d., the formless source of all form—filled with possibility before that potential energy is transformed into actuality.

As we come to sense this source of diversity as the plane of possibility, we can choose to develop the skill of accessing that which is already in each of us. Using meditative practices such as the Wheel of Awareness, built on a foundation of the interdependence of differentiation and linkage at the heart of integration, we can learn to access the plane of possibility, learn to access the love, the open awareness, and the connection that may be the interwoven threads of the tapestry of life revealed in this space of being.

A colleague of mine who struggled with a drive for certainty and control, manifesting in her life as alcoholism, found a way forward by accepting the Alcoholics Anonymous program's "Let go and let God" principle—despite the fact that her personal interpretation of God differed from the mainstream—by reinterpreting it for herself as "Let go and let the g.o.d."—the generator of diversity, the formless source from which all form arises; that is, the plane of possibility. This helped remind her that she could now access this space of being, and simply let life happen rather than trying to control her particular peaks with rigid, certainty-seeking plateaus.

So far, presenting the plane of possibility of the 3-P perspective as the generator of diversity, the g.o.d., has not been experienced as offensive or dismissive to any religious leaders I've had the privilege of dialoguing with, and instead has led to fruitful conversations and intriguing explorations of potential bridges between belief and science. The consilience with both theistic and non-theistic religious and spiritual traditions, as well as contemplative and Indigenous teachings, has been both fascinating and rewarding to witness over these decades of collaborative discussions. In your own narrative of life, how does the plane of possibility and the overall framework we are exploring feel to you? How do these perspectives find a fit or a mismatch with how you've come to live into your development to this moment in your life?

The wide-ranging consilience embedded in the 3-P framework is that consciousness may arise from a plane of possibility and that attention connects various states of probability as plateaus and peaks. From a mind perspective linked to physics, we can say that attention directs energy flow. This implies that the very act of intentionally shifting our focus of attention, linked with awareness as the bridge, brings us closer to the plane of possibility, freeing us to access a wider range of probabilities. In this way, the mental processes of attention and intention and the experience of awareness, from a 3-P perspective, are all about shifting energy flow, shifting our positions along a range of probabilities. From this framework, it seems clear that the human mind, along with the experience of being aware, shapes how mental processes arise—including our experience of self.

The mental capacity to shape perception, thought, and action would entail shifting how energy is moving along its probability dimensions, from open awareness in the plane, to states of mind and mood in plateaus, up to the actualization of thought, emotion, and memory, for example, as peaks. Mental life would then involve the flow of energy and the ability to monitor it and to modify it—to alter its probability state along these positions from plane to peak. The proposal of this 3-P framework of the mind is quite distinct from what seems to be a controversial interpretation of the physics research by some that the mind creates energy itself—that consciousness, for example, might construct a bougainvillea or the existence of an ocean: that is, the interpretation that the human mind creates reality itself. In contrast, our proposal is that mind shapes the experience of energy flow, in microstates or as matter; condensed energy. It doesn't create energy itself. As an implication of these alternative views, with seven billion human beings creating reality, how would we be able to walk down a street or swim in the sea with another person if each individual was constructing reality? While there is a tremendously exciting area of relevant research into the role of observation and consciousness on the energy states of electrons and photons, for example, it is a hotly debated and fascinating issue that should be acknowledged here, with respect. A conservative approach offered to the topic of energy and consciousness, to retain the consilience of this framework in its consistency with accepted physics and across the wide array of disciplines that seem to correlate with the implications of this approach to energy and the mind, is discussed in detail, for those who might want to explore more, in *The Developing Mind*.

It is important, as we go forward through our adult travels now, to ask how—individually and collectively—our minds' experience of self, identity, and belonging impact the world around us. The mind does not create energy so much as it shapes our experiences of energy flow, inside these bodies we are born into and outside them, in our connections with other people and with all of nature. This is a consilient perspective, grounded in accepted science and offering a framework for our sense of self that may be useful in bringing change into our waiting world.

CHOICE

As we approach the final segment of our journey through this book—from our relationship with space and time, through birth and development, bringing us to here, traveling the world in full adulthood—let's synthesize how far we've come and explore how we can choose ways of being and ways of doing in our lifespan voyage—how we can make choices in coming to understand our synergy of self, integrated identity, and broadened belonging to help us live a narrative of freedom, a story of our lives that can make sense both of reality and of how we might come to live fully, toward a generative way of being in the world.

We live in one reality, comprising the macro realm of our bodies and the micro aspects of our mental lives. We have explored the notion that our body, our macrostate, allows us to experience life with a set of properties that includes time and space as dimensions of separation of entities in the physical world in which we live. We have also explored how various shifts in our senses of that world, illuminated with reflective practices like the Wheel of Awareness, may give us access to the microstate realm of a quantum field, where we experience verb-like events instead of noun-like entities. In this realm, there is a sense of connection linking these events, emergence without the separation of time or space—a continuity of a massively connected whole.

The sense of awe in these open states of awareness—what we also experience by walking by a wide expanse of ocean, hearing a choir singing in harmony, or feeling a breeze dancing through a forest—enables us to transcend the close-up focus of our identity lens that is shaping our solo-self with its view of the self as only in the body. We feel the sense of something larger, the perspective of the greater world around us. With awe and the other "transcendent states" of gratitude and compassion, and perhaps with many other experiences suffused with love and connection, we come to realize the reality of a larger sense of life, a larger selfing that is broader than the body—one that, in this bodily form, can at first feel overwhelming, hard to understand, daunting.

And yet, when our sense of time and space relaxes its firm hold, we drop back into open awareness and let this sense of a synergy of self simply be a space of being. Even as a body form, who we are is something that is part of a system larger than the skin-defined boundaries would imply—we are part of the entire development of the universe from the beginning of time and into the infinite future, and we exist within the intricate space of the networks of life and the systems comprising the now of our universe, our planet, our lives, our connectome. These experiences remind us of the limitations of viewing the self as a synonym for the body. The whole we belong to is greater than the sum of its parts. Our identity becomes integrated, no longer constricted to the body alone, to the separate, isolated sense of a solo-self. A broader belonging and an integrated identity are experienced as both a Me, within these real bodies, and a We, within our connections to one another and within all of nature, across space and time: MWe emerges as a fully lived, intraconnected experience of self.

Synergy of self, integrative identity, broader belonging—these are ways to envision choosing how to be in life, how to live in ways that bring positive change to our personal loss of connection and to the many shared pandemics that plague our modern world. The basic premise we have been exploring throughout this journey, one echoed by the ancient teachings of Indigenous and of contemplative traditions, is that living with such an integrative identity will be a foundational shift in our contemporary human culture that will empower us to live a more generative life, with one another as a human family and within nature as a family of all living beings on Earth.

Self

You and I have a choice in how we sense our centers of experience, the foundational definition we've been exploring of this simple term "self." The synergy of the self is revealed in how the many components making up these centers intertwine as facets forming a functional whole. Naturally, at a small scale we have the many atoms that link with one another to form molecules, combine to make cells and their parts; cells collaborate to create bodily organs and entire systems, whose anatomy and function form the fabric of our bodily self. Part of that whole body is the embodied brain, a set of interconnecting parallel distributed processors that shape energy flow into streams of information, feeding the neural networks that help create the inner source of our mental lives, our emotions, memories, thoughts, hopes, dreams, and definitions of what we think the self is.

Shaped by an internal, survival-based drive for certainty, our inner mental life constructs categories, concepts, and symbols— sometimes beneath the surface of our consciousness, sometimes shared with our own awareness, and sometimes communicated with others—in an attempt to attain safety. In modern times, our contemporary culture shares the message that the sole source of self is the body-centered, solo-self. The default mode network (DMN) receives this message and is shaped by it, becoming overly differentiated. This may not only give us the "sense" of separation but also contributes to our experience of isolation, anxiety, and depression. In contrast, when the DMN is integrative—linking differentiated regions to one another—it is in balance with other aspects of our embodied brain, and it makes important contributions to our sense of insight, empathy, and compassion. Integrative experiences, such as meditation, can shape our brain's function, and thereby its structure, making the brain—and us—more integrated. The DMN becomes less a renegade and more a collaborative contributor to a now more harmonious whole.

Self is not just inside us, not just defined and confined by the skin's envelope that forms the boundaries of these bodies we are born into. We also have centers of experience that extend beyond the body: we are both inner and relational. We can choose which centers of experience to highlight in our day-to-day life. We feel this center as the subjective sensation, the perspective, and the agency of our self-experience. As we let that larger flow of a center of experience expand, we come to feel the emergence of something more than an isolated body, a separate part, the solo-self center of experience; we come to feel the synergy of self, its vitality, and a thrilling sense of our self-experience within the-whole-that-is-greater-than-the-sum-of-its-parts. Learning to expand how to directly sense this center of energy flow, to take on the perspective of that flow, and to take action on behalf of that flow empowers and expands our experience of selfing.

It's up to us to develop the skills of such an illuminated way of living. The awe, gratitude, and compassion of learning to live this way, with such an expanded and synergetic sense of self, are ours to let into our lives, if we choose.

Identity

How we choose to focus our lens of identity will determine which centers of experience we use to define our self and its characteristics. With a tightly focused lens, we see the singular body as the only source of the fundamental features of self, and we then contrast this identity to all "others." When we adjust this tight, body-based lens and expand our focus just enough to see self as plural—us—we include only those like-me, those with key elements (such as bodily features, bodily history, bodily embedded beliefs) that fit our view of identity. We've seen that the "self-construal" process can be independent with an individualistic perspective, and it can be interdependent, whether relational and connected to other individuals such as those members of a family or community, or collectivistic and based in affiliation with larger groups comprised of people who might share values and beliefs but whom we have never met. As we've seen, too, a metapersonal self-construal has been proposed that includes our relational connection to the whole of nature and the universe. Whatever academic controversies may exist about measurement details, the concept of a range of self-construal helps us envision the ways we construct our sense of self in various contexts and cultural settings. Yet our identity might also be seen as beyond these polarities of independent versus interdependent versus metapersonal, and we can envision combining the separate inner and the connected inter into an integrative identity—embracing the synergy that arises from being both an internal and a relational center of self-experience. Integration entails elements being differentiated and then linked; and within the linkage, the unique integrity of the parts is not lost in becoming part of the integrative whole.

Our external patterns of communication in modern societies, whether at home, in school, at work, or in the larger culture, often offer a message that the self is only identifiable as the body or, in its plural form, as an us that comprises only those bodies with features like our own. This leads to the development of a separate, solo-self, singular or plural. This constricted and highly differentiated social focus on a separated identity then becomes reinforced within the inner neural circuits, including the DMN, which now constructs this view of self-as-body to form our identity, to inform our ways of seeing the world, and to conform to continuing messages of the societal perspective on self. Energy then flows into disconnecting patterns of separation within our limiting connections to one another and within the neural connections within our embodied brain. The cultural and inner system of the solo-self becomes a pattern of self-reinforcing inter and inner flows of information that makes us accept the truth of this perspective without question.

How might we become empowered to choose a different way of being, to wake up from such a self-reinforcing, restrictive, constricting loop of external messaging and internal certainty seeking? One way would be to widen the focus of our lens of identity to include a broader range of centers of experience that together define what we sense as self. Knowing that we have a lens of identity enables us to choose to focus both close-up and wide-angle, giving us the tools to experience and embrace the many systems of energy and information flow in which we live: our body; our interpersonal relationships with family, friends, members of the community, colleagues, fellow citizens of Earth—the whole human family; and our fundamental relationship with all of nature. The systems of our identity are both within and between—our self is both inside the body and within the many layers of relational systems of our life that all form our multifaceted, intraconnected identity.

Belonging

We can choose to focus our lens of identity so that we can sense the energy flow that characterizes our experience of belonging—our sense of joining fully, of being a fundamental part, of having membership, of being connected. When our identity lens is focused close-up, we can use the experience of belonging to describe how we "feel connected" to our body itself. Widening our lens a bit, we come to sense that we belong to a personal family, have a deep connection with a circle of close friends; and if we widen our lens a bit more, we sense our connections to a widening set of circles of friendship, acquaintances, colleagues, neighbors, fellow citizens, and those who share our ancestral background in ethnic or racial identities, and those who share our belief systems and interests. And then we can choose to broaden our sense of belonging to all those in our human family; and broader still, we may sense a belonging even wider to embrace our connections within all of nature.

This is our journey: to integrate our relational self with our inner self—a journey we can choose to embark upon to escape the prison of modern culture's message of separation. This message is revealed in the sense of disconnection we too often feel, which imprisons us in the experience of a shrunken version of belonging as a solo-self. The great, empowering, hopeful, good news is that self-construal is an active, lifelong process, however we might measure and name it, shaped by messages we receive and concepts we believe. As Jane Goodall's work with hope in her Roots and Shoots activism message conveys, "Together we can, together we will" (https://rootsandshoots.org).

The world is not always kind, not always compassionate—not always integrative. Our human history of survival-based evolution leans us toward tribalism, and adding to this tendency is our genetically inherited, neurally mediated, socially reinforced propensity toward in-group and out-group evaluations. For these evolutionary and survival-based reasons, our species has culturally evolved with practices of exclusion that externally tell us to what and to whom we can belong. These cultural and genetic propensities, in our modern world, often hinder our sense of wholeness, robbing each other and the Earth of a generative way of living together. These are tendencies—propensities to construct particular patterns of transforming energy into information—that we can choose to push against. With realistic optimism and what Joanna Macy calls active hope, we can overcome these past patterns, if MWe work together toward this direction of change. MWe can alter modern culture's message of a solo-self construal and intentionally expand our experience as a synergy of self, an integration of identity, a broadening of our belonging.

Being connected in a healthy, positive way—what we are denoting as a state of acceptance and kindness in membership using the simple term "belonging"—is one of the most robust predictors of our well-being. Belonging is a birthright, not a luxury. In belonging, we retain our unique, individual features while being connected—we join, we are part of, we gain membership, we become a "we" without losing the "me." In these ways, the term "belonging" means the deepest facets of integrative joining—not merely fitting in or just going along to get along, and not losing our individuality under peer-pressure to become a part of a group. With such integrated belonging, we differentiate and we link to enable the synergy of MWe to be released: Me exists, We exists, and MWe is the intraconnected integrative whole within which we mutually belong.

Integration

We can choose to learn how to become aware, to take in the world around us and within us, and to sense when chaos or rigidity are filling our life and understand that these emerge from states of impaired integration. We can choose to understand how our own individual sense of differentiation or linkage may be blocked, and we can choose to become empowered with new skills and knowledge, to take the steps to develop and integrate our self as our centers of experience in our life. Integration, the linking of differentiated parts, is the basis for health in our lives—the life of our inner self and the life of our relational self in our connections with other people and with the planet: the intraconnection within all of nature. In the EMBODIED Appendix, you'll find an Embodied Integrative Practice that guides you through a mindful movement sequence that symbolizes nine domains of integration—including those of consciousness, memory, narrative, relationships, and identity.

We can cultivate this integration within our experience of self, close-up and wide-angle. With a flexible lens of identity and an expanded sense of belonging, we can choose to intentionally focus close-up on the body-based inner self's features—our personal history in this body's journey as a somatic form and our ancestral history across generations linking us in a familial line. And we can choose to focus our identity lens more widely, toward a broadening set of identifying features: I am not just alone in this body, I am not just identified with those who look like-me, my inner, individual self, singular or plural; I am also a relational self, related to the whole human family and to all of nature.

An integrated identity is our choice, no matter how the external world may marginalize our identity or insist on the view of a separate solo-self, based only in the body alone. An integrated identity differentiates the real facets of self as inner plus relational, in this simple identity equation: Me plus We are differentiated facets of self that can be linked within MWe.

The linking of differentiated components of self and identity does not erase our unique aspects as we experience the harmony of an integrative flow—an integrative identity embraces the distinct facets of our inner, individual self while also nurturing our relational self within the fields of connections created interpersonally and within nature. This honoring of differences—as me and as we—while synergetically integrating them as MWe, reveals how our many layers of identity contribute to our sense of self over time, over various states of being, and over a lifespan.

Cultivating the integrative nature of our identity as MWe reveals the power of the intraconnected whole to nurture its own systems intelligence, to honor and liberate the innate drive of integration at the heart of the self-organizational unfolding of complex systems. Living as MWe enables us individually and relationally to move toward harmony, freeing the natural emergence of integrative synergy and releasing the connection, awareness, and love at its source. All this we can feel within the integrated, intraconnected system we call "self."

Systems

We can choose to honor and acknowledge the many systems that flow through us as we flow through them. Energy flows in various forms, such as light, sound, and the electrochemical flow within our nervous systems, and energy flow can be shaped into information that symbolizes something other than itself—like these words we have been sharing along our journey and like the meanings of such terms as "self" and "system."

The gathering of energy into a network of interconnecting components is what we call a "system": a center of energy flow, with interwoven constituent nodes linked to one another across what we, in our Newtonian macrostate bodies, have named space and time, these everyday dimensions across which we share energy. In this way, we can see how, in a very real sense, a system is a form of self—self as centers of experience; experience as energy flow; interwoven energy flow patterns gathering as a system: system as self.

In the deep study of systems within mathematics, the term "self-organization" indicates that the system has innate propensities to regulate its own unfolding—its emergence as energy flow patterns. In complex systems, we see patterns of patterns, known as fractals; and we poetically refer to this sense of the intricate, enfolded nature of systems with such phrases as "the universe in a grain of sand" and "the drop reflecting the whole of the ocean." There is a sense of wholeness these mathematical implications suggest—we sense the system as a whole, with the perspective of the whole, acting on behalf of the whole. Subjective sense, perspective, agency—the intraconnected self.

As author Maria Popova and artist Ping Zhu state, "Emerging from this singular life is a lyrical universal invitation not to mistake difference for defect and to welcome, across the accordion scales of time and space, diversity as the wellspring of the universe's beauty and resilience" (Popova & Zhu, 2021). Integration entails the embracing of differences and the cultivation of compassionate, collaborative linkages in the emergence of the synergy of the whole.

Quantum physicist David Bohm (1980) explores these ideas:

> The word "implicit" is based on the verb "to implicate." This means "to fold inward" (as multiplication means "folding many times"). So we may be led to explore the notion that in some sense each region contains a total structure "enfolded" within it. (p. 149)

Bohm (1980) further postulates that

> the whole implicate order is present at any moment, in such a way that the entire structure growing out of this implicate order can be described without given any primary role to time. The law of structure will then just be a law relating aspects with various degrees of implication (p. 154) . . . . What is is always a totality of ensembles, all present together, in an orderly series of stages of enfoldment and unfoldment, which intermingle and interpenetrate each other in principles throughout the whole of space. . . . If the total context of the process is changed, entirely new modes of manifestation may arise. . . (p. 183–184). The implicate order gives generally a much more coherent account of the quantum properties of matter than does the traditional mechanistic order. What we are proposing is that the implicate order therefore be taken as fundamental. (p. 185)

When we sense, perceive, and act through a system-as-a-center-of-experience, the center of energy flow, we have the freedom to feel our many layers of self systems—beginning, but not ending, with the system of the body. What are the many systems of experience within which we exist? How does each one of those systems reveal a sense of wholeness? Is there a pattern of harmony, or is that system prone to chaos or rigidity? How do the distinct systems in which we live interface with one another? How do they reveal their distinct boundaries and patterns of energy flow? How might they be woven within the fabric of one another, perhaps revealing an implicate enfolding of a whole of what may initially have seemed to be quite distinct systems?

We have the choice to develop our own systems-sensing, -awareness, and -thinking that provide the foundations for our ever emerging systems intelligence. Combining this way of knowing in the world with our commonly taught linear thinking and conceptual intelligence allows us to link differentiated ways of knowing, within ourselves and with our relational others—the integration that underlies wisdom.

In *The Book of Hope* (2021), activist and scientist Jane Goodall is interviewed by activist and literary feng shui master Doug Abrams to explore how we can find hope by tapping into this natural state of wisdom. In their discourse, they cite Albert Einstein's words in this way:

> Doug: And then in a sense you become a channel—you open yourself to a wisdom that's greater than your own?
>
> Jane: Well, yes, for sure. There's a wisdom that's far, far, far greater than my own. I was so thrilled when I found that the great scientist Albert Einstein, one of the most brilliant minds of the twentieth century, came to the same conclusion based on pure science. ...It's in his book, *The World as I See It.* . . .
>
> [Einstein states], "The harmony of natural law ... reveals an intelligence that, compared with it, all the systematic thinking and acting of human beings is an utterly insignificant reflection." (p. 205)

Can we open to this capacity by opening our systems intelligence to recognize—to "bring back to mind"—the harmony of natural law, the innate wisdom of nature from which we all arose and continue to emerge? In this way, Indigenous teachings remind us of this fundamental truth that Einstein drew from scientific reasoning. As Wall Kimmerer (2013) states about the balance inherent to the Indigenous principles and practices that offer ways to cultivate harmony in the exchange of life for life known as the "Honorable Harvest":

> The Honorable Harvest asks us to give back, in reciprocity, for what we have been given. . . . Reciprocity is an investment in abundance for both the eater and the eaten. That ethic of reciprocity was cleared away along with the forests, the beauty of justice traded away for more stuff. . . . If the Earth is nothing more than inanimate matter, if lives are nothing more than commodities, then the way of the Honorable Harvest, too, is dead. But when you stand in the stirring spring woods, you know other-

wise. It is an animate Earth that we hear calling to us to feed the martens and kiss the rice. Wild leeks and wild ideas are in jeopardy. We have to transplant them both and nurture their return to the lands of their birth. We have to carry them across the wall, restoring the Honorable Harvest, bringing back the medicine. (pp. 184–195)

If the "wall" we must cross is business-as-usual in modern times, could we tap into our ESSENCE to enable the passion, the collaboration, the courage, and the imagination to envision and embrace the "wild ideas" from the wisdom of nature MWe need in order to proceed in an honorable way as we face the challenging times ahead?

Love and Linking

We can choose to express our sense of love and the joy it brings as we link among our circles of reciprocity, our mutual belonging. Perhaps the many variations of love—attachment love, romantic love, sexual love—are ways we express a fundamental life force among specific individuals, in specific settings, within particular contexts of relational connection. We can also have love for a specific thing or activity—a love of place, such as the mountains or forest; or a love of reading; or a love of hiking along the coast. Yet beneath and before this focus on particular individuals, places, or activities is a basic core state of being, this vital force of life, this fundamental potential suffusing the emergence of energy flow we may simply call "love."

What these all may share is the deep process of linking. When we love an individual in various ways, we link with them. When we love a place, we link with it. When we love an activity, we link with it. Linkage is a flowing into belonging, a membership, a joining that seems a natural aspect of love. In terms of resonance, linkage happens when differentiated individuals become connected—when they become integrated. Integration is the linkage of differentiated parts.

As a physician and as a scientist, the training I received never included discussions of love; and even mentioning the term was often met with disparaging comments and dismissive statements that speaking of love was "not professional" and "not scientific." Yet as a person in this world, trained as this body might be in these linear Western approaches to knowing, I cannot ignore the fact that thousands of reports from the Wheel of Awareness practitioners included the term "love" to describe the shift they experienced in the hub of the wheel, that metaphoric center of being aware correlating with the plane of possibility. From the strictly scientific reasoning perspective, this often-repeated expression of first-person experience becomes second-person data—the translation into what you and I hear they said of their subjective experience. We then examine third person data from "objective" empirical studies to see if there might be any overlap in findings between these reports and scientific data. To ignore these frequent findings would be unscientific. To accept the proposals blindly without contesting them would also be unscientific. And it is this process of challenging and examining that leads to the proposal that this experience of "love" might somehow relate to the deep potentiality of connection, of linking, of resting in the quantum vacuum, that sea of potential, the formless source of all form, the generator of diversity. This source of love would then be the plane of possibility, the portal through which integration naturally arises.

We can choose to be open to identifying and highlighting this linkage across boundaries of belonging that once disconnected us from one another and from nature. We can choose to be open to linking and differentiating, to integrating across all the domains that, from one perspective, are all expressions of love. This central, linking life force of love may just be a uniting thread, interwoven with presence and connection, in the tapestry of life.

The pairing of the term "love" with the term "linking" may help clarify this universal state of being, this fuel of our lives, this life force. If we look for examples in the self-extending emotions of awe, gratitude, and compassion, we can see them as emerging from a linking with, a linking in life. We expand our sense of "who we are" with awe, with being grateful for life, with compassionate resonance and action. Yet perhaps here is our vulnerability in a nutshell: We live in noun-like bodies, which tend to limit our perception and conception of who we are, making us prone to live as only noun-like, separate entities. An entity is defined as "a thing with a distinct and independent existence." With love, we realize we are more than an entity of separation. In Lynne Twist's words, "scarcity is the mindset of separation," and therefore sufficiency and natural abundance are the mindset of connection. In Robin Wall Kimmerer's terms, "reciprocity is an investment in abundance." Love is a state of being that liberates and highlights our reciprocal linkages, revealing the deeply intraconnected verb-like nature of who we truly are.

Love links us—when we release the mind from the top-down, constructed, macrostate filters of separation, we realize the reality of intraconnection. We do not need to "create" this connectivity; we merely need to reveal to ourselves the truth of our intraconnection by undoing the filters that create the illusion and delusion of separation, the separation that creates the solo-self.

But though this might be simple in concept, in these modern times this is rarely an easy task. Yet with community connection and reflective practices, our growing awareness of MWe permits us to embrace an integrated identity as both a "me" in a body and a "we" in our intraconnection with people and the planet. MWe do not need to be afraid of releasing any filters that keep us from being fully present and realizing the reality of our intraconnection—from empowering the healing, the making whole—that the linking of love creates.

Intraconnection

We can choose to open to the centers of experience beyond the confines of the solitary body, linking with love to ever-widening circles of connection, letting the natural, differentiated components of the many systems of energy emerge in our awareness, sensing into the implicate order of the whole—the enfolding, unfolding, emergent ways in which we experience the intraconnected reality of life. This choice moves us beyond a solo-self focus of our lens of identity to a broader belonging, a synergy revealing the wholeness of our subjective sense, perspective, and agency.

If a system is comprised of interacting elements, of nodes linked to one another, the solo-self perspective sees self as the node alone. What if a broader view—of the integrative, whole self—shows that the self is the entirety of the system, revealing that in modern times we've mistaken the nodes for the sole source of self?

Intraconnection is the sense, perspective, and agency of the self of the whole. In these bodies, we can choose to develop the identity lens we are given at birth, to maintain its flexibility of focus. Close-up, we sense the body as the center of experience; wide-angle, we sense our relational connections with people, and wider still, with the whole of nature, the whole of the universe; and taken together, we can feel the full range of our inner and relational centers as the intraconnected self.

Experience is energy flow. When that flow forms symbolic values, it is information—and with the modern DMN's sensitivity to social messages, the information we construct inside our brains supports the notion of the self as just in the body—the solo-self. Yet energy in fact flows beyond those midline cortical networks, not just throughout the wholeness of the brain but throughout the wholeness of the skin-encased body, and energy flows beyond the skull and skin— throughout all of the worlds of people and the planet, the wholeness of our relational lives. We share energy with the sun and its solar system and with our Milky Way galaxy—and in these ways, the widest-angle lens of identity lets us perceive that the center of who we are, at its broadest belonging, is not just in the body but within the whole of the universe and the generator of diversity, the mathematical space of the sea of potential. In this way, we are both the emergence of energy from possibility into probability and actuality and we are that formless source of all form. MWe are the intraconnected whole, from possibility to actuality.

We now know that experience, a flow of energy, involves two realms: 1) macrostate accumulations of energy with the properties of noun-like, separate entities such as molecules, bodies, and planets, that interact with one another across the familiar, classical Newtonian dimensions of time and of space; and 2) microstate properties of units of energy, such as the quanta of electrons and photons that manifest as probability fields, verb-like happenings that have no arrow of time and have massive connectivity across dimensions of the ever-changing movement from possibility to actuality—the flow of energy's trajectory. Who we are is both realms at once: macro and micro, noun and verb, time-bound and timeless, separated and differentiated, while also connected and linked. MWe are intraconnected, an abundant whole of reciprocity woven in a tapestry of connection, open awareness, and love.

Interconnection

Living in a body entails a macrostate realm of noun-like existence as an entity, a body separated within the sea of matter by our skin, separated across space from other bodies, separated across time from those who went before and those who will come after. When these entities interact, we are prone to thinking in linear terms: A interacting with B leads to C. Interaction has a sense of something that is here impacting something that is there, like a billiard ball interacting with other balls on the pool table. The term "interconnection" implies something more than "acting between"; it refers to a "connection between" yet still implies that there are two things that are connected—whether they are entities of mass or events, like flowing energy patterns.

As we have seen, related terms, such as "interdependent" and "interwoven," each retain this "betweenness" of something. Recognizing this connected nature of our existence—the ways we are, from the point of view of the part, interconnected—is an important starting place for moving from the linear notion of interaction to the more systems view of interconnection. Recognizing the interdependence of all things is a deep teaching of Indigenous knowledge and contemplative practice; respecting the interconnected nature of contexts, influences, impacts, and actions are crucial to seeing the systems solutions for the many problems we face. We can choose to move beyond the linear thinking of interaction to more systems sensing, systems perceiving, and systems thinking—to systems intelligence—by honoring the deeply interconnected nature of reality.

We can embrace both the reality of interconnection and the reality of intraconnection as terms that reveal our sensation, perspective, and agency of both the parts and the whole. Integration is honoring difference while promoting compassionate linkage. We integrate our lives as a MWe when we sense the interconnection of "me" and "we" as well as the intraconnection of MWe.

Our Noosphere

We, together, can choose how to create the atmosphere of knowledge—in what philosopher Pierre Teilhard de Chardin (1959) named our noosphere—in which we live the stories of our individual and collective lives. Often, this culture into which we are born is not of our choosing; we soak in its messages about how the world works, what has meaning, who we are, and how we should live, often without even being aware of them. Yet we can choose, with intention, to influence the noosphere in which we live. We can shape the story of you, the story of me, the story of us. Sometimes we might even need new words to say what we mean, terms like MWe and intraconnected. These linguistically-shaped narratives are how we make sense of our lives, constructing both an inner and shared world view with meaning, and they are the story-based scaffold of how we live our lives, determining how we interact with others and how we, in turn, contribute to the atmosphere of knowledge, our culture's narrative.

As we change the story of our identity, we help move cultural evolution forward. While genetic evolution unfolds over many generations, culture evolves at a relatively rapid rate, shaped by how we interact with one another as we enact our shared narratives and by the messages we create to form the noosphere of our shared conceptual space.

We can choose to shape our noosphere in an integrative direction. The specific steps we take individually can be inspired by our own proclivities, passions, and skills. No one else can dictate how we find meaning in this life, yet together we can make meaningful contributions to our shared world of knowledge. Our noosphere can be cultivated with compassion and kindness at its core. We can come to see that, beyond interaction, we are interconnected, and, as a whole, MWe are intraconnected.

We can collectively wake up to the illusion and delusion of the isolated, solo-self; we can awaken ourselves individually and collectively to these vulnerabilities of our modern human perception and conception of erroneously viewing the self as separate. Parallel to what Indigenous and contemplative wisdom have suggested for millennia, and as we've explored along our journey, we can wake up and live our lives as layers of self-experience: an inner me, a relational we, and the integrative, intraconnected whole of MWe.

The pandemics of racism and social injustice are violent examples of the dehumanization that arises from in-group/out-group division, the antithesis of an integrative way of honoring and thriving with differences and cultivating the compassionate linkages of living in harmony, with a reciprocity of belonging, caring for one another because MWe are one another. The pandemic of polarization and misinformation comes from excessively differentiated bubbles of information, driven by fear and hate, perpetuating their own divisiveness. The pandemic of attention-addiction draws us to focus on digital distractions that keep us disconnected in our relational lives. And our pandemic of environmental destruction, too, emerges from the isolation of humanity from its intraconnected place within all of nature.

The collaboration we need to deal with a viral pandemic invites us to embrace the reality of interconnection and interdependence— what we do here and now influences others here and in the future: it influences others across time and space. We can be courageous enough to dissolve the toxic, lethal lie of the separate, solo-self and choose a new integrative path forward, embracing the fundamental, intraconnected whole as our identity and belonging.

Adult Development and the Resistance to Change

As we move along in our lifespan journey, through adolescent development and the experience of its ESSENCE as an emotional spark, social engagement, novelty-seeking, and creative engagement, we've now entered the time commonly known as "adulthood." Findings from a range of empirical studies, from neuroscience and the discovery of the lifelong neuroplasticity in the brain, to the psychological studies of individuals' sense of self and changes in mental life in maturity, reveal that we continue to develop in adulthood—given the right conditions. In many ways, though, while we can change, we often don't, even if we want to. This truth has kept me busy as a psychotherapist over the last four decades. The resistance to change has direct relevance for how we approach the practical implications of what we've come to understand about how people develop in adulthood and how we might nudge cultural evolution to move toward a more integrative way of living.

Adulthood may be filled with a resistance to change; a kind of psychological momentum as a tendency to stay on the same business-as-usual course, to avoid alterations in the way things are. While we can look deeply at human development and say an individual can change, we can also look at history and anthropology and see how whole populations can also change with cultural evolution. As we examine the adult process of change and the resistance to it, let's keep both the individual and the collective in mind.

In her book *The Gift of Presence* (2020), mindfulness author Caroline Welch suggests that being mindful—developing those three pillars of focusing attention, opening awareness, and cultivating kind intention—enables us to identify and live with purpose, to pace ourselves wisely, note times in need of change, and then pivot when we need to make an intentional modification in the course of our lives. Welch notes:

> Pivoting has origins in Old French and dates back to 1605–1615. The noun pivot means "any thing or person upon which we depend vitally," as in a rock or an anchor. The anchor is a key feature of Pivoting, just as in basketball when we keep one foot anchored while passing the ball, and the person we are depending upon is ourselves. We're all likely familiar with the day-to-day Pivoting that allows us to meet the ever-evolving demands of our work, family, and friends . . . . There's also "crisis Pivoting" that's required when emergencies arise and demand our full, immediate attention—such as a serious illness, unexpected loss of a job, or the death of a loved one. When these life events occur, we drop everything to deal with them. (pp. 133–134)

Within the pivoting array is also what Welch calls "proactive Pivoting," in which we can plan for how to make changes before a crisis has arisen. If the many pandemics we face now are each caused by or intensified by the modern cultural view of the solo-self, is this a crisis, or an impending crisis? Is the pivoting we need to consider—whether proactive or crisis-mode—the anchoring of our inner self as a vital starting place, and then expanding that modern cultural emphasis on independence to include not only our interdependent self-construals, but the wider relational connection of self-experience to all of nature as well? In this way, we can move forward with cultural evolution as an intentional pivot—holding on to the me while also embracing the we—to live as an intraconnected MWe.

Psychological researchers Robert Kegan and Lisa Laskow Lahey (2009) have proposed and extensively studied a framework of adult development that includes changes in "mental complexity," and a process that tends to keep things the same, an "immunity to change." While these discoveries explore adults in the workplace—in business, government, schools—we can build on their work to imagine how cultures, as systems of individuals, may also have a resistance to change based on similar mechanisms in the mind of the adult. After all, a culture is comprised of a system of individuals communicating in patterns of energy and information-sharing. The shift in the collective of culture will be intimately interwoven with the shift in individual minds.

In this mental complexity framework, three stages of adult psychological capacity are identified: the socialized mind, the self-authoring mind, and the self-transforming mind. The socialized mind prioritizes the attention to others' expectations in the form of both interpersonal and collective (group) allegiances. In some ways, this seems parallel to the findings of the interdependent self-construal research and its overlap with relational and collective features. The self-authoring mind, in contrast, can step away from these inputs from the social world and construct a self-authorized way of prioritizing one's own individual values and behaviors. This perhaps has overlaps with the independent self-construal findings. The next step in the evolution of the self in this model is the self-transforming mind in which a broader perspective on values and behavior is taken that enables the individual to embrace paradox and contradiction, and the capacity to consider the importance of others' perspectives, not merely one's own lens on reality. As Kegan and Lahey (2009) state about this self-transforming stage of mental complexity: "Our self coheres through its ability not to confuse internal consistency with wholeness or completeness, and through its alignment with the dialectic rather than either pole" (p. 17).

Their research has found that each successive stage builds on the prior one, so that the mental filters used to organize one's thinking and feeling move along with increasing complexity. The socialized mind values others' points of view, the self-authorizing mind takes these into account but prioritizes the filter of that individual's views, and the self-transforming mind knows its own filters, but widens a perspective to include multiple viewpoints from the social world and one's own internal processes. In Kegan and Lahey's (2009) words: "The way information does or does not flow through an organization—what people 'send,' to whom they send it, how they receive or attend to what flows to them—is an obviously crucial feature of how any system works" (p. 17). For this reason, the way assemblies of individuals—from families to organizations to our larger human cultures on Earth—will reflect the stage of mental complexity achieved by its members. Perhaps the coherence of the self, embracing the seeming poles of inner and inter as seemingly contradictory sources of self, can be facilitated by weaving another option—that of the integration of inner and inter, the me and the we, as the MWe of self-transformation. Integration may be at the heart of a self-transforming mind's enhanced mental complexity.

Drawing on the work of their colleague and friend Ronald Haifetz (1998), who distinguishes between "technical" and "adaptive" challenges, Kegan and Lahey identify a process they call the "immunity to change," in which the mere addition of technical skills and knowledge is insufficient to adjust or adaptively pivot in response to a challenge. Instead, an adaptation of new mental complexity is required to modify thinking, problem-solving, and behavior to effectively adapt to a challenge. Before we look at what Kegan and Lahey's research reveals about what steps may be needed to move past this resistance to change and growth, what do you think might be the changes called for in responding to the array of current pandemics we face? Is the acquisition of new technical abilities enough to address these challenges? Do we also, or instead, need the adaptive change of acquiring new mental states? If that new mental state is the increased complexity in the construction of a self, then perhaps our journey to this point into how self, identity, and belonging develop has provided us with what we might call the integrative adaptation we need to face what we might then consider as modern "adaptive challenges."

Kegan and Lahey (2009) suggest that "optimal conflict" is what produces greater mental complexity. Building on extensive research from other scientists, they suggest that their assessment process of creating what they call an "X-Ray" into the immunity to change reveals this optimal conflict, one that has the features of

> The persistent experience of some frustration, dilemma, life puzzle, quandary, or personal problem that is. . . . Perfectly designed to cause us to feel the limits of our current way of knowing. . . . In some sphere of our living that we care about, with. . . . Sufficient supports so that we are neither overwhelmed by the conflict nor able to escape or diffuse it. (p. 54)

Is our solo-self pandemic just such an optimal conflict? It is persistent, pushes us to the limits, and is the inner sense of self that we care so much about. If we do this together, facing this conflict could have the sufficient supports to help us effectively pivot, to make the integrative adaptation that we need to move our selves to the next level of what we might call cultural complexity.

The immunity-to-change process reveals how often our efforts to make a shift in how we live comes up to a brick wall, halting us in our tracks despite every intention to make progress. Kegan and Lahey (2009) note that working with this immunity system requires a reconceptualization of the challenge to change, a potential for the development of new capacities for mental complexity, and the ongoing emotional regulation of anxiety.

> When we overcome an immunity to change, we stop making what we have come to see is actually a bad bargain: our immune system has been giving us relief from anxiety while creating a false belief that many things are impossible for us to do—things that in fact are completely possible for us to do! . . . Thus, the immunity we have uncovered is not just an explanation of why people have so much difficulty bringing about a change they dearly want to make. It also shows us a whole system at work. The immune

system is a way of managing an extraordinarily powerful feature of emotional life—the deep sense, often well founded, that life is dangerous, and that any sensible person must attend to the human version of national security. (p. 50)

The three components of this immune system involve 1) a "change-prevention system" that, often without awareness, blocks necessary adaptation to challenges in order to meet the needs of some hidden assumption based on survival-based factors; 2) a "feeling system" that monitors and modulates emotions, such as fear and anxiety; and 3) a "knowing system" that constructs a perception of the world and makes meaning of experience. In the X-Ray image created in over-coming this immunity to change, an assessment of visible commit-ments to change is outlined, as well as what is being done—or not done—instead of these commitments; hidden commitments that compete with the visible ones, and the "big assumptions" about what will keep the individual safe.

We call them "big assumptions" because they are not currently viewed as "assumptions" at all. Rather, they are uncritically taken as true. They may be true, and they may not be, but as long as we simply assume they are true, we are blind even to the question itself. (p. 58)

Might avoiding the exploration of what "self" is in modern times be an example of the unasked question, the unexamined presumption of the truth of separation, a blind acceptance that keeps us from ques-tioning this non-integrative, unhelpful nature of the solo-self? Might the scarcity mindset of separation be driving us into survival mode so that our "big assumption"—that separation will keep us safe—is how we, individually and collectively, are trying to manage our anxiety, to downregulate our fear, to feel at ease and soothe our distress as best we can as these pandemics plague us? If the answer to these questions is yes, then expanding our mental complexity, individually, and our cultural complexity, collectively, so that we embrace a more flexible, integrative experience of self may be what the next stages of cultural evolution require.

Complexity increases in a complex system when it combines differentiation on the one hand with linkage on the other. The fundamental balance of this differentiation and linkage, as we've been exploring throughout our journey, is the process of integration.

Adult development research on self and mind suggest we can change. Studies of cultures suggest that collectively we can evolve. If we have the adolescent ESSENCE of passion, collaboration, courage, and imagination still with us (and if we don't, we can regain it) then we can have the cognitive and emotional resources, the inner fuel and drive, to approach this optimal conflict we now face together with an adaptive cultural change. We can pivot and cultivate integration as a core principle that drives our change in humanity. If modern times have been built upon a big assumption—an unquestioned view about reality—that who we are is the solo-self, singular or plural, a self only in the body or bodies "like ours," then this excessively differentiated perspective is blocking integrative living for us as individuals, as a human species, and as a member of life on Earth.

The immunity to change approach empirically reveals how examining these big assumptions and dispelling their myths while honoring the need to be in touch with what we fear can be the steps needed to overcome this resistance to adaptive growth. When released from the fear the big assumption attempts to protect us from, we are freed to make an adaptive step in our development, to make a significant change in our lives. And it is adaptation we now need, not merely the acquisition of more technical skills or knowledge, to create the intra-connected cultural complexity that can guide our way forward.

The fear of losing the experience of certainty by letting go of the nounified construction of the solo-self may be at the heart of what has been keeping us stuck. By clinging to that flimsy fantasy of certainty, we do not wander, nor do we wonder. We stay stuck in a fantasy of our own making, a fantasy that is based on a lie. We do not need to constrict and control to survive; we can let go of that drive for certainty and connect with one another as part of a larger self-organizing system that thrives with differentiation and linkage, optimizing complexity with integration. Such reciprocity is the seed of abundance. If this is the big assumption about certainty that keeps us from the freedom and potential of the plane of possibility, that generator of diversity, then our immunity to change will continue to keep us stuck. To liberate us from this resistance to change as we move toward this conflict of excessive differentiation in our separation from other people and from nature, we will need the courage to illuminate the fear of letting go of our flimsy fantasy that certainty is both attainable and a guarantee of survival. With an integrative approach, MWe can embrace uncertainty to free ourselves—literally, our selves—from the understandable but misguided protective illusion of our big assumption that in modern life is blocking us from adaptive change.

With passion, collaboration, courage, and imagination, with our ESSENCE fully a resource we can tap into, we can move into our adult development and adaptively respond to this optimal challenge. Whether we see this as preparation for a challenge or full crisis-mode, together we can pivot toward an integrative way of living on Earth. By moving through the resistance to change by identifying the big assumption, we can embrace the freedom that comes with opening to the wide-angle view of what the self actually includes. We do not need to discard individuality to achieve relationality. Integration embraces the whole of who we can be, inner and inter. Who we are is a me in these bodies, a we in our relationships: with people we know, people we align with in our values, with all of humanity, and all of nature. Together, our self can be experienced as a MWe in the intraconnected whole of this precious life; living with reciprocity, sufficiency, and abundance.

HOPE

The modern, Western-derived cultural view of the self as separate and as encompassing the totality of one's identity is responsible for much suffering, as internal chaos and rigidity and as relational turmoil and disconnection. This individualistic self-construal, when taken to its extreme without being integrated within a larger sense of self, cannot help but contribute to the pandemics we are currently facing: the infectious diseases running through populations due to our failure to honor the differentiation of the wilds of nature; the dehumanization and marginalization of out-groups by in-groups; the environmental destruction of the Anthropocene era; the misinformation and polarization that is possible due to bubbles of isolated information; and the loss of a sense of meaningful connection and the compulsion to attend to digital distractions. How do we address such daunting challenges?

The 3-P diagram (Figure 11.1) provides a simple summary of one possible, practical framework that may offer a path forward to approaching these challenges and conflicts of our modern world. Hope is not wishful thinking, but a realizing of the possibilities beyond the actualities we now experience. With hope, we can be realistically optimistic—finding the path forward to a positive outcome in a real world of choices. When we draw on the resource of hope, we can be practical idealists seeking potential directions that may not yet be visible with a narrow lens focus but can be seen with a wider-angle view. With hope, we have the courage to challenge our big assumptions that may be blocking us from change. Hope is the steward of justice, the fuel for making the invisible visible. It is my deepest hope that this journey you and I have been on will provide the tools to access that wider lens, and help us be more prepared to address whatever conflicts we face, helping liberate us from the immunity to change, and then to effectively pivot to address the adaptive challenges ahead.

To synthesize and integrate where we've come along our lifespan journey, in this final chapter let's review the fundamentals of this view of our mental life as emerging from a range of probabilities, from the potential of possibility to actualization as certainty. From the 3-P perspective, a sea of potential—the plane of possibility—gives rise to probabilities as plateaus, which establish the "ground rules" for our states of mind and the story of our selfhood. From these narrative plateaus arise certain peaks of actuality, appearing to us as thought, emotion, and memory.

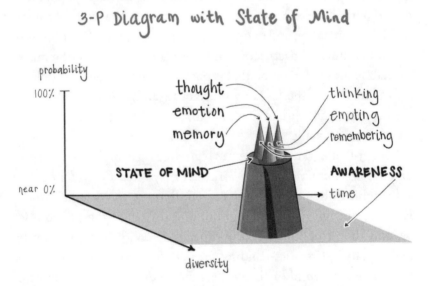

Figure 11.1 Summary of the 3-P system.

Energy flow, then, is the movement from the plane of possibility to peaks manifesting as actualities. For self-experience—the sense, perspective, and agency we know as "self"—this flow can emerge as bottom-up sensation in the experience of life, as close to subjective sensory reality as we can muster. This is the conduit capacity of the mind to experience, as best we can, the direct flow of energy in our lives. Yet perspective—the point of view we take—is a constructive process, and agency builds on the mind's top-down constructive processes of thinking, believing, and choosing action in the world. The perspective and agency of self-experience are constructive top-down processes serving as the foundations of the narrative of self: we first sense life, and we then turn that sensory subjectivity into mental models of reality and ultimately narratives of who we are, which directly mold our perceptions and actions. Sensation emerges directly from uncertainty—from the plane of possibility. Perception and agency are our attempts to achieve certainty—they are the plateaus of mental models, narratives, and our states of mind from which the peaks of our actualities may often arise.

Whatever the level of mental complexity in the development of the self, these plateaus can be envisioned as how we filter the ways we construct a view of the world, and how we behave in it. The socialized mind would soak in filters from others; the self-authoring mind would have tall plateaus strongly filtering which thoughts and emotions are given priority; the self-transforming mind would have more access to the plane of possibility and more flexible use of its filtering plateaus—of which plateaus to use and when to use them. In this way, the mental complexity we have will shape our experience of self and how we come to narrate who we are in the world.

The stories of our lives are not only what we say, in our mind and to others, but also how we live our lives. The layered stories of our life become embedded in the actions we carry out in the world. When as a community we share the foundations of these stories—when the values and meanings, interpretations and beliefs, are conveyed collectively in communications with one another—culture is created.

If our modern cultural narrative collectively molds us to live as disconnected entities, then our experience will arise from those filtering plateaus, defined by the categories, concepts, and symbols of separation. With our vulnerability to asking who is like me and who is not, we are at risk of dehumanizing those not like-me in an effort to cling to our intensified drive for certainty, including the certainty of separateness. With the threat of scarcity, separation is intensified. Sadly, this gives us insight into how humans, throughout history can carry out genocide against those deemed not like-me—those in the dehumanized out-groups across the globe.

As antiracist scholar Ibram X. Kendi (2017) suggests, racism, the stance that one group has essential features that make it better than another group, gives rise to the idea of race. Believing these constructed stories of innate superiority and inferiority may be a desperate attempt to attain that flimsy fantasy of certainty, to reduce anxiety—and we run the risk of building social structures that have foundations in how we believe these narratives to be true, even though they are based on fear, and based on lies.

Two thousand years ago, my ancestors were slaves. After a centuries-long journey throughout Europe of escape, desperation, and dehumanization, they arrived in America at the beginning of the twentieth century. The white color of their skin gave them, and me, privilege in what some consider an American caste system that oppresses People of Color. As Pulitzer Prize–winning journalist Isabelle Wilkerson (2020) reveals, the Nazi government even came to the United States prior to the second World War to study how the United States treated Black people so that they, too, might learn how to effectively marginalize and ultimately destroy a whole group of "others," in this case, the millions of "non-human" Jewish people they were about to systematically slaughter.

As a person with white skin in a white-dominant society, whatever my cultural ancestry, I can accept and embrace that it is my responsibility to recognize this position of privilege within such nonintegrative cultural practices and that it is my responsibility to identify, in myself, how I might be carrying out racial bias in action or thought.

Then I can awaken to ways to help reduce, even eliminate, such ways of being, both internally, within my inner self, and relationally, in the connections I have with those with whom I interact. As Nobel Laureate Archbishop Desmond Tutu taught us, there is no neutrality when it comes to injustice. We either are working against it, or we are supporting it. Our modern narrative of humanity constructs levels of superiority or inferiority that are the basis for dehumanization and injustice; we can come to change, with these words of recognition, by identifying the false nature of this big assumption of separation and superiority, by a widening in our lens of identity, by growing our mind toward integration—the basis, we can suggest, of living with justice, care and connection. When we come to realize our place in the larger family of humanity, and within all of nature, we come to experience the truth that integration made visible is kindness and compassion.

As discussed in the LEAVING HOME chapter, studies of mindfulness meditation that incorporate compassion training to build kind intention—not just in surface words but in the deep mental practice of authentically focusing on our connections—may offer preliminary insights into how we can reduce implicit racial bias. Becoming aware and being open to these common but often hidden prejudging beliefs—these unfortunate plateaus that can keep us far from the connection, open awareness, and love of the plane of possibility, filters that shape our perceptions and emotional reactions—is essential for us to change the status quo. We can learn to drop beneath the illusion of certainty that our plateaus of constricted identity convey and learn to find comfort and connection in the open plane of possibility, letting uncertainty become a sanctuary, not a feared, unpredictable place with lack of control. We can live the reality of the synonyms for uncertainty: freedom and possibility.

The 3-P perspective reveals a pathway with purpose: beneath the narrative of our plateaus rests the plane of possibility. We need to acknowledge the individual histories each of us has, those differentiated plateaus and peaks of our particular personal identity. You are distinct from me. My immediate ancestors had their own particular journeys; yours had theirs. Living in clusters of communities across the generations, they have population characteristics of skin color, facial features, bodily dimensions, and other characteristics we might use to say we belong to this or that group. And as our populations lived in isolation from each other, these differences intensified over time.

And yet, though we may have some genetic variations across populations, some bodily features that are distinct and histories anchored in the land in different regions of Earth, there is no essential, innate difference from one group to the next. We are a heterogeneous mixture of populations and peoples from disparate regions of the globe. Any human can mix and mate with any another human, blending the population variations each partner brings to the union. No matter our histories and our characteristic population features, you and I are of the same species—we are all of the same human family.

Our life narrative can begin with our personal history with our family and move outward into layers of identity as we shift our lens from close-up to wide-angle. If you consider your own life stories, how do your layers of self help shape those narratives? What is your subjective sensory experience of being alive here in this life, in this moment, right now? How has it emerged in your life within the family in which you grew up? What is your point of view, your perspective in current times, and how was this molded by your family? How is your action, your agency, influenced by your life stories of where you've come from, who you are, where you are going?

These types of inquiries can also be applied to a wider set of identity features—not just your family, but outward to friends, school, profession, religion. As philosophy professor Kwame Anthony Appiah (2018) has said, we have the layers of creed, culture, color, class, and country all as part of our identity in what he calls the "lies that bind"; lies in that we make them up; bind in that they enable us to belong to one another:

> My main message about the five forms of identity . . . is, in effect, that we are living with the legacies of ways of thinking that took their modern shape in the nineteenth century, and that it is high time to subject them to the best thinking of the twenty-first. (p. xiv)

This revision, Appiah suggests, would mean seeing the fundamental ways our worlds shape our identity from the beginning:

> In each of my five test cases, we fall into an error . . . of supposing that at the core of each identity there is some deep similarity that binds people of that identity together. Not true, I say, not true. (pp. xv–xvi)

Could we let go of even the need for identity? Appiah (2018) doesn't think so:

> There's no dispensing with identities, but we need to understand them better if we can hope to reconfigure them, and free ourselves from mistakes about them that are often a couple of hundred years old. Much of what is dangerous about them has to do with the way identities—religion, nation, race, class, and culture—divide us against one another. . . . We need to reform them because, at their best, they make it possible for groups, large and small, to do things together. They are the lies that bind. (p. xvi)

Our stories connect us across past, present, and future as they help us make sense of our identity and belonging. How wide and far-reaching or close-up and narrow does your lens of identity tend to be? How broad or narrow is your belonging? Learning to adjust that lens is how we learn to integrate our identity and belonging, to bring more coherence and vitality to our narratives of who we are, and to sense, perceive, and act with more freedom within our experience of selfing.

Appiah (2018) offers these relevant insights:

> Social identities connect the small scale where we live our lives alongside our kith and kin with larger movements, causes, and concerns. They can make a wider world intelligible, alive, and urgent. They can expand our horizons to communities larger than the ones we personally inhabit.... When it comes to the compass of our concern and compassion, humanity as a whole is not too broad a horizon.... We live with 7 billion fellow humans on a small, warming planet... our common humanity is no longer a luxury; it has become a necessity. (pp. 218–219)

He concludes his fascinating treatise with a poem from the dramatist Publius Terentius Afer, better known as Terence, a Latin interpreter of Greek comedies and a slave from Roman Africa who called himself "the African":

> Homo sum, humani nihil a me alienum puto.
> I am human, I think nothing human alien to me.

And Appiah (2018) responds with: "Now there's an identity that should bind us all" (p. 219).

We have many layers and levels of self-experience that shape our identity and influence our belonging from the inside, and our culture has its own ways of seeing our identity, welcoming us or not. Our position in our culture influences our relational shaping of our experience of self. Yet we are not so helpless that we must just accept this cultural input as accurate or unchangeable. Hidden big assumptions based on survival reactions and the scarcity-separation linkage can be identified and dissolved, helping us directly address the immunity to change and giving way to an adaptive pivot toward a more integrative way of living. Our inner reflections can help us make sense of the effects those external inputs have on how we experience and express our self to be. Learning ways to access the plane of possibility, to drop beneath the internal and external factors that have shaped the plateaus that limit our narrative perspective and agency, frees us from these self-reinforcing plateaus, with their particular thought, emotion, and memory peaks, to liberate the dynamic making-sense processes of our narratives to then arise more directly from the plane of possibility. Embracing uncertainty, we come to see more clearly. We learn to live "from the plane"—learning, loving, laughing, and leading from this open place of connection and awareness. When we drop beneath those plateaus that limit our experience of self, as they determine "who is like-me" and "who is not like-me," we come to join in a mutuality of belonging, emerging from a place of commonality, the plane of possibility.

We've learned from attachment research that repair of the ruptures in our connections—when we don't experience our four S's of being safe, seen, soothed, and secure—is both possible and important, but it needs to be initiated by those that create the rupture. In the case of the cultural ruptures of slavery, racism, and the genocide of Indigenous people in the United States of America, the repair needs to be initiated by those in the dominant group: those who identify as white, particularly those who identify as white, cisgender males. In this body called Dan, I am a member of this subgroup. And it is my hope that this conversation you and I are having is part of that repair and restoration.

If we have ruptures in the fulfillment of our human need for security, might we develop shame as a result of this nonsecure relationship we have with society? Can we engage in the repair process, taking responsibility—honoring differences and promoting compassionate linkages—for actions that were not integrative and, in that way, have thwarted a secure attachment within our communities, within our culture? Part of that repair process is finding ways to engage in a conversation, together. And key for that conversation to be effective is to find how to communicate, both nonverbally and verbally, the means to reach across the illusions and delusions embedded in our prior narratives and their big assumptions about separation and superiority. We can harness hope's goals, agency, and social support and have the fortitude and skills to embrace the uncomfortable and inconvenient.

How can we work together to make this pressing transition and pivot from the solo-self of contemporary times to a synergy of self in a new era? As we leave the familiarity of business as usual, realizing it will lead to what Joanna Macy (2021) calls a Great Unraveling, can we find the passion, collaboration, courage, and imagination to cultivate instead what she has named as a Great Turning? This would be turning toward a living together, a mutuality of belonging, a world of harmony which environmental philosopher Glenn Albrecht (2014) calls the Symbiocene in contrast to the Anthropocene which Diane Ackerman (2015) explores in *The Human Age*.

As we are intraconnected within a complex system, so can we look to the science of complexity, which suggests a system unfolds over time in four basic phases. As a complex system begins a repeating cycle of organization, disorganization, and reorganization, it has a growth phase, in which new assemblies form and give rise to ways these differentiated component parts connect and interact with one another. This initial growth is then followed by a conservation phase, with stable, if temporary, interactions that may be prone to rigidity, resistant to change, as they persist in their established patterns. The system then shifts past a tipping point of these accumulated factors and enters a release phase; the prior stability of the conservation phase is disrupted, and the system enters a phase transition. The ensuing reorganization phase has an increased potential for the rearrangement of components and their interactions, giving rise to a new growth phase; and the cycle continues. We've been exploring a lifespan approach to our development of self, and now we are examining a systems development view of how our larger intraconnected self may be emerging. Which phase do you think we as a modern culture and we as living beings in the complex biosystem of life on Earth may be experiencing at this moment?

When we see that we live both in and as complex systems and that these systems have a natural cycle, shaped by the forces of self-organization, we get a sense of how our inner- and our inter-selves shift and change over time. We can then release our systems intelligence to support these natural cycles among the systems we are intraconnected within. Might we now be in a reorganization phase, an opening in which our intentional actions may help reduce, or eliminate, blockages to the system's natural reorganization toward more complex states of integration? Might these VUCA times (with volatility, uncertainty, complexity, and ambiguity)—as painful and terrifying as they are—also be a window of opportunity to pivot away from business as usual and take on a more productive and collaborative path forward? In recognizing that we, as human beings, have created these impediments to the natural drive for optimal self-organization, and in recognizing that we as a species have excessively differentiated and minimized the linkage of connection, we might choose to intentionally move ourselves from the solo-self of the Anthropocene to the synergy-self of the Symbiocene by empowering the collaborative, integrative work of a Great Turning.

As journalist Andy Revkin's webcast at Columbia University's Earth Institute (https://www.earth.columbia.edu/videos/channel/sustain -what) suggests in its very title, *Sustain What?*, how can we move beyond merely sustaining systems that are already in such a challenged state to instead consider how to cultivate regeneration of life?

Is there a way to take the optimism, abundance, and regeneration principles Figueres and Carnac-Rivet (2020) suggest and use that "OAR" to make an adaptive pivot in our lives? Joanna Macy (2007) offers us a vision of the path forward by stating that the Great Turning is a

> revolutionary transition we need to make from the industrial growth society to a life-sustaining society. Basic to this revolution is the arising of an ecological identity, "the greening of the self," as well as a readiness to persevere for the long haul. (p. 12)

Macy goes on to suggest that "a quantum leap of consciousness is required if complex life forms are to survive on Earth" (p. 13). A Great Turning may be one way to name how our modern culture can evolve to nurture our collective lives here on this fragile and precious home we've named Earth.

In speaking with people in our human community across the globe, the feeling arises that the time for a change is now. As we've discussed, Albrecht and colleagues (2007) suggest that we have "Earth emotions," such as solastalgia, akin to eco-grief or climate grief, that involve a deep sense of loss about a diverse and thriving world of nature that we know is no longer here. The grief he describes is resonant with the grief work of reconnecting with one another and with nature that Macy (Macy 2021; Kaza, 2020) suggests is essential to helping us move in a more collaborative direction. The symbol and meaning of MWe embodies the teachings of how to move collectively forward in our sense of self, identity, and the mutuality of belonging at the heart of Macy's approach. Religion and environmental scholar Stephanie Kaza (Macy, 2021) powerfully states, "Macy invites us to experience the ecological self, the way each of us is an expression of much larger self-organizing patterns" (p. xiv).

Perhaps the Great Turning invites us to integrate our lives, embracing the fullness of reality. A Great Turning may be the cultural evolutionary step of reorganization.

Organizational consultant Margaret Wheatley (180 Studio & Saunders, 2020) reminds us to see the foundations of this often-hidden sense of connection that does not typically become a part of our modern human story:

> In the quantum world, relationship is the key determiner of everything. . . . In this world, the basic building blocks of life are relationships, not individuals. Nothing exists on its own or has a final, fixed identity. We are all bundles of potential. Relationships evoke these potentials. We change as we meet different people or are in different circumstances. (p. 139)

Each of the pandemics we face provides pressing reasons for change. As group facilitator Adam Kahane (180 Studio & Saunders, 2020) states, "If we want to change the systems we are part of, we must first see and change ourselves" (p. 267). What makes this so challenging, Kahane suggests, is that

> problems are tough because they are complex in three ways. They are dynamically complex, which means that cause and effect are far apart in space and time, and so are hard to grasp from first-hand experience. They are generatively complex, which means that they are unfolding in unfamiliar and unpredictable ways. And they are socially complex, which means that people involved see things very differently, and so the problems become polarized and stuck. (p. 265)

A simple strategy to approaching solutions for these complex challenges we've suggested is to understand the isolated solo-self as a myth of modern times and as both the underlying cause of and the exacerbating factor worsening our pandemics that plague the world.

This myth is an erroneous narrative of our times, a violation of epistemic trust. Dispelling this myth might just be the revolution in consciousness that a Great Turning is inviting us to catalyze in our culture. The truth is that the potential exists for sufficiency and abundance, to live with reciprocity in a regenerative way as a system of life on Earth, if we have the courage to make the adaptive changes we need to liberate us from the lie of the solo-self. This is a moment of optimal challenge for us individually and as a humanity. Can we get our acts together to make the adaptive pivot these times are calling for to advance the Great Turning? Opening our inner awareness to the reality of intraconnection might be the key that helps move us in an integrative direction as a human family on our fragile planet.

As we prepare to say goodbye, for now, in our discussion of these important issues of our time, let us reflect on our journey into the intraconnected nature of reality and on the position of the human mind's construction of the solo-self as the vulnerable place in humanity's current moment in cultural evolution. Before energy ever manifested as matter, potentiality existed in a space of being, which we've been exploring as the plane of possibility: that sea of potential, a formless source of all form, the generator of diversity. The journey from possibility into actuality is the flow of energy, the basis of experience. As potentiality formed into matter, billions of years ago, the universe formed as galaxies and solar systems and our own home, planet Earth. An arrow of time, the directionality of change, was created with the macrostates of matter moving ever forward toward entropy—toward disarray. Our experience of that directionality of change we would come to call "time," something we could measure with a clock, something we'd often come to feel we were running out of. Nothing really is flowing like a river; change happens and fills us with experience. Energy from the sun provided input to matter here on this planet to form life hundreds of millions of years ago. Across a wide array of life forms, the biosystem of Earth enabled more and more complex beings to arise—plants, fungi, animals—into which we, connecting with these words, were formed. As we experience this energy flow called "our lives" in these moments of having a body, the clock-time of our macrostate human bodies and the spatial appearance of separation are but one realm of reality; we also have available to our awareness the timeless, deeply connected microstate realm that is equally real, simply another facet of experience—of energy flow.

How we come to differentiate and link these distinct realms of reality in the flow of energy and information will shape who we are and even our sense of why we are here. As complex systems, we arise as flow that is greater than the sum of its parts—a process we name as emergence or synergy. Who we are is more than our body, something beyond its skin-encased boundaries, broader even than the fully embodied brain. Energy flow is not limited by skull nor skin. The natural flow of a complex system's emergent property of self-organization is to maximize complexity, a state of flow in which the differentiation and linkage of its parts enable the most flexible, adaptive, and energized states to arise. This is the state of harmony; and this integration is the basis of health. In many ways, cultivating integration, bringing kindness and compassion into our world, brings purpose and meaning into the flow of our lives. Dropping into the plane of possibility—the hub of the Wheel of Awareness—can let this sometimes overwhelming and darkening world of our Newtonian realm find the light of possibility in that generator of diversity; learning to live from that sea of potential brings hope alive.

Since the earliest years of our bodily lives, each of us has been on a journey in which the inner, core self of affectivity, agency, continuity, and coherence is shaped by our attachment experiences. We can have avoidance and disconnection from within and between, in which our core self is isolated and learns to adapt by minimizing the drive for connection. We are then left, literally, with a leaning to the left side of the brain, the left mode of processing energy into information with its narrow focus of attention and its disconnection from both the internal sensory world of the body and the rich reflective sense of an autobiographical narrative self-experience. Or, we may have emotional confusion and develop ambivalence as an adaptation, wherein we rev up our drive for connection. With ambivalence, the inconsistent and sometimes intrusive behaviors of our caregivers build in us a core self that is confused when around them. Or we can have a disorganized attachment, if terror in response to our unrepaired interactions with a caregiver drives us both away from and toward the same people—our attachment figures—the result being a fragmented core self when we are around those people and the disintegrating adaptation called dissociation.

As we've seen, these early attachment experiences shape our sense of self, our identity, and our belonging. As we grow and move out into a wider world beyond the family, we then activate similar patterns in our experiences with teachers and peers, friendships and romantic partners. This self-reinforcing loop literally reinforces the secure, disconnected, confused, or fragmented core self we developed with our caregivers early in life—and the relational self that has learned patterns of being a part of a "we," or not, in our earliest years. We then become a self-fulfilling set of recurrent patterns of interacting.

If we see the plateaus and peaks as our way of visually depicting the neural and subjective mechanisms of various states of mind, then we can envision how a secure core self would entail fluid access across peaks, plateaus, and the plane of possibility—enabling a broad range of perspectives as they arise from the plane. With this way of living, each energy configuration, each probability position, is enabled to be differentiated and linked—an integration of peak, plateau, and plane as a wholeness we can feel and share.

Our sense of sharing and reciprocity, the abundance of belonging in the world—feeling membership, an experience of joining in our connections with those around us and with nature—is shaped by our identity, our experience of being alive, our sense of self. In our journey here together we have explored the experience of human development, of becoming who we are—how we cultivate a sense of self, of belonging, and of identity. Within the realms of reality, we dance as patterns of energy that enable us to resonate as the harmony of life.

Isolated as a solo-self, our identity is constricted, our belonging constrained; our drive to be certain and survive coupled with a mindset of control and division. When we widen the lens of identity and broaden our belonging, we experience the sense, perspective, and agency of selfing in a more integrative flow. The wonderful news is that from infancy through adulthood, we can grow and change. Even facing the immunity against trying on new ways of being, we can harness the passion, collaboration, courage, and creativity to move from resistance to resilience. We can shed light on our protective but false assumptions, realize the fears of threat we may experience, and find solace in the connections we cultivate within our deep awareness and within the relationships with our human family and all of nature. Instead of viewing these impediments to integration as overwhelming and dreaded threats that perpetually activate our reactive states of alarm, we can take them on together as challenges, welcoming them each day as dance partners with whom we can find a way to connect, engage, and facilitate growth. This is how we can actively move toward regeneration and a Great Turning while minimizing our vulnerability to exhaustion given our courage to care. We can learn to let life happen as we both differentiate and link, liberating the connection, open awareness, and love of that plane of possibility to guide our ways of living, together, with harmony. By discovering and empowering the true nature of our intraconnected self, we can widen our lens of identity and transform our experiences to live healthier, fuller, freer lives across the entire range of belonging, with enhanced personal health and shared planetary well-being. Together, MWe can make this integration of self, identity, and belonging our common ground, linking timeless wisdom with timely action in our magnificent, intraconnected world.

APPENDIX 1

Wheel of Awareness Practice:
A Brief Summary

The Wheel of Awareness is a metaphoric image of the mind in which the central hub of the wheel represents the experience of being aware—of "knowing"—and the rim represents that which we are aware of—the "knowns." A single metaphoric spoke symbolizes attention. The Wheel drawing has helped young children visualize how they can be empowered to "rest in the hub" and not respond to impulses on the rim. In this way, the hub allows for a pause between impulse and action, permitting choice and change. For adolescents and adults, the Wheel can be used to guide a reflective practice. If you'd like to explore this directly, the Wheel of Awareness as a practice can be found on my website, https://drdansiegel.com/resources. If you would like to explore more in-depth discussions about these ideas and this practice, I've dedicated two books to this topic: *Aware* (2018) and *Becoming Aware* (2021).

Throughout *IntraConnected*, we've explored a consilient proposal that the mechanisms of mind may be envisioned as a diagram of probability. That view was initially inspired by the collective responses of individuals throughout the world who took part in workshops in which they practiced the Wheel of Awareness and described their

Basic Wheel

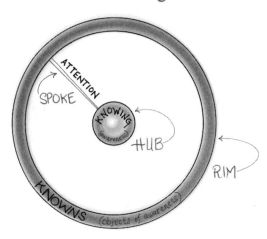

WHEEL OF AWARENESS

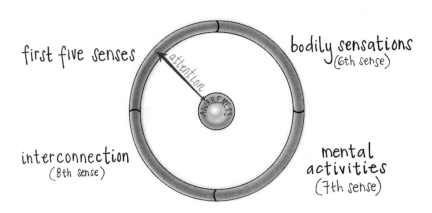

Figure Appendix.1a and Appendix.1b: The Wheel of Awareness and its basic components.

subjective experience, their perspective, and their mental agency during the practice. In this sense, their experience of self shifted during this "integration of consciousness" reflective exercise that differentiates the elements of the knowns from the knowing and then links them. One way to envision the correlation between the metaphoric integration of consciousness practice and the 3-P diagram is seen in this image:

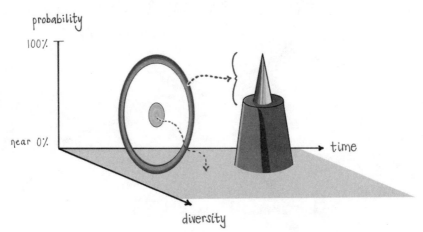

Figure Appendix.2: Hub of the Wheel correlates with the plane of possibility.

As individuals (including this person named Dan) practice the Wheel, the acquired skill of distinguishing the hub from the rim seems to correlate with the capacity to access the plane of possibility. As reviewed in the discussions here and in *Aware* and *Mind: A Journey to the Heart of Being Human,* this learned skill to "live from the plane" generates the ability to tap into a deep inner source again and again—in this way a vital "re-source"—that is filled with possibility, connection, open awareness, and love. In 3-P framework terms, we learn to sense the plateaus of states of mind and their particular peaks of thought, emotion, and memory as mental activities, developing the capacity to not become swept up in overidentifying with them as the totality of our identity. In this way, the Wheel of Awareness as a practice, or even as a metaphoric image of mind, helps us to go beneath the learned, top-down plateaus of the limited solo-self view of who we are in order to access a direct means of sensing, perceiving, and acting on behalf of the intraconnected whole.

APPENDIX 2

Integrative Movement Series

Welcome to a movement series that embodies many of the fundamental principles of integration we've been exploring along our journey together. This practice involves nine domains of integration, each of which has direct implications and applications to the integration of self, identity, and belonging:

1. Interpersonal integration
2. Temporal integration
3. Identity integration
4. Memory integration
5. Narrative integration
6. State integration
7. Bilateral integration
8. Vertical integration
9. Consciousness integration

Below, for each domain, I offer a concise summary followed by a description of flowing physical movements designed to represent the integration of each domain. I'll then provide some short commentaries about how that domain directly relates to our journey to explore intraconnection and that serve as a review of many of the areas we've touched on, directly or indirectly, in our journey together. This brief immersion into these integrative physical movements offers a way to experientially ground your journey with the synergy of integration into the body.

If we choose our path forward from a place of integration, we can then draw on our personal propensities and proclivities to find our own unique, differentiated way of living in the world and bring more integration into our lives. It is my hope that this movement series encourages a sense of integration within you in your many centers of experience of self in the world.

These movements, inspired by modern dance, jazz dance, ballroom dance, and ballet, combine lessons from the practice of tai chi chuan and qigong to weave conceptual notions of the domains of integration together with symbolic movement forms.

From my personal perspective, this body I live in has had several injuries that make the practice of more challenging movements in various disciplines, including yoga, quite difficult, so I've tried to create a set of movements that, for myself and now many others, are quite comfortable. Please make your own careful assessment of what your particular body can and cannot handle—feel your body's signals for what feels healthy to do and what does not, and please care for your inner, bodily self and modify your movements accordingly.

Warming Up

Let yourself stand comfortably, arms at your sides. If this not accessible for you, you can sit or lay down flat. And if no movement at all is possible, imagine carrying out these movements, as this may be beneficial— imaging studies suggest that imagining motion activates similar brain regions as actually performing the same motion.

With gentle movement, alternately move one hand to the opposite side, gently touching the lower back with the back of the hand. After six to eight rounds, let the swinging hand move up to the opposite shoulder, palm touching the shoulder, for six to eight rounds. Then move one hand down the outside of the opposite arm, make your palm touch gently and briefly, then up the inside of that arm. Repeat this sequence on the same arm, then repeat the same sequence, moving twice down and up the other arm.

Now let one hand pat down the outside of the opposite leg, toward or all the way to the ankle, and pat back up on the inside of the leg to the abdomen and then the center of the chest. Do this twice, then do this sequence on the other side. If you have a vulnerable back, as I do, try lifting your leg up toward your hand instead of bending at the back, and don't worry about reaching all the way to the ankle.

Grounding in the Energy Center

Various traditions describe energy flow through the body, and often they identify nodes of the system of this somatic life force, this body energy, as including a center between the belly button and the pubic bone. If you are not yet familiar with this energy center, try placing your hand there and feeling—with the inside of your palm, close to where your fingers meet your palm itself—a sense of something. Some describe it as a fullness, a slight heat, a tingling, a buzzing, an energy—sometimes subtle, sometimes intense—emanating from this anatomic location.

Let's refer to this as your energy center, or your EC. Studies of acupuncture and meridians of energy flow suggest that there may be something happening there that is identifiable in Western medical terms, but no one has ascertained what this life energy really is. Eastern medical traditions view the state of this energy flow as part of a healthy life, to enable this flow be "balanced" or "released"—what we might call "becoming integrated"—as the basis of well-being.

To center our selves in this source of energy, to become grounded, let both palms gently rest over your EC. Try first with left over right hand, then right over left. Which gave you a clearer feeling of the EC? You can try different ways of sensing this life force, this energy.

Now let your hands move upward, a short distance from your body, palms angled up, fingers overlapping at their tips as they slowly move up your abdomen toward your chest. Then turn your hands to face slightly downward, at a comfortable angle, and move them back to the EC. Try this gentle up-and-down movement with your hands just a small distance from your body and see if you can feel energy moving inside your body, in your hands, or both. If you are familiar with breath practices, you can try coordinating the in-breath and out-breath with this upward and downward movement in whatever ways feel most balancing, but this is not necessary.

Do a set of six to eight movements, up and down—and this is a useful number, as well, for each of the domains' sequences we'll be trying out. When you complete these, let your palms rest facing your EC. Let your eyes close, if they were open, and rest here for a bit. Now that you've completed the warm-up and energy grounding, we'll begin the symbolic practice itself. Each of the following nine sets of movements can be done directly and without any thoughts about what they represent as a domain of integration. You can even try them out that way—just do the movement without reading the descriptions that precede and that follow that instruction in the second section. Then you can read each of the section's summaries—the first is related to the domain in general, the third applies that domain, briefly, to our journey of intraconnection.

Interpersonal Integration

The domain of interpersonal integration: We give to the world of people—the inter between our body and other bodies, other individuals—with generosity and humility. We receive from other individuals with gratitude and openness. This is the core of interpersonal integration and healthy social relationships.

The sequence for embodiment of this domain: Let your hands rise from the EC to about chest level, let them extend forward, palms up, out to almost your arms' full extent, and then slowly reverse direction and bring your hands, palms up, back toward your chest. Repeat (for each motion, repeat as many times as you can, up to eight or so).

The domain's relevance to intraconnection: {The gestures of palm up reaching out represent the giving to the world; the flow back to the body is the symbol of receiving.} We begin life, as babies, needing connection for survival, and we take the adaptations we've learned from those attachment experiences out into the world of interpersonal relationships. Learning to be a "we" in our personal family of origin may directly impact our experience of widening our lens of identity to embrace a larger set of relational connections—belonging to others in romance, friendship, community, and the world of nature. We come from the inner Me, as the body-based identity, and then connect to other individuals in our social relationships as We.

Temporal Integration

The domain of temporal integration: Across seemingly contradictory opposing aspects of experience, we embrace each apparent polarity, such as time and timelessness; finite and infinite; a longing for permanence, predictability, certainty, and immortality despite the reality of impermanence, unpredictability, uncertainty, and mortality. We sense these opposing aspects across time—temporal integration—linking the differentiated reality and the longing for its opposite.

The sequence for embodiment of this domain: With your hands at your chest, reach upward toward the ceiling or sky, elbows out to the side. When you reach the top, let your hands and arms slowly move downward and out to your sides, palms facing down toward the ground at the bottom of the movement. Then bring your hands together toward the middle as they move back up to your chest. Repeat.

The domain's relevance to intraconnection: {Reaching toward the sky represents the ideals we aim for; reaching toward the ground grounds us in the practical, embracing reality as the real while we also long for the ideal.} We've explored much about the ideas and ideals underlying a view of the whole as intraconnected, and this domain reminds us of the importance of being both idealistic—to have a vision of where we may need to go in our human family and our family of nature—and practical—to envision doable steps as to how we might most effectively get there. This domain also reminds us of the two realms of reality: the time-bound Newtonian macrostate realm of seemingly separate noun-like entities that our body is based in and the timeless quantum, or microstate, realm we may access with open awareness in which even physical separation does not impede the verb-like interweaving of deeply connected events.

Identity Integration

The domain of identity integration: The lens of identity can focus close up on our inner mind, our inner self as Me, and that same lens can focus out on our inter mind, our relational self as We. To link these differentiated inner and relational selves, Me plus We equals MWe is the integrative equation.

The sequence for embodiment of this domain: With your hands resting on your chest, extend your elbows out to your sides, and let your hands follow, slowly arcing forward and ending extended fully out to the sides, encircling a wide expanse. Let them meet in front of your body, forming a circle with your arms. Then move each hand toward the opposite side of your body, your left hand crossing over to rest on your right shoulder, and your right on your left shoulder. Repeat.

The domain's relevance to intraconnection: {The encircling gesture represents the We; its starting place at your torso represents the Me; and the whole sequence combined represents MWe.} Integration is the basis of well-being, and we've seen in our journey that we can differentiate an inner, bodily based center of experience—of energy flow—from an inter center of that flow—our relationships. This is how we differentiate Me from We and then link them in integrative wholeness, the intraconnection of MWe.

Memory Integration

The domain of memory integration: We live in bodies that remember experiences across the flow of energy, a flow of change in this macrostate realm we've named "time." What happens at one time influences the probability of something happening at a later time. This is the origin of what we call past, present, and future: each are moments of happenings, of now-events, that occur across a space–time block of experience. We connect these moments in the body with memory systems, consisting of connections in networks involved in implicit encoding, storage, and retrieval, which take the form of somatic sensation, perception, emotion, and behaviors. These networks also prime us for what we anticipate might happen next and to make generalizations as mental models or schemas—the plateaus acting as filters to construct our perception. This is how bottom-up conduition of sensation becomes top-down construction of perception, conception, and action. Memory integration is about linking these differing aspects of implicit memory into explicit forms of factual knowledge and autobiographical memory of the self across episodes of experience, across our lifetime.

The sequence for embodiment of this domain: Begin with your hands at your shoulders, move them toward the EC, and in a sweeping motion left to right, right to left, let one hand lead away from the EC, but at that level—with the back of this hand facing away from the body, following the elbow leading the way—as the other hand follows, elbows bent, with palm facing toward the leading hand, in a slow, wave-like motion to the furthest extent and back. Now, reverse the sequence, and then repeat the entire set.

The domain's relevance to intraconnection: {The wavelike motion at the level of the EC, passing back and forth over this bodily source of life vitality, represents memory in that the leading elbow is how we move into the future, the hand is the present moment, and the following of the other arm in the sequence represents the past. Memory integration links past, present, and future.} We have implicit memory for the wholeness of "being at one with the uterus"—and we may have some form of implicit knowing of the plane of possibility, that generator of diversity or sea of potential from which we all arose as manifestations of actuality from possibility. Our explicit memory will not have either of these two states of being at one, of being whole; yet we may have an implicit longing for that which we cannot name—it is this drive for coherence that is the motivation of the integration of memory and its inner sense of "going home" and "making the world right" to remind—bring back to mind—the intraconnected wholeness of reality.

Narrative Integration

The domain of narrative integration: Woven from experiences encoded and stored as memory, the stories of our lives are constructed not only in the retrieval of explicit memory but also in the plotlines of our stories from the implicit mental models—our life schemas or worldviews—that summarize and symbolize our view of self. Just as we have many facets of self-experience, we may have many life-story lines as well. Making sense of these narratives across selves and across experience is the organizing, constructive process of narrative integration. We not only tell ourselves, or others, our life story but also come to live life through our narrative integration.

The sequence for embodiment of this domain: With the same back-and-forth flow as the memory integration sequence, shift your forward-moving hand and leading elbow up to the level of your chest, but keep your lower hand, palm facing forward, sweeping across at the level of the EC. Reverse your hand positions and repeat, as with each of the domains, for about eight cycles.

The domain's relevance to intraconnection: {Narrative can create a sweeping direction not only to how we make sense of life, but also to how we live our lives, day to day. The movement of that sweep is embodied in the sequence of the waving flow of the arms, which are now higher than in the memory sequence position.} As stories structure how we live, the modern cultural narrative of the solo-self is constraining our lives not only as a human family, but in our destructive impacts on all living beings on Earth. Narrative integration is a vital component of how our integrative movement toward MWe can be one path that may have deep and lasting impacts on our individual, interpersonal, and biosphere's health as we move ahead in the near future. Narrative can transform cultural evolution, and it is here that living a more integrative story of who we are as an intraconnected whole may make important inroads into liberating us from the prison of the modern story of the solo-self.

State Integration

The domain of state integration: Energy flow can enter states of activation, reinforced as waves, oscillating harmonics that link differentiated zones, connecting them as resonant energy fields. This rhythm of differentiated activations coupling into a functional whole can be called a state. A state of mind can be internal, relating to the activations of the embodied brain. A state of mind can also be relational, the social field as part of a system of interacting individuals and their resonating inner states. State integration focuses on the reality of these differentiated states and how together they form a whole flow of life. Envision these as the many facets or parts or layers of our self that can be woven within a given state for inner-integration, woven across time or between states as cross-state integration, or the linkage with others' states into a system of relational state integration.

The sequence for embodiment of this domain: Begin with the position from the sequence for narrative integration. Raise the leading arm higher still, to the level of the head, keeping the lower hand following at the level of the EC, and move with a wavelike flow, back and forth, alternating left and right elbows leading at their respective heights. Reverse the arm positions and repeat.

The domain's relevance to intraconnection: {As a state takes over our moment-to-moment experience, the higher and wider motions of this sequence symbolize the connection to memory and narrative that underlies our states of mind. The flow represents the interweaving of these in the construction of our present moment filters of experience.} Shifting our identity lens from narrow to wide enables us to shift our state of mind. It is this flexibility of the human mind to embrace an array of self-states, from personal in the body to interpersonal in our social connections to being an intraconnected part of all of nature, that empowers us with state integration.

Bilateral Integration

The domain of bilateral integration: In modern academic neuroscience circles, speaking about the differences between the left and right sides of the brain is often discouraged, mostly to avoid oversimplification and misinformation. Nonetheless, research on the vertebrate nervous system reveals millions of years of differentiation of the two sides of the brain. Both the limbic region and the cortex are separated, left and right. The right side of the cortex develops earlier, is active more than the left in the first few years of life, and takes in the signals of the body more directly, making an integrated map of the body's inner state. The right cortex also specializes in nonverbal signals, both reception and expression, as well as in the autobiographical form of explicit memory—storing recollections of the self across time. In contrast, the left cortex develops later, has less direct input from the body, and specializes in explicit factual memory and encoding linguistic expression and reception. The left loves lists, logic, and literal thinking. In general, "right-mode" processes specialize in a broad focus of attention, and "left-mode" processes utilize a narrower, detailed focus of attention. Bilateral integration honors the value of each of these left-mode and right-mode processes, regardless of which brain areas are ultimately involved. These modes are distinct in their functions, yet one side is not better than the other. Linking them together allows more creativity, connection, compassion, and collaboration to arise in our lives as we honor the differences, cultivate these differences, and then link them together into a synergetic integrative whole.

The sequence for embodiment of this domain: Position your right hand in front of your forehead, fingers pointing down and palm facing right. Position your left hand at your EC, fingers pointing up and palm facing left. Now begin to move your hands toward each other, fingers pointing in the direction of movement, here right moving down, left moving up. Make your hands cross, back to back, somewhere around where your abdomen meets your ribs, the back of each hand moving past the other, and return them to their opposite starting points—top hand facing up to the sky above its shoulder, bottom hand facing down to the ground at the level of the hips. Then let your palms face their respective sides again and move passed the center of the body, continuing down or up each side. Repeat.

The domain's relevance to intraconnection: {This movement combines the symbolism of distinct left and right actions with a crossing of arms in the middle to represent the fluid differentiation and linkage of these important two modes, enabling them to be integrated.} The narrow focus of the left mode may make us prone in these modern times to focus on the parts rather than the whole, which is what the right mode's wider focus of attention permits. The logic and linear thinking, based in linguistic symbols, of the left mode may also contribute to the "analytic" ways we break a system into its parts. There is a role for both the left and right modes, for the details of parts and the synergy of the whole.

Vertical Integration

The domain of vertical integration: This form of integration involves linking the lower regions of the anatomically distributed embodied brain with the higher regions, honoring the important signals of the body and the subcortical regions—the heart and gut areas and the limbic and brain stem areas—and linking these with the cortically mediated experience of consciousness. When we are aware of these deep patterns of energy and information flow within the body, we call this "interoception"—the perception of our interior, our sixth sense. Studies suggest that the more we can develop and use this somatic sense, the more insight and empathy we cultivate. Vertical integration is the embodiment of the experience of our intuition, the taking in of the important heartfelt sense and gut feelings that arise as energy flow from these organs of the body.

The sequence for embodiment of this domain: With one hand at your forehead and the other at your EC, bring together the fingertips of each hand, including the thumb, as if each hand was encircling a small ball. Keep your lower hand anchored just at or beneath the EC, and move your upper hand slowly downward to meet the tips of the fingers of the lower hand.

Now flip their positions, the upper hand becoming the lower, while maintaining the contact of the fingertips. While holding your hands in front of your EC, twist your fingers back and forth in a rotating manner, as if polishing a jewel being held between the fingertips of each hand, grinding the energy just at the level of your EC. After a few seconds of twisting, let your hands rest in place.

Now imagine the sensation of a rubber band connecting your two sets of fingers. Let your upper hand move slowly up toward the forehead, sensing the stretch of the rubber band as your hand slowly pulls it upward, with your lower hand grounding that stretch at your EC. Once your hand reaches your forehead, pause, feel the stretch, and then slowly relax the tension as you move your upper hand back down to your EC. Switch your top and bottom hands and repeat; then repeat the entire sequence the usual six to eight times or so.

The domain's relevance to intraconnection: {This motion links a grounding in the body with the higher processes of consciousness to represent vertical integration.} The wisdom of our nonrational mind—emerging from the whole of our "embodied brain"—may be able to tap into the intelligence of nature and feel into the synergy of the intraconnected whole of reality that we've been exploring in our journey. In this way, vertical integration can be a window into this nonrational, intuitive sense of how the invisible is real—patterns of the interconnection of parts underlying the intraconnected whole.

Consciousness Integration

The domain of consciousness integration: Consciousness includes the experience of knowing—of being aware—and those things of which we are aware: the knowns. When we differentiate the various knowns from one another and then link these knowns to the differentiated experience of being aware, of knowing, we integrate consciousness. Like the Wheel of Awareness practice, this movement sequence also has the three pillars of mind training that have been shown, in independent practices, to lead to positive changes in the brain and body. Inspired by the tai chi ball practice, we symbolize the integration of consciousness and the 3-P framework with this movement.

The sequence for embodiment of this domain: Place the lower hand from the prior movement at the EC. Move your upper hand down to the EC. Let both hands meet, with fingers cupped as if holding a small sphere, the size of a tennis ball or an orange. Now rotate your hands slowly as if turning this imaginary ball clockwise, counterclockwise, clockwise, over and over.

Soon, with each turn you may begin to feel a sense of energy making your hands separate from each other, as if the imaginary ball between them is inflating with air. You may feel energy pushing your hands apart as the imaginary ball or balloon gets bigger and bigger with each rotation, back and forth, as your hands form a larger circle, your arms a larger sphere, with each turning.

At some point—whatever timing works for you—your hands will feel at their maximal extension. Continue rotating your hands and arms this way, then that. When it feels right, make each turn slowly start to compress that energy again. Feel your hands move closer to each other with each rotation, and finally come back together as if holding a small round object.

Then, after a few more rotations, imagine placing that sphere of energy into your EC, keeping your hands over that source of energy, which you may now feel streaming into and then through your whole body. Focus on this sensation, resting in it as you feel grounded.

The domain's relevance to intraconnection: {The symbolic sense of this movement is of potential energy, representing the plane of possibility, expanding within us. As this energy symbolically expands outward, energy flow is the movement from possibility to actuality.} Throughout our journey, we've seen that the hub of the Wheel is the metaphoric representation of the plane of possibility. In the consciousness integration domain, we see that accessing this plane beneath learned plateaus of separation—including the view of the isolated solo-self—can be an important step in integrating the self's experience of subjective sensation, perspective, and agency.

Take the time you need to let these nine domains rest in your awareness as you conclude this practice. You are learning to adjust an identity lens from narrow to wide; you have now learned to focus on nine named domains of integration. Each domain, as we've seen, has direct applications in our journey into living as an integrative self, identity, and belonging as MWe realize the wholeness of intraconnection.

You've now grounded yourself with the nine domains of integration: interpersonal, temporal, identity, memory, narrative, state, bilateral, vertical, and consciousness. Thank you for choosing to try out this integrative movement series and for being on this journey.

References, Resources, and Readings

I used the following sources in constructing this narrative, our journey together from twinkle to twilight. I've also included resources you may find helpful as you continue your journey of exploring self, identity, and belonging, of widening your lens to incorporate the plane of possibility and our collective experience as MWe.

180 Studio, & Saunders, E. (2020). Seed and spark: Using nature as a model to reimagine how we learn and live. 180 Studio. https://seedandspark.live

Ackerman, D. (2015). *The human age: The world shaped by us.* Norton.

Albrecht, G. (2014) Ecopsychology in "The Symbiocene." *Ecopsychology, 6*(1), 58–59. doi: 10.1089/eco.2013.0091

Albrecht, G., Sartore, G.-M., Connor, L., Higginbotham, N., Freeman, S., Kelly, B., Stain, H., Tonna, A., & Pollard, G. (2007). Solastalgia: The distress caused by environmental change. *Australasian Psychiatry, 15*(S1), S95–S98. https://doi.org/10.1080/10398560701701288

Appiah, K. A. (2018). *The lies that bind: Rethinking identity—Creed, country, color, class, culture.* Profile Books.

Bateson, G. (1972). *Steps to an ecology of mind: Collected essays in anthropology, psychiatry, evolution, and epistemology.* University of Chicago Press.

Baumeister, R. F. (1998). The self. In D. T. Gilbert, S. T. Fiske, & G. Lindzey (Eds.), *The handbook of social psychology,* 4th ed. (pp. 680–740). McGraw-Hill.

Boell, M., and P. Senge. See website for more information: www.systemsawareness.org

Bohm, D. (1980). *Wholeness and the implicate order.* Routledge.

Breger, L. (1974). *From instinct to identity: The development of personality.* Prentice-Hall.

Challenger, M. (2021). *How to be animal: A new history of what it means to be human.* Penguin.

Chester, J. (Director). (2018). Biggest Little Farm [Film; documentary].

Clark, A. (2016). *Surfing uncertainty: Prediction, action and the embodied mind.* Oxford University Press.

Damasio, A. R. (2010). *Self comes to mind: Constructing the conscious brain.* Pantheon/Random House.

Damasio, A. R. (2018). *The strange order of things: Life, feeling, and the making of cultures.* Pantheon.

DeCicco, T. L., & Stroink, M. (2007). A third model of self-construal: The metapersonal self. *International Journal of Transpersonal Studies, 26*(1), 84–108.

DiAngelo, R. (2000). *White fragility: Why it's so hard for white people to talk about racism.* Beacon.

Dweck, C (2006). *Mindset: The new psychology of success.* Random House.

Einstein, A. (1950). Letter in the New York Times (29 March, 1972) and the New York Post (28 November, 1972).

Einstein, A. (2014). *The world as I see it.* CreateSpace Independent Publishing Platform.

Epel, E. (2022). *The stress prescription: 7 days to more joy and ease.* Penguin Random House.

Ertinger, I. & Roebers, T. (2020). Rooted messages [Documentary]. Retrieved on November 13, 2020, from https://rootedmessages.com

Figueres, C., & Rivet-Carnac, T. (2020). *The future we choose: Surviving the climate crisis.* Knopf/Borzoi.

Fuller, R. B. (1975). *Synergetics: Essays on the geometry of thinking.* Macmillan.

Gambini, B. (2021, April 13). Mindfulness can make you selfish. But there's a way to help prevent it. University of Buffalo Daily Health Check. University of Buffalo Study by Poulin, Gabriel, Morrison, Naidu and Ministero, *Psychological Science,* 2021.

Gibas, D., Giraud, T., Le Conte, J., Rubens, L., Martin, J.C., & Isableu, B. (2016). Attempt to validate the self-construal scale in French: Systematic approach and model limitation. *European Review of Applied Psychology, 66*(2), 85–93.

Glück, L. (2012). *Collected poems: 1962–2012.* HarperCollins.

Godfrey-Smith, P. (2016). *Other minds: The octopus, the sea, and the deep origins of consciousness.* Farrar, Straus and Giroux.

Goodall, J., & Abrams, D. C. (2021). *The book of hope.* Sounds True.

Graeber, D., & Wengrow, D. (2021). *The dawn of everything: A new history of humanity.* Farrar, Straus and Giroux.

Grant, A. (2021). *Think again: The power of knowing what you don't know.* Penguin Random House/Viking.

Hanh, T. N. (2013). *The other shore: A new translation of the heart sutra with commentaries.* Palm Leaves Press.

Hanh, T. N. (2007). *Chanting from the heart: Buddhist ceremonies and daily practices.* Parallax Press.

Hawken, P. (2017). *Drawdown: The most comprehensive plan ever proposed to reduce global warming.* Penguin Random House.

Hawken, P. (2021). *Regeneration: Ending the climate crisis in one generation*. Penguin Random House.

Heifetz, R. (1998). *Leadership without easy answers*. Harvard University Press.

Human Rights Campaign. (2022). Glossary of terms. Retrieved February 3, 2022, from https://www.hrc.org/resources/glossary-of-terms

Katz, R. (2017). *Indigenous healing psychology: Honoring the wisdom of the First Peoples*. Healing Arts Press.

Kaza, S. (Ed.). (2020). *A wild love for the world: Joanna Macy and the work of our time*. Shambhala.

Kegan, R. (1982). *The evolving self: Problems and process in human development*. Harvard University Press.

Kegan, R. (1994). *In over our heads: The mental demands of modern life*. Harvard University Press.

Kegan, R. and Lahey, L. L. (2009). *Immunity to change: How to overcome it and unlock potential in yourself and your organization*. Harvard Business Press.

Kelly, G. A. (1955). *The psychology of personal constructs* (Vols. 1 & 2). Norton.

Keltner, D. (2016, May 10). Why do we feel awe? *Greater Good Magazine*. https://greatergood.berkeley.edu/article/item/why_do_we_feel_awe

Keltner, D., & Haidt, J. (2003). Approaching awe, a moral, spiritual, and aesthetic emotion. *Cognition and Emotion, 17*(2), 297–314.

Kendi, I. X. (2019). *How to be an anti-racist*. One World.

King, D. B., & DeCicco, T. L. (2009). A viable model and self-report measure of spiritual intelligence. *International Journal of Transpersonal Studies, 28*, 68–85.

Kornfield, J. A. (2009). *The wise heart: A guide to the universal teachings of Buddhist psychology*. Penguin Random House.

Lent, J. (2021). *The web of meaning: Integrating science and traditional wisdom to find our place in the universe*. New Society Press.

Levine, T. R., Bresnahan, M. J. & Park, H. S. (2003). The (in) validity of self-construal scales revisited. *Human Communication Research, 29*(2), 291–308.

Macy, J. (2007/2021). *World as self world as lover: courage for global justice and planetary renewal* (30th anniversary edition, 2021). Parallax Press.

Macy, J., & Johnstone, C. (2012/2022). *Active hope: How to face the mess we are with unexpected resilience and creative power*. Revised edition. New World Library.

Mara, C., DiCicco, T., & Stroink, M. (2010) An investigation of the relationships among self-construal, emotional intelligence, and well-being. *International Journal of Transpersonal Studies, 29*(1), 1–11.

Markus, H. R., & Kitayama, S. (1991). Culture and the self: Implications for cognition, emotion, and motivation. *Psychological Review, 98*, 224–253.

Markus, H., & Sentis, K. (1982). The self in social information processing. In J. Suls (Ed.), *Social psychological perspectives on the self* (pp. 41–70). Hillsdale, NJ: Erlbaum.

Marsella, A. J., DeVos, G., & Hsu, F. L. K. (Eds.). (1985). *Culture and self.* London: Tavistock.

Menakem, R. (2017). *My grandmother's hands: Racialized trauma and the pathways to mending our hearts and bodies.* Central Recovery Press.

Milton, J. P. (n.d.). Way of Nature. www.wayofnature.com

Murthy, V. H. (2020). *Together: Loneliness, health, and what happens when we find connection.* Wellcome Collection.

Neihardt, J. G. (2014). *Black Elk speaks: The complete edition.* University of Nebraska Press.

Nisbett, R. E., & Miyamoto, Y. (2005). The influence of culture: Holistic versus analytic perception. *Trends in Cognitive Sciences, 9*(10), 467–473.

O'Brien, K. (2021). *You matter more than you think: Quantum social change for a thriving world.* CHANGE Press.

O'Donohue, J. (2000). *Conamara blues.* Double Day (The poem, Fluent, page 41).

O'Donohue, J. (1998). *Anam cara: Soul friend.* Double Day.

O'Donohue, J. (2008). *To bless the space between us: A book of blessings.* Double Day.

Ogude, J. (2019). I am because we are: An interview with James Ogude [Interview]. IDEAS; Consortium of Humanities Centers and Institutes. https://chcinetwork.org/ideas/i-am-because-you-are-an-interview-with-james-ogude

Panksepp, J. & Biven, L. (2012). *The archaeology of mind: The neuroevolutionary origins of the human mind.* Norton.

Popova, M. (2017). Flatland revisited: A lovely new edition of Edwin Abott Abbott's Classic 1884 allegory of expanding our perspective—On the absurdity of truth by consensus, and a gentle invitation to consider how our way of looking at the world limits our view of it. Retrieved February 2, 2022, from https://www.themarginalian.org/2017/12/20/flatland-epilogue/

Popova, M., & Zhu, P. (2021). *The snail with the right heart* [Back flap copy]. Enchanted Lion Press.

Poulin, M., Ministero, L., Gabriel, S., Morrison, C., & Naidu, E. (2021, April 9). Minding your own business? Mindfulness decreases prosocial behavior for those with independent self-construals. https://doi.org/10.31234/osf.io/xhyua

Revkin, A. (2022). Sustain what? [Webcast]. Earth Institute, Columbia University. https://www.earth.columbia.edu/videos/channel/sustain-what

Roth, G. (1998). *Maps to ecstasy: A healing journey for the untamed spirit.* New World.

Scharmer, O. (n.d.). See his website: www.ottoscharmer.com

Schwartzberg, L. (2022). Gratitude Revealed [Documentary].

Siegel, A. W. (2016): Good Leg. Alex Siegel Music/Alexsiegel.com

Siegel, D. J. (2007). *The mindful brain.* Norton.

Siegel, D. J. (2010). *The mindful therapist: A clinician's guide to mindsight and neural integration.* Norton.

Siegel, D. J. (2012). *Pocket guide to interpersonal neurobiology: An integrative handbook of the mind.* Norton.

Siegel, D. J. (2014). *Brainstorm: The power and purpose of the teenage brain*. Tarcher/Penguin Random House.

Siegel, D. J. (2017). *Mind: A journey to the heart of being human*. Norton.

Siegel, D. J. (2018). *Aware: The science and practice of presence*. Tarcher/Penguin Random House.

Siegel, D. J. (2020). *The developing mind: How relationships and the brain interact to shape who we are*. (3rd ed.). Guilford.

Siegel, D. J. (2021). *Becoming aware: A 21-day mindfulness program from reducing anxiety and cultivating calm*. Tarcher/Penguin Random House.

Siegel, D. J., & Hartzell, M. (2003). *Parenting from the inside out: How a deeper self-understanding can help you raise children who thrive*. Tarcher/Perigee.

Singelis, T. M. (1994). The measurement of independent and interdependent self-construals. *Personality and Social Psychology Bulletin, 20*(5), 580–591.

Smith, S. M., Nichols, T., Vidaurre, D., Winkler, A., Behrens, T., Glasser, M., et al. (2015). A positive–negative mode of population co-variation links brain connectivity, demographics, and behavior. *Nature Neuroscience, 18*(11), 1567–1571.

Stern, D. (1985). *Interpersonal world of the infant*. Basic Books.

Stern, D. (2004). *The present moment in psychotherapy and everyday life*. Norton.

Stevenson, B. (2019). *Just mercy: A story of justice and redemption*. OneWorld.

Stone, E. (2017, April 27). The emerging science of awe and its benefits. *Psychology Today*. https://www.psychologytoday.com/us/blog/understanding-awe/201704/the-emerging-science-awe-and-its-benefits

Teilhard de Chardin, P. (1959). *The future of man*. Double Day.

Twist, L. (2017). *The soul of money: Transforming your relationships with money and life*. Norton.

Villamil, A., Vogel, T., Weisenbaum, E., & Siegel, D. J. (2019). Cultivating well-being through the three pillars of mind training: Understanding how training the mind improves physiological and psychological well being. *Open Access, 4*(1), 1–11.

Wall Kimmerer, R. (2013). *Braiding sweet grass: Indigenous wisdom, scientific knowledge, and the teachings of plants*. Milkweed.

Welch, C. S. (2020). *The gift of presence: A mindfulness guide for women*. Tarcher.

Wilkerson, I. (2020). *Caste: The origins of our discontents*. Random House.

Wilson, E. O. (1998). *Consilience: The unity of knowledge*. Penguin/Vintage Books.

Yunkaporta, T. (2020). *Sand talk: How Indigenous thinking can save the world*. Harper One.

INDEX

Note: Italicized page locators refer to figures; tables are noted with a *t*.

ABOUT THE AUTHOR

Daniel J. Siegel received his medical degree from Harvard University and completed his postgraduate medical education at UCLA with training in pediatrics and child, adolescent, and adult psychiatry. He served as a National Institute of Mental Health research fellow at UCLA, studying family interactions with an emphasis on how attachment experiences influence emotions, behavior, autobiographical memory, and narrative.

Dr. Siegel is a clinical professor of psychiatry at the UCLA School of Medicine and the founding codirector of the Mindful Awareness Research Center at UCLA. An award-winning educator, he is a Distinguished Fellow of the American Psychiatric Association and recipient of several honorary fellowships. Dr. Siegel is also the executive director of the Mindsight Institute, an educational organization which offers online learning and in-person seminars that focus on how the development of mindsight in individuals, families, and communities can be enhanced by examining the interface of human relationships and basic biological processes. His psychotherapy practice includes children, adolescents, adults, couples, and families. He serves as the medical director of the LifeSpan Learning Institute and on the advisory board of the Blue School in New York City, which has built its curriculum around Dr. Siegel's Mindsight approach.

Dr. Siegel's unique ability to make complicated scientific concepts exciting and accessible has led him to be invited to address diverse local, national, and international groups including mental health professionals, neuroscientists, corporate leaders, educators, parents, public administrators, healthcare providers, policy-makers, mediators, judges, and clergy. He has lectured for the King of Thailand, Pope John Paul II, His Holiness the Dalai Lama, Google University, and London's Royal Society of Arts (RSA). He lives in Southern California with welcome visits from his two adult children.